A BIOGRAPHY

J. P. FUSI

Translated by Felipe Fernández-Armesto

Preface by Sir Raymond Carr

1817

HARPER & ROW, PUBLISHERS, New York
Cambridge, Philadelphia, San Francisco, London
Mexico City, São Paulo, Singapore, Sydney

First published by Ediciones El Pais, Madrid 1985

First U.S. Edition

Library of Congress Cataloging-in-Publication Data

Fusi Aizpurúa, Juan Pablo, 1945–
  Franco: a biography.

  (Icon editions)
  Translation of: Franco.
  Bibliography: p.
  Includes index.
  1. Franco, Francisco, 1892–1975.   2. Spain—History—
1939–1975.   3. Generals—Spain—Biography.   4. Heads of
state—Spain—Biography.   I. Title.
DP264.F7F8713   1987   946.082′092′4 [B]   87-45820
ISBN 0-06-433127-X

88 89 90 91 10 9 8 7 6 5 4 3 2 1

Contents

Preface

The Francoist era – though those who suffered persecution under it will find such an interpretation an insult – was a realm of mutual fantasies. The fantasy of its creator was that a system forged by a 'clerical reactionary' – as the German Ambassador called Franco during the Civil War – could contain and rule what by the 1960s was an increasingly secular society, and that what Franco had once termed a totalitarian regime could survive in a democratic Europe. The fantasy of its opponents was that, before the dictator died in his bed, they could overthrow a regime which had brought prosperity after the 'hungry years' of the 1940s and which enjoyed widespread, if passive, support.

The great virtue of J. P. Fusi's book is that he writes as a historian not given to applying the taxonomic labels of political scientists to a political system which, as Franco insisted, was unique. During the Civil War and its aftermath the regime claimed to be totalitarian and the influence of Germany and Italy, allies in the Civil War, was apparent. Apart from these early Fascist leanings, Fusi sees Francoism as the personal rule of an authoritarian conservative soldier whose conception of his function as ruler of Spain was derived from his reflections on the destructive role of liberalism in modern Spanish history. Spain needed unity and order. Catholicism had to be re-established as the moral basis of the state.

If in the 1970s a sort of quasi-legalized dissent was tolerated, opposition to the Caudillo and his rule was regarded as mutiny. Franco was not by nature a cruel man. He was an officer who believed that the punishment for mutiny was the firing squad.

Franco had been given by his fellow generals 'all the powers of the new State'. He thus became the most powerful Spanish ruler since Philip II. But whereas Philip II was a civilian ruler and a discriminating patron of the arts, Franco was a middle class soldier, given, like so many of his subjects, to watching Match of the Day on TV and filling in the pools. Nor was he, like Philip II, a workaholic, poring over his secretaries' memoranda; Spain, he declared in one of his occasional disconcerting asides, was easy to govern.

Francoism was, Franco himself claimed, 'a novel solution'. In outward show it was a curious mixture of the formal paraphernalia of a royal court and populism, of ceremony and an adulation that reached what now seem comic heights. Ceremony was designed to create a distance between the Messiah and those he had come to save. The dictator's speeches and public appearances were intended to shorten that distance. Personal rule was legitimized in the eyes of the ruler by what I called the democracy of the plaza: the assumption that the acclamation of a mass audience of enthusiastic and committed supporters implied the consent of the governed. Like Primo de Rivera, Franco, until stricken by illness, was an assiduous travelling salesman. The sales talk, delivered in his piping voice, varied. The pompous rhetoric of national socialism became what Fusi calls 'the arid language' of the statistics of development. His public image was refurbished. The victorious general on his white charger became the grandfather who had given peace and prosperity to his extended family, the Spanish people.

As Fusi points out, it was precisely the development that Franco presided over and took pride in that undermined the social foundations of Francoism. The society that was the result of the relative prosperity of the 1960s and 1970s had outgrown the carapace of a system invented to conquer the demons of the 1930s. Franco to the end ranted about the ancient enemies – masonry with which he was obsessed and communism which he regarded as a conspiracy to destroy Spain – in order to conceal the failure of his regime to come to terms with the fact that Spanish society increasingly resembled that of the European democracies that surrounded it. The contrast with the 1930s and the early years of the Second World War is dramatic. Then it seemed that the totalitarian dictatorships might defeat the 'decadent' democracies. After 1945, Spain – Portugal apart – stuck out in democratic Europe like a sore thumb. International ostracism in the 1940s and again in the 1970s was presented as an attack, not on Francoism, but on Spain and Western Christian civilization.

The essential inner contradiction of Francoism, Fusi maintains, was its 'bad democratic conscience'. He is quite right. For all the Caudillo's hatred of pluralist democracy as practised in Spain under the Second Republic of 1931–36 when unpatriotic political parties and liberalism opened the gates to communism, the regime was conscious that it lacked democratic legitimacy. Hence its semantic juggling with phrases like 'real democracy', 'organic democracy' and its experiments with specious democratic devices that allowed Franco to argue that the rigged referendum of 1947 supplied his regime with the necessary democratic credentials.

It was the search for this elusive democratic legitimacy that accounts in part, for Franco's delays in 'institutionalizing' his regime by giving it a permanent political structure and a head of state to succeed him. His propagandists lauded his 'magisterial inertia' but his closest advisers, as Fusi points out, were alarmed when his vaunted prudence – a favourite word – seemed only to cloak a stop-go policy, an incapacity to decide between the competing formulae put forward by the political families of the regime which he manipulated with considerable skill, changing their relative strength in his ministries. But this political legerdemain could not hide the fact that he had not, as he boasted, 'tied things down' within a political framework that would outlast him to ensure that the institutions of Francoism would survive an ageing dictator as loyal Francoists hoped. By the 1970s it was evident that the system was in trouble. Hence the struggles within the regime between 'openers' (*aperturistas*) – those like Manuel Fraga who saw quite clearly that the regime was doomed if it did not change – and the apostles of 'continuism' for whom, as Carrero Blanco was alleged once to have put it, to offer political change to Spaniards was like offering a drink to a confirmed alcoholic. Both were correct. The regime would not survive without a degree of democratization; yet democratization could not be reconciled with its fundamental premises. No amount of semantic manoeuvring would square the circle. The result of Fraga's press law, however limited its application, was to make the conflicts of Spanish society – strikes, terrorism, university riots – public property and the leaders of the opposition known at least to a public that could buy and read a weekly like *Cambio 16* in the 1970s.

The prolonged disintegration of the regime was paralleled by the physical decay of the Caudillo himself. Fusi's description of the final dissolution is moving in its macabre detail. Franco bore the onslaught of pain as he bore the burdens of government; stoically as a soldier. His agony symbolized the Spain of the last epoch of his rule: an authoritarian technocracy that sought to maintain the traditional Catholic values in a Spain of secular consumerism. Subjected to every horror of modern medicine, Franco died with the Mantle of the Virgin of Pilar and the arm of Teresa of Avila by his bedside.

Fusi's book is far and away the most balanced and intelligent exposition of Francoism that has appeared, magisterial in its account of the origins of Francoism and its adaptation to new circumstances, reflected in ministerial reshuffles that 'resolved' crises – for instance that of 1956 when in Fusi's words 'it appeared that the whole edifice was in danger of falling down'. It will raise the hackles of the opposition because hitherto – except for the works of his adulators – the history of Francoism has so often been written as if it were merely the history of the opposition. Fusi gives that opposition credit for its bravery and does not underestimate the contribution made by the clandestine parties and unions, the democratic (i.e. non communist) opposition, the Basques and the Catalans to the erosion of Francoism's moral credibility and the undermining of the system. He shows Franco's petulant irritation with Don Juan and his claim to a crown that would reconcile in a democratic monarchy Spaniards divided by the memories and blood of the Civil War. He believed Don Juan to be counselled by a clique of aristocratic courtiers – the Caudillo had few aristocratic tastes apart from his obsessive pursuit of birds and fishes. But Fusi cannot neglect the fact that opposition failed to overthrow the regime. He quotes the Italian Communist Rosanna Rossanda who came to Spain in 1962; she found a depoliticized society with a clandestine opposition 'which fed on its own fantasies. . . . It was not a silenced political society but apparently a non-political society, not gagged but empty'. This was no longer true in the 1970s; hence the failures of Arias Navarro gagged by the Francoist bunker. The opposition and the *aperturistas* within the regime had flung up a politicized intellectual élite to confront a bankrupt political system. But opposition was paralyzed by the expectation that death would end Francoism without running the appalling risks of revolution. When nature did remove the Caudillo, his chosen successor, King Juan Carlos, and the political élite of a new generation could destroy the political structure whose origin lay in a meeting of generals on a Salamanca aerodrome in September 1936.

His rule, he claimed, would be 'for life'. And so it turned out to be. But 'the novel solution' could not outlast its architect. There was no Francoism after Franco.

1987   RAYMOND CARR

Introduction

In length and purpose this book is a biographical essay, not a biography in the strict sense of the word. It is intended as a short critical survey of Franco's life. It is not – and is not meant to be – a definitive study based on comprehensive original research, such as might yield spectacular revelations. Rather, it is an attempt to interpret what we already know. Any interest it may have must therefore arise from the persuasiveness of my interpretation or the usefulness of the method I have used (which, by the way, is that of the historian).

In calling the book an essay in historical interpretation, I want to avoid eulogy and calumny alike. Both approaches are equally valueless to an historian. Francoist hagiography has always evaded the Franco regime's most interesting problem: its lack of genuine moral legitimacy, in the eyes of the liberal and democratic world, due to its origins in military insurrection and civil war and its authoritarian, repressive character. Anti-Francoist demonology – often, despite appearances, a kind of academic escapism – evades equally disturbing problems of its own, such as the willing and sincere acceptance of Francoism by a very broad spectrum of Spanish society, the system's almost inviolable stability over several decades, the weakness of the opposition and the remarkable transformation of Spain and the Spanish state between 1939 and 1975.

It is neither pleasant nor easy to write about Franco. I have tried to avoid two obvious temptations. The first is to write not about Francoism but about the opposition to it – a common and unacceptable confusion. The second is to let one's own views take over from historical analysis. I start from the assumptions that history – including the story of Franco – is not a proper field for expressions of personal opinion, and that historians should limit themselves to conclusions drawn from the evidence, not from their own preferences and sentiments. I have at least tried to follow Weber's advice and put the ethic of objective responsibility above personal conviction in the scale of values which underlies this book.

J.P.F.

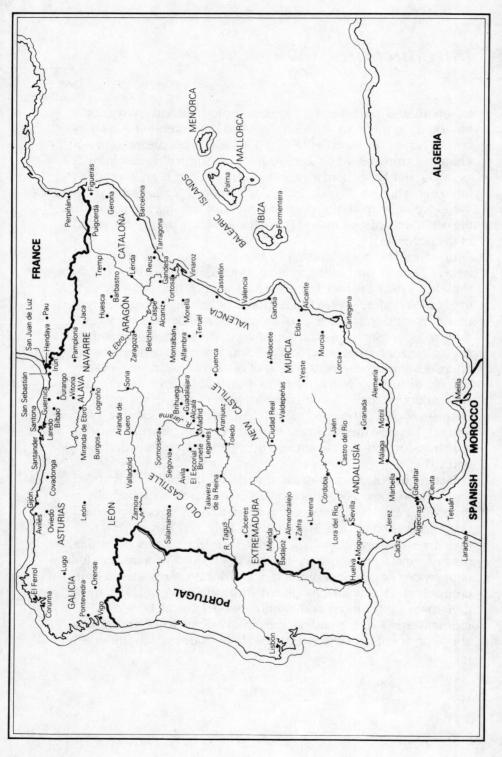

The Spanish Mainland

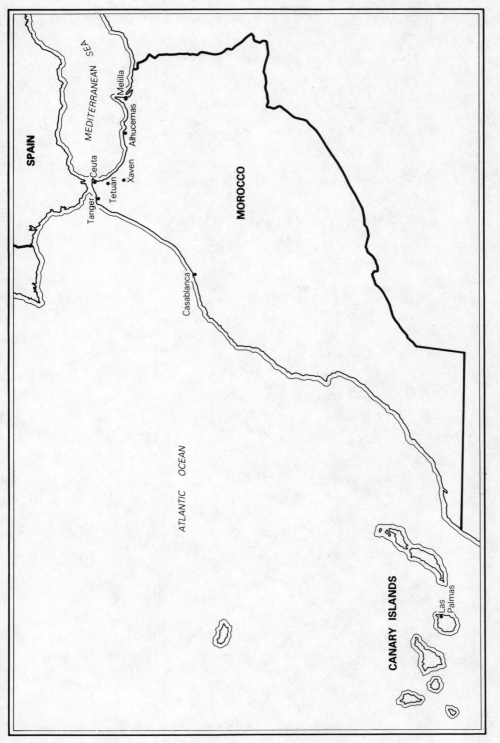

Morocco

1
The Soldier from Africa

In an election address given in Cuenca on 1 May 1936, the socialist leader Indalecio Prieto referred to the discontent in the army and the current rumours of a possible military rebellion against the republic. And in particular, he declared, 'Owing to his youth, his talents, and the range of his connections in the army, General Franco is the man who, given the opportunity, could lead such a movement, with all the enormous advantages which accrue from his high prestige'.[1]

As is well known, Prieto's forecast was fulfilled shortly afterwards on 18 July 1936, when Franco and other well-known officers, led part of the army in an insurrection, which, after three years of bitter Civil War, put an end to the democratic experiment of the Second Republic. A personal and authoritarian regime was then established which would last for forty years until 20 November 1975 under Franco's own lifelong leadership. It is worthwhile, therefore, to stress what Prieto pointed out in Cuenca: Franco was a soldier of renown and it was his prestige in army circles which marked him out as the military leader longed for by the Spanish right. What was more, Prieto was not inspired by mere caprice: he was voicing a widely held opinion.

Franco was forty-three years old in 1936. He had been born in El Ferrol on 4 December 1892 to a family with naval traditions, whose circumstances – 'modest, but decent and honourable' in his cousin's words – were typical of a middle class household with four children (Nicolás, Francisco, Pilar and Ramón).[2] After a colourless childhood and early schooling locally, he went to the Military Academy of Toledo in 1907 to begin one of the most rapid and conspicuous ascents in the history of the Spanish army in this century. For although his work as a cadet was only mediocre – he passed out in 1910 with the rank of 2nd Lieutenant and was placed 251st out of the 312 officers who graduated with him – his subsequent rise was meteoric. In 1912 he became a lieutenant; in 1915, captain; in 1917, major; in 1925, colonel, and in 1926 – at 33 years old – brigadier-general.

Franco spent virtually the whole of his military career from 1912 to 1926 in Africa, save for three short interludes: for 17 months when he was posted to El Ferrol between August 1910 and February 1912; followed by three years which were spent in Oviedo between May 1917 and September 1920; and a further six months when he was back in Oviedo between January and June 1923. All his promotions, except for the first, were for achievements in combat. He won, moreover, no fewer than thirteen medals, crosses and honours – not including, however, the highest award of all, the Order of St Ferdinand (which he was to bestow on himself at the end of the Civil War). In each and every one of these incidents, his undeniable gifts of calm, courage and competence were acknowledged. What was more, Franco was lucky: despite being in the front line in a huge number of encounters (a reputed total of 47 between June 1918 and November 1924 alone) he was only wounded once, on 29 June 1916, at El Biutz, near Ceuta. And this was in a war which cost the lives of 915 officers and 16,000 soldiers between 1916 and 1926.

Franco felt that it was the years 1920–25, when he was second-in-command in the Foreign Legion – the elite corps of shock troops formed in 1920 by Millán Astray – that saw the 'tempering' of his character.[3] His prestige was established and the basis of his popular reputation was laid in these years, thanks chiefly to the part he played in the recovery of the district around Melilla in the latter part of 1921, after a devastating attack on Annoual in July by the rebel forces of Abd el Krim. The débâcle of Annoual resulted in the rout of the Spanish forces under General Silvestre, the loss of 9,000 men and the collapse of the main strongholds in the Melilla area, and was the worst military disaster for Spain in the entire Moroccan War.

Franco had joined the Legion in Africa in October 1920 – after three long years of duty in Oviedo – and early in 1921 took part in frequent operations in the Xaven area with forces led by Colonel Castro Girona. After Annoual, the Legion formed the vanguard of the expedition despatched under General Sanjurjo's command to relieve Melilla and Franco and his men took part in the recovery of a number of positions around Melilla. Subsequently after the Dar Drius (*Driouch*) offensive, completed by early 1922, and actions at Taferhsit, Bu Hafora and Tizzi Azza that October, which would be remembered as some of the most daring and impressive in the history of the Legion, almost all the territory lost to the rebels the previous year was regained. Numerous Spanish newspapers singled Major Franco out as 'the hero of the Moroccan campaign'. A few months later, in June 1923, he was gazetted Lieutenant-Colonel and appointed to be the new Commander-in-Chief of the Legion, in succession to Lieutenant-Colonel Valenzuela, who had been killed in battle shortly before.

Franco still had three more years to serve in Africa. He continued the fighting role which he had played so far and was rewarded for his part in numerous actions between 1 August 1923 and 31 December 1924 by promotion to colonel on 7 February 1925. When he became a brigadier general on 3 February 1926, the citation dwelt particularly on his part in a large number of actions connected with the withdrawal from Xaven in the closing months of 1924. This was clearly well deserved, since Franco and the Legion had the job of covering a risky manoeuvre in which 2,000 men were killed. Franco had, moreover, been opposed to the action, because he saw it as evidence that General Primo de Rivera (who had come to power following a coup d'état on 13 September 1923) intended to adopt a policy of withdrawal in Africa.

This did not in fact happen, owing in part to the lobbying of the Army of Africa, in which, as we shall see, Franco took a hand. The war went on and even intensified until 1927, when the Spanish forces felt satisfied with the pacification of Morocco. The decisive moment was the landing in the bay of Alhucemas on 8 September 1925. Franco and the Legion had been the last to leave Xaven: now they were the first to land on the beaches of Alhucemas (*Al Hoceima*). Franco at Alhucemas – carrying on the fight beyond the beach-head until the end of the month – evinced the same bearing as he had shown in the past: that of an outstanding and brave assault-force chief. The sort of operation that was mounted at Alhucemas, with 40 French and Spanish warships without counting the tugs and landing craft, 76 aircraft including seaplanes, and 15,000 men, was beyond his proper sphere of command. The sort of war which would subsequently be waged in Morocco – reflecting modern ideas, requiring the establishment of long lines and continuous battle-fronts and involving a strategy of broad outflanking manoeuvres – was outside his experience. In Africa, Franco was a great leader of men, not a strategist. He did introduce some tactical innovations, but he was by no means up to date with the modern style of warfare brought to Morocco in 1926 by General Manuel Goded, the Chief of Staff of the Army of Africa, which Sanjurjo continued to command.

Nonetheless, Africa provides the key to understanding Franco's life. Franco was basically a solider, as demonstrated by mere mention of his main postings between his return from Morocco in 1926 and the outbreak of the Civil War: Director of the General Military Academy from 1928 to 1931; Military Commandant of Corunna in 1932; Captain General of the Balearic Islands in 1933 and 1934 (this and the previous command having been gazetted under the Second Republic, proclaimed on 14 April 1931); overall Commander of the Spanish forces in Morocco in the first half of 1935; Chief of the Central General Staff from 17 May 1935 to February 1936, and Captain General of the Canary Islands from February until 18 July of that year. Franco was – I repeat – a soldier, and a particular kind of soldier: one of the *Africanistas* or 'Africanists' who had served in Africa and identified with the African cause. He belonged to what has been called the military 'generation' of 1915, composed of those born around 1880–95, men such as Orgaz, Goded, Mola, Varela, Aranda, Vigón, Kindelán, Rojo and Martínez de Campos.[4]

From his military and African backgrounds, Franco derived a handful of strong, basic convictions which would never leave him. Essentially these were as follows. First he had an overriding sense of nationalism geared to military values and saw the army as the incarnation of patriotism and the ultimate guarantor of national unity. Simultaneously he felt disgust with the constitutional monarchy of 1876–1923, which he held responsible for the decline of Spain symbolized by its defeat by the United States in the Cuban war of 1898. Secondly, he believed that war in Morocco would restore the prestige the army had lost in 1898 and would rekindle the ideals of Spanish patriotism. Thirdly he felt that Spanish history vindicated the army's record of political interventions in the interests of the united Spanish state and as the last line of defence in 'the survival of the fatherland'.

The African dimension of Franco's thought was made abundantly clear not only in his own military record but also in a book he wrote in 1922, *Morocco: the Inside Story of a Fighting Force* (*Marruecos: diario íntimo de una bandera* – a 'bandera' being the basic unit of the Legion) and in the many articles on the Moroccan war which he published in a variety of military journals. *The Inside Story of a Fighting Force* was a diary of the Foreign Legion's operations from its arrival in Morocco in the autumn of 1920. The first part described the campaign around Tetuan until July 1921; the second, activities in Melilla immediately after the Annoual débâcle and until April 1922.

It would be wrong to classify Franco's *Inside Story* as a political work. It hardly mentioned the author's future obsessions – communism, freemasonry and political parties. But under the austere technical and direct language of a campaign diary the book concealed some important revelations. It was a celebration of military and nationalist values and a defence of Spain's Moroccan war. Franco suggested by implication that to discard the ideals of heroism, valour and patriotism would lead irremediably to Spain's undoing.

At the very moment when Madrid seemed to be considering making Morocco a protectorate under civilian administration, Franco was arguing that the pacification of the Moroccan Protectorate would be impossible without armed sanctions and that force had to be applied by an army suitably encouraged and equipped by a committed government and public. That was why in his *Inside Story* he decried the indifference with which the nation beheld the 'sacrifice' of the army and its officers; he even rejected the creation of a colonial army separate from that of metropolitan Spain, as was favoured in some circles within the service. Franco could see that Morocco was the best training ground for the Spanish army. He wanted it to be schooled there and he believed that to combine civilian rule in the Protectorate with an exclusively colonial army would lead to 'a very dangerous erosion' of military morale. While war correspondents, writers and politicians were presenting the Moroccan war as damaging the armed forces for the sake of futile or shabby objectives, and while a campaign to apportion blame for the Annoual disaster was being mounted at home and in both houses of the *Cortes* – the Spanish parliament – Franco drew attention to the war's great importance to the army and dedicated his book as an epic of the heroism and valour of the Legion.[5]

Thoroughly identified with the African cause, Franco was naturally opposed to the 'Army Committees' (*juntas militares*). These resembled unionized groups of army officers on the home front and first appeared in 1917. Their influence on politics was a decisive factor in the growing crisis of the liberal monarchy which led to General Primo de Rivera's coup d'état of 13 September 1923. They were against promotion on grounds of active service – what in English is called a brevet rank – and would have preferred civilian rule in Morocco.

For the same reason, Franco also opposed the policy of retrenchment and withdrawal which Primo de Rivera initially espoused on his assumption of power in 1923 and which took effect in operations like the evacuation of Xaven in 1924. Franco took various opportunities to let his superiors know his views. In an incident which says a great deal about him, he told Primo de Rivera of them to his face. On 19 July 1924, at a meal at the Legion's camp at Ben Tieb – in the Melilla area, not far from Annoual –

Franco explained to the dictator the officer corps' distaste for planned withdrawals. When Primo de Rivera replied by demanding 'iron discipline' from the army in Africa, one of the officers present – the future General Varela – shouted out his disagreement. The atmosphere was fraught with tension and the meal broke up quickly. Franco took the responsibility for his officer's conduct. The incident went no further and relations between the dictator and the commander of the Legion returned to normal at a further meeting held a few days later at Melilla. But the episode had shown that Franco was not just the 'modest, naïve and straightforward' writer of the *Inside Story* – to quote the comment of a Madrid newspaper:[6] his terse speech and sparing gestures were supported by great willpower, which could be asserted defiantly on behalf of what he believed should be done.

His passion for the African cause had a clear formative influence on the way Franco perceived Spanish politics in his day. He was consistently hostile to the liberal and constitutional monarchy that prevailed in Spain between 1876 and 1923, although he never said so explicitly before the Civil War. He blamed the monarchy for the loss of 'the greatest fragments of our homeland', as he said in Barcelona in January 1942, referring to the defeat of 1898 and the loss of Cuba, Puerto Rico and the Philippines. He regarded the '98 war as an act of treason by civilian rulers against the army and believed that, with more resources, the war could have been won. He was convinced that nineteenth-century liberalism had precipitated Spain's decline. As he said on 13 July 1960 when he unveiled a monument to Calvo Sotelo (the leader of the Spanish right assassinated on the eve of the Civil War) the history of the nineteenth century was that of a 'sordid and degraded Spain, degenerate in spirit, incapable of retaining the leadership of an empire or of supporting the weight of a glorious tradition.' The century that ran from 1833 to 1931 was one which Franco would have liked to expunge from the national record.

Franco's hostility to liberalism was a basic defining feature of his idea of what Spain was and of his political notions. It was a conviction from which he never wavered and which he voiced repeatedly throughout his forty years as head of state. For instance, as late as 17 November 1967, inaugurating a session of the *Cortes* he again pointed out the familiar record: between 1833 and 1868 there had been 41 governments, 2 civil wars, 2 regencies, 3 constitutions and 15 military insurrections; between 1868 and 1902 there had been a further 27 administrations, 2 monarchies, a republic and one civil war and the remnants of Spain's empire had been lost; and in the reign of Alfonso XIII (1902–31) Spain had experienced another 29 governments, while two prime ministers had been assassinated and various revolutionary threats had arisen.

He thought Alfonso XIII had been a distinguished king, but felt that he had erred in 1930–31, first in dismissing Primo de Rivera and then again in not calling in the army to resolve the subsequent crisis. The conservative populist Antonio Maura was the only politician of the entire restoration period (1876–1923) who Franco sympathized with. Evidently, he understood neither how liberal politics worked nor what a parliamentary and constitutional system was. He saw liberalism as politics without the authority, unity and continuity which, he thought, were vital for effective government.[7]

Franco must therefore have contemplated Primo de Rivera's putsch of 13 September 1923 with satisfaction, even though, like the rest of the army in Africa, he recoiled from the dictator's early strategy of withdrawals. When this was reversed in 1925, Franco served the regime loyally until Primo de Rivera's fall in 1930 and the proclamation of the Second Republic on 14 April 1931. He did so in the significant capacity of head of the General Military Academy of Saragossa – an institution which had been created anew in 1927, having been closed down in 1893 – to which he was appointed on 4 January 1928.

Franco steered clear of all political áctivity and, of course, of all conspiracies against the dictatorship, although these soon attracted the prominent participation of his younger brother Ramón, the flying ace who became a popular idol in 1926 after piloting the *Plus Ultra* to Buenos Aires from Palos, Columbus's departure point near Moguer. When asked by a journalist in 1926 if he had any political views, Franco replied simply, 'I'm a professional soldier.'[8] As such, he would always remember General Primo de Rivera and his regime with pronounced sympathy. He considered that during the seven years of the dictatorship, peace, order and progress had prevailed; the General had pacified Morocco and had sought greatness and new vitality for Spain.[9] Franco would, however, later voice certain reservations which had probably not yet been formulated in the dictator's time but which may have taken shape subsequently, when Franco was thinking about the structure of his own regime: Primo de Rivera, after all, had not abolished the liberal constitution of 1876 and had not created a new political order. And Franco even deduced a further lesson: the dual leadership of king and dictator, which had continued from 1923 to 1930, had been instrumental in the failure of the dictatorship.

As a soldier in Africa, Franco had not only been brave and efficient but also tough and decisive. He would later remind his cousin of how he ordered the shooting of a legionary who had not shown proper respect for a superior officer in connection with some minor mealtime irritation.[10] At the Saragossa Military Academy, he introduced a traditional concept of the army, which stressed – as ideal values for the cadets – patriotism, arduous training, rigorous discipline, chivalrous behaviour, and the virtues of duty, responsibility, self-denial, valour and sacrifice.[11]

As Director of the Academy, he was already an anti-communist and a conservative. At Saragossa, he subscribed to a periodical, published in Geneva, on Comintern affairs and became convinced that communism was already at work in Spain.[12] In the 1933 general election he voted for the CEDA (*Confederación Española de Derechas Autónomas*) the electoral confederation of Catholic parties led by José María Gil Robles. As well as an anti-communist and a conservative, Franco was becoming increasingly religious, something he had not been when young: in the Legion he had been known as the man who was three Ms short: fear (*miedo*), women (*mujeres*) and Mass (*misa*).

This change owed a great deal to his marriage, on 22 October 1923, to Carmen Polo Martínez Valdés. Marriage brought Franco emotional stability, for he was a man of apparent sexual austerity who was not known to have had other than entirely innocent relationships. Furthermore, because the Polo family was relatively well off, Franco found that his social ambitions were advanced. At Saragossa, he was already a practising Catholic and, what was of greater political significance, he now believed that the Catholic faith had been 'the formative feature of Spanish nationhood', as he said at the presentation of credentials by the papal nuncio on 24 June 1938.

On the eve of the Second Republic, Franco was a professional soldier who had scarcely uttered a single political idea in public. Political matters seem to have caught his attention after his return from Africa, although he was to claim much later that his concern for social issues had begun in 1917, when he was stationed in Oviedo and observed the unrest of August of that year. (Despite his later claims he took no part in the suppression of this unrest.)

Franco, however, could hardly fail to notice what was happening in Spain – both because of the job he was doing and because of the particular crisis of 1930–31. To judge from what he said later, Franco believed that Alfonso XIII acted unfairly in dismissing Primo de Rivera on 29 January 1930. He thought it was a mistake to appoint General Damaso Berenguer to head the new government in Primo's place, because Berenguer's position was highly vulnerable – public opinion had singled him out as chiefly to blame for the Annoual disaster of 1921, when he had been High Commissioner of the military government in Morocco and Commander-in-Chief of the Spanish forces. Finally, Franco believed that Alfonso XIII should not have handed over power as he did on 14 April 1931. He felt that the monarchy rather than republicanism had won the elections of 12 April – the local elections on which Alfonso had staked his crown – and that the army was united and ready to defend the throne, and would indeed have done so had the Commander-in-Chief of the Civil Guard, General Sanjurjo, given the command.[14]

From all that has been said it was entirely predictable that Franco viewed the proclamation of the Second Republic with extreme suspicion. He submitted to the new regime and served it in positions of responsibility which have already been mentioned; but he never fully endorsed the new state of affairs. 'I never gave a cheer for the Republic,' he told his cousin in May 1964, 'not even when I was in command of the Army of Africa, appointed by Lerroux's republican government. I always refrained from uttering "Long live the Republic!" when I felt nothing of the sort in my heart.'[15]

Indeed, after the proclamation of the Republic on 14 April, he neither struck the royal standard nor hoisted the republican tricolour over the Military Academy until ordered to do so in writing by the new republican authorities on 20 April. The following day, after rumours that the new regime was going to make him military governor of Morocco, Franco published a letter (dated 18 April) in the daily newspaper *ABC* in which he denied the rumours and stressed the loyalty with which he had served the monarchy: 'The provisional government cannot have contemplated any such thing,' he wrote, 'nor would I have felt able to accept any position, which could in any sense be construed either as signifying approval on my part of the newly introduced system of government or as evidence of any tepidity or reserve whatsoever in the performance of my duties or in the allegiance which I owed and performed to those who, until yesterday, represented, in their persons, the Spanish nation under the monarchy.'

It was a letter of undeniable courage and dignity – for Franco could have stayed quiet or, like many others, come to terms with the new situation – and it clearly marked him out as a dissident from the new regime. This was emphasized shortly afterwards, on 14 July 1931, when he took his leave of the cadets of the Saragossa Military Academy, which had been closed by government decree a few days before. His farewell speech was harsh and bitter; after praising the work done at the Academy and the martial virtues inculcated there, he appealed for discipline in obeying even capricious and incorrect orders – an unmistakeable allusion to the republican government's decision to close the Academy. Moreover, Franco ended by calling for three cheers for Spain in order to avoid mentioning the republic: this was to imply a significant distinction. The War Minister, Manuel Azaña, asked his advisers to study the speech to see if it contained any indictable material. He even signed a warrant for the General's arrest, which remained on file until Franco was appointed, by Azaña himself, to command the XVth Infantry Brigade and the garrison of Corunna.

From then on, Franco, though hostile to the republic, served it obediently until 18 July 1936. He did not want to take advantage of Azaña's reforms, which allowed serving officers to retire into the reserve without loss of emoluments. Franco preferred to follow his profession. Only in 1933 did he seem to hesitate when he was offered the chance of standing in the general election as a CEDA candidate. In the end, however, he did not accept. He remained at his post in Corunna until February 1933; in the same year he was appointed to a new command at a higher rank as Captain General of the Balearic Islands, a move he regarded as a kick upstairs.

Franco had nothing to do with the failed coup attempt on 10 August 1932 by pro-monarchists under General Sanjurjo, his old chief from the days in Africa. Undoubtedly, however, he must have been sounded out. He had lunch with Sanjurjo in Corunna on 13 July, when the conspiracy was already under way. Later, towards the end of the month, he went to Madrid ostensibly to choose a regulation mount, and had a meeting there with Sanjurjo and Generals Varela and Goded, who were also involved in the coup. He told them candidly that they could not rely on him for support in any sort of military plot. Franco was later to claim that he did not even consider rising against the republic until he became aware of a slide towards communism in 1936. On 10 August 1932 Franco was at his post in Corunna, although to his great indignation he was linked by rumour to the conspirators, and Azaña warned the state security agency to keep a close watch on him because he was regarded as 'the most dangerous' general of all.

The events of 18 July 1936 were to prove that Azaña was not far wrong in his view. In the immediate circumstances, however, he was mistaken. Nor did Franco join the Spanish Army League (*Unión Militar Española* – UME). This secret organization of monarchists in the army was created at the end of 1932 and was at the centre of a series of plots (of which Franco was kept informed).

Franco was even unwilling to defend Sanjurjo in the trial at which his former chief was arraigned, though the latter asked him to do so. What is more, Franco's response reveals the chilling side of his character, which was becoming increasingly apparent. It seems that he told Sanjurjo, on visiting him in prison, 'I have to tell you that in my view, your insurrection and its failure have won you the right to die.'[16]

The centre-right's triumph in the elections of November 1933 helped Franco's military career. The successive governments of the so-called 'two black years' of 1934–36, all grouped around Lerroux's Radical Party (*Partido Radical*) with the support of Gil Robles's CEDA, reversed the defence policy which had been followed since 1931. To pilot the new course they relied on the African veterans whom Azaña had dismissed to the sidelines in the previous two years. Franco, in particular, was made a divisional general as early as March 1934, while continuing for the time being at his post in the Balearics. A friendly relationship grew up between him and the radical War Minister of January–November 1934, Diego Hidalgo, whom he met in February of that year in Madrid. It was a particularly distressing time for Franco, who had just lost his mother. Hidalgo at once formed an extremely favourable impression of Franco and of his military opinions and sought his counsel. When a rebellion, provoked by CEDA's admission to the government, broke out at dawn on 5 October, organized by the socialists and the Catalan left, and centred in the mining districts of Asturias and in Barcelona, Hidalgo called Franco in to act as his adviser.

It was Franco, in effect, who directed operations against the Asturian miners from the War Ministry in Madrid, with no other title than that of adviser to the minister. The result was the defeat of the rebellion in a pincer movement which started from Galicia, Santander and León to converge on Oviedo, the chief city of Asturias, using naval units and troops from Africa under the command of General López Ochoa. It was all over in little more than a week.

This episode set the seal on Franco's character for good. He did not see his role as an act of service to the republic – much less as a defence of democracy and constitutionalism. Not for a moment did he pause to consider the reasons which impelled the workers of Asturias to rebellion – reasons which included, no doubt, the fear that the state would gradually yield ground to fascism. Since 21 June 1934 he had been enrolled in the *Entente Internationale Anticommuniste*, and he saw the Asturian rising as an attempted communist revolution; all he knew or wanted to know was that the left and the Catalanists, who had decreed a short-lived Catalan Republic, were acting outside the law. In a note in the archives, Franco was to write that the Asturian and Catalan rebellion opened the eyes of the officer corps. In his own case, at any rate, the effect was to confirm his existing prejudices and convictions. It did one thing more for him: it made him the top general in the army and the favourite of the Spanish right. Evidence that this was happening was the letter written to him a few days before the outbreak of the revolt, on 24 September, by José Antonio Primo de Rivera, leader of the Falange – the Spanish edition of European Fascism – warning him of what was about to happen and inviting him to give some thought to the imminent danger.[17]

No doubt Franco thought that the army had saved Spain from revolution. The government decorated him with the Grand Cross of Military Merit and on 15 February 1935 appointed him to command the army in Morocco. But Franco was to spend only three months in Africa. In May, when CEDA and the Radicals formed a new government with Lerroux as Prime Minister and José María Gil Robles as Minister of War, Franco returned to Spain to take up the most prestigious job in the army: Chief of the Central General Staff. He would spend the next ten months in the job, until new elections in February 1936 brought the Popular Front to power.

Franco, who teamed up in the ministry with other African veterans unreconciled to the republic – men like Generals Fanjul, Goded and Mola – did his job in a thoroughly professional and technical fashion. His main concern was to revitalize the armed forces, to procure new equipment, to improve training, to modernize the coastal defences and airstrips and to foster war industries. He remained on the sidelines of political life, save in so far as he belonged to a ministry headed by the most representative member of the Catholic right, Gil Robles, with whose work Franco was thoroughly identified. Not once, however, did he comment on the political position in Spain as he saw it.[18]

It was obvious enough that the formation of the Popular Front in particular, worried him – the coalition of the entire Spanish left, from Azaña to the communists, organized to fight the elections of February 1936. Franco failed to see the Popular Front for what it really was: an electoral alliance called into being by factors in domestic politics and based on the Socialist and left Republican parties. From reading the newsletters of the *Entente Internationale Anticommuniste* Franco got the impression that the Popular Front was a Spanish version of an international communist manoeuvre inspired by the Soviet Union: this may have been true as far as the Communist Party's adherence to the Front was concerned, but was not true for the other participants.

Despite his concern, Franco does not seem to have taken any clear or firm decision on what ought to be done. Although he very probably did talk over the possibility of intervention by the army with his colleagues in the ministry (Fanjul, Mola and Goded, who was at the heart of every anti-republican plot), Franco was still, at the end of 1935 and early in 1936, in favour of respecting the legality of the republic. In December 1935, for instance, when with Gil Robles's consent, Fanjul (Under-Secretary of War at the time) asked him about the possibility of a coup in response to the refusal of the President of the Republic to allow CEDA to form a government, Franco denounced against the idea; he had done the same on a similar occasion when Fanjul and Goded had approached him a year previously in November 1934.

Yet, obviously Franco was to some extent privy to what was being planned. He himself told Major Antonio Barroso, Spain's military attaché in Paris, when they travelled to London together in January 1936 for George v's funeral, which Franco was to attend as Chief of Staff, that the army would have to be ready for the worst if the Popular Front won the elections; if he, Franco, were to leave for Africa, that would be a signal that a decision in favour of an uprising had been taken. On the other hand, Dr Gregorio Marañón, who saw Franco in Paris at about the same time, remained convinced that while he was afraid of a communist victory in the elections, Franco was not willing to go along with a coup d'état.[19]

This was borne out in a sense by the events of Sunday, 16 February 1936, when the electoral results confirmed that the Popular Front had won. In his alarm, Franco, still Chief of the Central General Staff, wanted the government of the centrist prime minister Portela Valladares, who had been in power since December of the previous year, to declare a state of war. He refused, however, to countenance an alternative suggestion from Generals Fanjul and Goded, supported this time by Rodríguez del Barrio, that he should sound out the feelings of the garrison in Madrid with a view to a possible initiative by the army without reference to the government. Franco was firmly in favour of declaring a state of war – something widely desired on the right – but wanted it to be done by the lawful head of government, Portela. This was his motive for meeting Portela on Monday, 17 February. He had already had an interview with General Molero, who was then Minister of War, and the head of the paramilitary Civil Guard, General Pozas, whose views were quite distinct from Franco's. When Portela suggested as a counter-proposal that the army alone, without the government, could take the action they wanted, Franco demurred.

And so it was, despite rumours that Franco and Goded were about to lead a military coup (categorically denied by Portela), that the leader of the Popular Front, Manuel Azaña, was able to form a government on 19 February 1936. Franco can have had few illusions about the future. Nevertheless, the new government appointed him to a post that was by no means negligible, as Captain General of the Canary Islands. Such was his alienation from the government of the Popular Front that Franco saw his new command as a kind of exile.

From about that time, the die was cast. On 8 March, before leaving for Tenerife, Franco had two meetings. The first was at the home of his brother-in-law, Ramón Serrano Suñer, with the Falangist leader, José Antonio Primo de Rivera: this proved counterproductive, as the two instantly disliked each other, and later, in April, Primo de Rivera would veto Franco's nomination as a candidate of the Right at a second round election in Cuenca. The other meeting was more important. It was held at the home of José Delgado y Hernández de Tejada, known as a CEDA man. Generals Mola, Orgaz, Fanjul, Varela, Kindelán, Saliquet, Villegas, Rodríguez del Barrio, Galarza and González Carrasco were there with Franco: Goded had left for his new command in the Balearic Islands a few days before. They agreed to have a plan of armed intervention ready, to be implemented only when they were certain of the absolute need. They must have been convinced that their moment had arrived by the end of April, when Mola took charge of the conspiracy that was to launch the insurrection of 18 July 1936.

Thus when he sailed from Cadiz on 10 March, Franco was a party to the military conspiracy. He probably never had any doubt of the army's moral, historical and quasi-constitutional right to step in to safeguard what the professional soldiers saw as the essential interests of the fatherland. Franco was a believer in an army-centred nationalism that saw the army as the defender of the nation's unity. In a letter to Gil Robles, dated 2 April 1937 and published in the nationalist organ, *El Diario de Burgos*, in the very midst of the war, Franco stated that the army 'has the right to rise up in a cause as sacred as that of the fatherland in peril.' 'It is not lawful,' declared Franco to the monarchist paper *ABC* in Seville on 19 July 1937, 'for the army to resort to arms against a party or a constitution just because it doesn't like them, but it has a clear duty of resistance in defence of a fatherland threatened with extinction.'

These were not mere excuses. Franco and many other Spanish

servicemen strongly believed what he was saying. He often recalled the doctrine in speeches he made as head of state. As late as 29 October 1970 he could still call the army 'the zealous guardian of the nation's conscience.' Franco, as a professional soldier nurtured in the military virtues such as obedience, discipline and honour, never absorbed the constitutionalist and democratic conception of the army's role as subservient to legally constituted authority. For Franco, the army had a duty to maintain an obedience of a higher order to the supposed essential and immutable nature of the fatherland.

If Franco failed to understand the liberal parliamentary regime of 1876–1923, much less did he grasp the reality of the Second Republic of 1931–1936. He saw it as a regime ill adapted to the character Spain had formed in the course of her history and, in consequence, as a system which had aggravated beyond endurance the processes that threatened Spain with disintegration. Franco called it a 'tragic' excess. 'The republic that lasted from 1931 to June 1936,' he later stated in a speech to the Cortes (on the occasion of the nomination of Prince Juan Carlos as his successor on 22 July 1969), 'combined all the instability, anarchy and indiscipline implied by its record: two presidents, 18 governments, a constitution frequently suspended, recurrent religious persecution, acts of arson against churches and religious houses, continual outbreaks of public disorder, communist infiltration, attempted separatism in two regions – a series of events which culminated in the murder, on the government's own orders, of the leader of the parliamentary opposition, Señor Calvo Sotelo.' Franco never uttered a single generous or understanding word about the republic, apart from such justice as there may have been in his account of its shortcomings. He was utterly insensible, if not actually hostile, to the democratic values which the republic represented, and incapable of appreciating the deep sense of history and of morality which inspired the ambitious programme of reform that republicans wanted to carry out in freedom and democracy.

In the spring of 1936, Franco's immediate anxieties were taking a different turn. He had none of the optimism of his fellow-conspirators and was afraid that the army would fail to act in unison – as, indeed, happened – and that the government would act to abort the plot. He doubted whether the garrisons of Madrid, Barcelona and Valencia would join the uprising and must have feared, for this reason and others, that the conspiracy would trigger off a long and hard-fought civil war. This was why, as late as 23 June 1936 – in spite of the fact that on 11 June Mola, Kindelán and Jorge Vigón had agreed on how to transfer Franco to Africa to take command of the colonial army – Franco wrote a letter to the prime minister, Casares Quiroga. The very act of writing the letter was surprising, because it seems unusual for a general involved in a conspiracy to warn the government – as Franco did – about the discontent and ill feeling in the army. The content was surprising too, because of the calculated ambiguity with which it was written. No reader could be sure whether it was intended as an ultimatum or as a last gesture of reconciliation. On the one hand, the writer warned that the state of the army was highly dangerous, and, on the other, said that the army was not implacably opposed to republicanism. He gave it as his opinion that divisions within the armed forces threatened 'future civil conflict' but argued that this could readily be avoided by a calm and just policy. Franco seemed to be threatening the government with dire consequences if it took any unreasonable and violent steps against the leaders of the military malcontents; yet at the same time he offered a helping hand by urging consultations with non-political generals and officers 'known for their love of the army': among them, no doubt, though he did not say so, he included himself.

Even so, by that time Franco had consented to the uprising and Mola was in a position to confirm this to Fanjul on 6 July. The day before, the proprietor of *ABC*, Juan Luca de Tena, had ordered his paper's correspondent in London, Luis Bolín, to hire a plane, a de Havilland Dragon, to be in Casablanca on 12 July and Las Palmas on the 15th; Franco was to use it to transfer from Las Palmas to Tetuán on the 18th. Meanwhile, on 13 July, the assassination of the leader of the opposition, José Calvo Sotelo, precipitated events. On 17 July, at one o'clock in the afternoon, the garrison of Melilla rebelled; Colonel Solans took charge of the stronghold 'in the name of Franco'. Soon afterwards, Yagüe took control of Ceuta, and Colonels Sáenz de Buruaga, Asensio Cabanillas and Beigbeder took Tetuán.

Franco, who had gone from Tenerife to Las Palmas on the 16th, signed the orders for the uprising at 1 am on 18 July. The Madrid government (now led by Diego Martíjnez Barrio of the Radical Party after Casares Quiroga, incapable of meeting the crisis, resigned in sudden despair) may have expected to contrive some sort of compromise with the rebel generals, along the usual lines of the nineteenth-century *pronunciamientos*. Such hopes, however, were dashed before nine o'clock that morning by General Mola's uprising in Pamplona. At 1 pm on the 18th Franco left Las Palmas in the Dragon, slept in Casablanca and arrived in Tetuán at

7 am on the 19th. There he assumed command of the army of Africa.

By 1936 Franco's character showed the traits that would remain with him throughout his life. He was held to be a cold man, remote, reserved, distrustful, cautious, yet at the same time courteous with polished manners and an occasional pleasant conversationist who even had some sense of humour. He was a proud man, although he did not seem so, thoughtful and unlikely to take a decision without mature consideration, a process which could sometimes absorb a good deal of time, so that by the end of the process his real opinion was sometimes concealed. As has been seen, he was a professional soldier with a high reputation, but he can hardly be said to have fitted the charismatic mould. He was very short (1.64 metres), a poor public speaker afflicted by a piping voice, and by 1936 he no longer had the slight, lithe frame of his years in the Legion but showed a tendency to put on fat, which deprived him of presence. The German admiral, Wilhelm Canaris, who was his country's secret service expert on Spain, told Hitler that Franco 'was no hero to look at, but a short little man'. Don Juan de Borbón, the pretender to the throne, said after an interview with Franco in August 1948, that nothing about him seemed lively or shrewd 'except for his eyes'.

Franco had taken his time in siding with the uprising against the republic. When he did so, he justified his action and that of the army by classifying a soldiers' coup against a legally constituted regime as a 'national rising' – an expression he used from the outset – in self-defence against what he saw as a combination of anarchy, public disorder, attacks on the honour of the army, the destruction of national unity, disrespect for the laws and institutions of government and communist infiltration. All these appeared in his address to the Spanish people, released in Las Palmas at 1 am on the morning of 18 July but written in Tenerife two days before.

The first job was to destroy the republic. Neither Franco nor his comrades in arms had any settled plans about the type of state or political system they would erect after victory. In an attempt to resolve the differences they had among themselves, Franco proposed at their preparatory meetings that their movement should be simply 'pro-Spanish and pro-Catholic'. Probably they all had in mind some period – variously long or short – of army rule, after the model of Primo de Rivera's dictatorship. Franco was always worried that the failure of Sanjurjo's rising of 1932 would be repeated. He knew that, in any insurrection, an officer's life and career were on the line. He was afraid that civil war would break

out and, if so, that it would be excessively long. He was unsure of
his own prospective role in the military power structure that might
emerge from a successful rebellion. At the outset, it was General
Sanjurjo, in exile in Portugal, who was, at least nominally, to be
charged with the leadership of the generals' movement, even
though he had played no part in preparing it.

For the time being, Franco was back in Africa from 19 July 1936.
His return tended to confirm what Ortega y Gasset had said about
Morocco in *Invertebrate Spain*: that the war had 'gathered the
scattered fragments of army morale in a fist clenched and raised
for the punch'. As Franco told the journalist, Manuel Aznar, on 1
January 1939, 'Without Africa, I wouldn't have been able to begin to
understand myself'.

2
Caudillo of Spain

On 27 April 1968 Franco explained to his cousin and colleague from his days in Africa, Lieutenant-General Francisco Franco Salgado-Araujo, that, as 18 July 1936 approached, it was his belief that 'a professional solder who turns his weapons against his lawful government can expect no right to pardon or pity and must therefore be ready to fight on to the end.'[1]

That was what happened in his own case. Franco took arms in the summer of 1936 against a lawful government and continued his fight against it to the bitter end, until final victory, which was not attained until 1 April 1939. As he had feared, the rising had initially succeeded only in parts of Spain: in the Canary Islands, Morocco, Galicia, Old Castile and León, Navarre, Álava, the three main cities of Aragon, western Andalusia and the provinces of Cordova and Granada, with their chief cities, the Balearic Islands (except Minorca), Cadiz and a few isolated cities such as Oviedo. In the rest of the country it had failed: Asturias, Santander, Vizcaya, Guipúzcoa, Catalonia, the Valencia region, eastern Andalusia, Murcia, Albacete, Badajoz, Minorca and New Castile. The armed services and security forces had split almost down the middle. Officers of known sympathies had been shot on both sides in the opening phase of the conflict. Of the rebels, Fanjul and Goded, among others, were shot, while of generals loyal to the republic, the same fate befell Núñez de Prado, Batet, Campins – Franco's old colleague at the Saragossa Academy – and Romerales. The Civil War became inevitable and irreversible. For Franco, the war was to bring, among other things, his elevation to supreme command and head of state – *Caudillo* or leader was his favourite and official designation – in the rebel zone, soon called the 'national' zone. On his investiture, on 1 October 1936, Franco became responsible for military and political affairs in 'national' Spain. His objective was twofold: to win the war and to construct a new state.

As far as the war was concerned, Franco had overall strategic control of all the operations of the nationalist forces. The responsibility went far beyond the experience he had built up in Morocco and during the suppression of the Austrian revolt in 1934. How Franco's conduct of the war should be judged will soon emerge. But it may be useful to point out at the start the main features that Franco was to display as a strategist: he proved to be cautious, ponderous, opposed to improvization, full of admiration for the French army and its methods, pre-occupied accordingly with logistics and positional warfare, hostile to the establishment of excessively long battle-fronts, always keen to concentrate his forces at strategic points with strong cover of their lines of communication, and therefore little inclined to the mechanized warfare of rapid movement which, because of new weaponry and technology, would be favoured by the younger generation of European officers in the 1930s and was put into practice by the Germans and Italians in the Second World War.

In its broad outlines, the strategy of the rebel generals was based on a joint attack on Madrid by the armies of the north, led by General Mola, and those of Morocco and the south, led by Franco. This division of the command was decided on 25 July by the National Defence Council (*Junta de Defensa Nacional*), which had been formed in Burgos the previous day by all the major figures in the uprising except Franco, who was only brought into the Junta on 30 July.[2]

At the time of this decision, Franco was sitting in Morocco with 47,127 men of the best fighting force in the nationalist armies – the army of Africa – under his command. The strategy adopted meant that he had to get them across the straits of Gibraltar immediately. He had neither 'planes nor ships'. 60–65% of air force personnel had sided with the republic, together with most of the navy. Franco therefore took a crucial decision, and asked for permission to get transport planes from Germany and fighters and bombers from Italy. In other words, he advocated calling on Europe's totalitarian powers for help. The response was favourable. On 29 July the first German Junkers arrived in Morocco and the next day the first Italian fighters followed. In July and August alone, Franco was able to take some 10,500 men over to Andalusia and on 7 August 1936 he set up his headquarters in Seville.

Franco had called on what he expected to be the most effective potential sources of help; in this he agreed with Mola, who had made similar overtures without success. Any ideological sympathy he may have had with Hitler or Mussolini existed only in a highly modified form, but his choice was nevertheless politically significant. Franco knew that only totalitarian dictatorships like Nazi Germany, Fascist Italy and the corporatist Portugal of Salazar would uphold a military insurrection against a democratic regime such as the Second Spanish Republic. He took his decision in full awareness of what he was doing and in the full knowledge that the consequences would colour, in various ideological, political, economic and diplomatic ways, the future of the regime which would have to be created in the course of the war and after the victory.

Once on the mainland of Spain, the armies of Morocco and of the south carried out their appointed task – the march on Madrid – with spectacular and unexpected speed and efficiency, in contrast to fate of the army of the north, detained at Somosierra in the mountains of Madrid from the end of July. Franco was criticized for approaching Madrid via Extremadura instead of by the most direct route through Cordova, Ciudad Real and Toledo. But by 3 September 1936, when Franco's columns under Yagüe, Asensio Cabanillas, Castejón, Barrón and Tella arrived at Talavera de la Reina, the criticisms were forgotten and Franco's prestige manifestly strengthened. They had covered 500 km in a month, capturing Llerena, Almendralejo, Zafra, Mérida and Badjoz on the way. Nowhere, save at Badjoz, did the republican forces seem to have any idea of how to put up effective resistance or exploit their advantage in the air; they did nothing except retreat slowly, though this did not detract from the acclaim the rebel general enjoyed.

By 22 September, Franco was in Maqueda (province of Toledo), where he took his next controversial decision – controversial, at least, to General Kindelán, his air force chief, and Colonel Yagüe, commander of the assault corps who was removed from his command for his dissent and replaced by General José Enrique Varela. The decision was to relieve Toledo, where Colonel Moscardó with several hundred soldiers, Civil Guards and civilians had been besieged since July in the ancient fortress of the Alcázar. The alternative would have been a determined attack on Madrid. Varela's men took Toledo on 27 September; but the detour may well have prejudiced the chances of a successful march against the capital. Franco's choice fell on Toledo for reasons which combined propaganda objectives with symbolic and sentimental motives: Toledo was a city of considerable fame all over the world; the republicans had invested a great deal of effort in suppressing resistance there; the Alcázar housed the Infantry Academy, where most officers on both sides, including Franco, had studied; and Toledo had a peculiar importance in Spanish history as an ancient 'capital' and primatial see. Propaganda would soon turn the story of Toledo's resistance into a legendary saga. With the raising of the siege of the Alcázar Franco scored a point of enormous publicity value which he exploited cleverly.

It happened at a momentous time. The nationalist generals were about to take a final decision on the unification of command and, therefore, on the nature of the political power to be exercised in the 'national' zone. The problem had remained unresolved since 18 July. Sanjurjo, the nominal head of the generals' movement, had been killed on 20 July in a plane crash en route from Cascaes in Portugal for Spain. On 24 July the National Defence Council had been formed in Burgos, with General Miguel Cabanellas as chairman; by the end of September, all the important generals on the nationalist side belonged to it. But the junta had been called into being amid an air of temporary expediency – or, at least, without being thought of as the raw material of a new state. It had done nothing to resolve the problem which most concerned its original members: how to ensure united control of the war effort.

This was the problem addressed in September 1936. Franco and Mola – the visible leaders of the generals' movement, had probably discussed it at meetings held at Seville and Burgos in mid-August and subsequently at Cáceres. Franco seemed the best qualified, even the obvious candidate. He enjoyed exceptional prestige on account of his time in Africa and at the Saragossa Academy; his rank was higher than, for example, Mola's; the consistency of his public stance was incomparably greater than that of say another possible candidate, General Queipo de Llano, renowned as a soldier but mercurial in his politics. Franco's claims were also supported by the quality of his victories since 18 July (here the capture of Toledo was of some importance since it balanced Mola's success in taking San Sebastián on 13 September); and the importance of the armies of Morocco and the south in the make-up of the nationalist forces counted for a great deal. Franco had, furthermore, taken charge of the war effort and of foreign relations from the start in his sphere of operations; foreign negotiators seem to have treated with him accordingly and accepted him as supreme commander, as did some of the media, some of his army colleagues and the people of many of the cities and towns captured by his troops. Even the republicans gave him a higher profile than his fellow rebels, by making him the main target of their counter-propaganda.

Thus the decision the leaders of the rising took at their conclaves at the air force base of Salamanca on 21 and 28 September came as no surprise. Franco was named 'Generalissimo of the

National Forces' on land, sea and air and 'Head of Government of the Spanish State' in the words of the decree promulgated by the junta on 29 September 1936. It was unsurprising and it caused no serious dissent or opposition, even though those present at the Salamanca meetings may not have liked everything that had happened.

Franco's chief supporter was General Kindelán, and his only opponent was the chairman of the junta, the veteran General Cabanellas, who knew Franco from Africa and on that basis preferred a collective system of command. Mola, whose opinion could have been decisive, confined himself merely to expressing concurrence in Franco's appointment.

The demonstration organized on 27 September in celebration of the relief of Toledo and glorification of Franco, at Cáceres, where Franco's headquarters had been located since 26 August, cannot have given his electors much pleasure. Nor did the orchestration by Franco's men (his brother Nicolás and Colonel Yagüe) of an elaborate ceremonial in Franco's honour, involving Falangists, Carlists and soldiers, in Salamanca itself to coincide with the decisive meeting on Monday, 28 September. Both operations were designed to put pressure on the junta to force through Franco's nomination. This seemed to run counter to the impression Kindelán had gathered from the future dictator, whom he had found initially unwilling to accept supreme command. The reluctance was probably genuine. But once Franco had made his decision, he demanded and obtained not only control of the war, which no one seems to have sought to deny him, but also investiture with all the powers of the new state, without any limitations. Kindelán had wanted Franco to take on the headship of state just for the duration of the war probably hoping that this would be no more than an interval preceding the restoration of the monarchy. Yet in the final text of the decree, drawn up by friends of Franco, no restrictions of any sort appeared.[3]

Thus Franco became head of state on 1 October 1936, at the Captain General's Residence at Burgos, after a short ceremony at which the chairman of the junta handed over his powers. A year later, on 25 November 1937, he would tell the correspondent of the Japanese paper *Asahi* that he would resign as soon as his mission was accomplished. 'I shall retire to the country to resume family life in peace.'[4] In view of what was to happen, one might think this was a cynical joke on the general's part, yet Franco was not being consciously ironical when he said, as he often did, that political life had no appeal for him. He even came to believe that the headship of state was a responsibility and a duty conferred upon him for reasons that transcended his own wishes. In any case, he never admitted that his mission was over: he died, still in office as head of state, on 20 November 1975.

From 1 October 1936 Franco possessed absolute power, though it is doubtful whether he had any clear idea of what to do with it. Since 18 July he had uttered or issued in public a fair number of proclamations, speeches and statements. These amounted to little more than a series of patriotic harangues in the military tradition of no very exact political content save what might be inferred from Franco's repeated definition of the army's rebellion as a 'national movement' and a 'crusade' – almost in a religious sense – against communism and in favour of the greatness of Spain. On 15 August he had raised the old red-and-gold flag in Seville, but it would be imprudent to read any explicit political programme into that gesture: Franco held the flag to be that of the nation, rather than the monarchy. He appeared somewhat less vague in his early statements to the press. He declared to the Portuguese journalist, Leopoldo Nunes of *O Seculo*, again on 15 August 1936, that he would introduce 'a brief military dictatorship', after which the military men would invite others to take part. 'The business of government,' he said, 'will be entrusted to experts, not to politicians, with the aim of giving the nation the organic structure, properly Spanish in character, which is absolutely essential'. He used similar language to Luigi Bargina of *Il Popolo d'Italia*: he was going, he said, to give Spain 'a strong government, a well organized, modern dictatorship'.[5]

Franco apparently had the model of Primo de Rivera's dictatorship in mind or, at any rate, a system similar to the Portuguese 'new state' of Oliveira Salazar, which appealed to Franco's sensibilities in a number of ways. Thus on 26 October he appointed a 'Technical Council of Government' (*Junta técnica de gobierno*), rather than a cabinet of ministers, summoning men of proven professional competence and little political significance, some of whom had worked with Primo de Rivera.[6] At the suggestion of his brother Nicolás, who worked as his political secretary, he also gave some thought to the problem of creating a political organization in which to integrate the various forces which had combined in the rising of 18 July: the Falange, the Carlists, the Alfonsine monarchists and the Catholics. He said as much to the German Counsellor from the Lisbon embassy on 6 October 1936 at a reception in Salamanca, where Franco had taken up residence in the bishop's palace at the time of his installation as head of state.

The speech Franco made in a broadcast on 1 October 1936 to

mark his investiture as head of state contained more politically significant material than all his previous pronouncements put together. For the first time, Franco spoke of how the new state was to be organized. He said that it would take shape 'within a broadly totalitarian framework'; he affirmed 'the adoption of the most rigorous standards of authority'; he emphasized that regional peculiarities would be respected, but only in the service of 'uncompromising national unity' and that municipalities would be reorganized along centralist lines; he took the opportunity to rule out democratic forms of participation and indicated that the national will would be expressed through 'vocational and corporate bodies' organized on a national basis; he rejected class-based trade unionism, but looked forward to social measures designed to guarantee wages and workers' benefits and perpetuate the progress that had already been made; he added a few generalities about support for small farmers and economic co-operation with other nations, except the Soviet Union, with which he ruled out any sort of contact; and finally, he hoped for a concordat with the Catholic Church, with the proviso that the state would have to remain non-confessional.[7]

Clearly, this was a revealing statement of principles, which his regime was to follow down to 1975 in many ways, but much was still left vague. Nothing was said about the structure of the state, nor the functions of government, nor the political order which would be adopted. No hint was given of what the institutions of the future would be, nor of the forms which the legislature and judiciary would take, nor was there any mention of whether any opposition parties would be permitted or of whether there would be a single party. It is likely that Franco had not thought or, at least, not decided about these matters. One thing which he seems to have been sure about from 1 October 1936 onwards was his determination to assume full personal responsibility in the exercise of the power conferred upon him and, from the very first moment, to take upon himself a personal and authoritarian (*Caudillista*) style of government, evidently inspired by totalitarian models. Soon enough, this would spawn an ill-controlled personality cult which accorded ill with the austerity and simplicity of Franco's conduct in his private life.

Franco also had at his disposal an important fund of ideological and political notions which would be particularly useful to him: the teaching and thought of the Catholic Church. Opposed by the anti-clerical spirit of the Second Republic, disadvantaged by its legislation and persecuted in the republican zone of the country (except for the Basque Country), the Church threw all its weight behind Franco. First came the pastoral letter of Bishops Olaechea of Pamplona and Múgica of Victoria on 6 August 1936, in which the rising was described as a movement 'of soldiers and civilians' in defence of the faith. Next was the pastoral letter of the Bishop of Salamanca, Enrique Pla y Deniel, on 30 September, the day before Franco's solemn investiture as head of state. Describing the war as 'a crusade for the faith, for the fatherland and for civilization', Pla y Deniel handed Franco the best propaganda argument which he had so far had at his disposal; at the same time, he provided an essential framework and terms of reference for Franco's future policies and régime. For Franco still had no clear plans for these in mind, and probably did not do so until his brother-in-law, Ramón Serrano Suñer was able to escape from Madrid and reach Salamanca: this was not until the end of February 1937. A few days earlier Franco had told the Italian ambassador, Roberto Cantalupo, 'The state I want to establish will be the opposite of what the Reds want.'[8] Probably, that was still one of the few things he was sure about.

On the military front his ideas were crystal clear.[9] Madrid remained the focal point of his strategy at least until spring 1937 though there were other ancillary objectives, and other fronts to concentrate on – and even after 1937 Franco did not give up on this main goal.

The assault on Madrid, which had already suffered occasional bombing raids, began in earnest at the beginning of October 1936, escalated appreciably in November and was called off on the 23rd of that month when Franco realized that a frontal attack on the city was impossible. The first phase of the offensive was well conceived: a triple enveloping manoeuvre from the Tagus and Toledo against Pozuelo, Alcorcón and Getafe, villages close to Madrid. The nationalists accomplished that stage of their plans by 6 November despite fierce resistance, greatly superior to what the army of Africa had met on its march through Extremadura to Toledo. On 6 November, the proximity of Franco's forces – Varela was already in Carabanchel and Villaverde was practically on the outskirts of Madrid – forced the republican government (headed by the socialist Largo Caballero since 4 September) to flee from Madrid for Valencia. The defence of the capital was left in the hands of a *junta*, chaired by General Miaja with Lieutenant-Colonel Vicente Rojo as Chief of General Staff.

The second phase of the assault – a frontal attack on Madrid through the Casa de Campo and the University Campus – was a mistake. The nationalists launched their attack at points where, thanks to the course of the River Manzanares, the terrain most favoured the defence. After heavy blows on every front and at every point of the battle, Franco's troops, led by his most favoured officers – Varela, Barrón, Asensio, Tella, Delgado Serrano – where thwarted at the Franceses Bridge. After Miaja had counter-attacked effectively on 19 November, Franco called a meeting of his generals at Leganés, where he acknowledged that the Madrid offensive had broken down and began to outline new plans to bring about the submission of the capital by other means. He did, however, leave a portion of his forces wedged against the Manzanares on a line that was not to change again until the end of the war.

The battle of Madrid had demonstrated a number of things: the republican forces evidently had greater potential in both attack and defence than had been supposed; victory was not going to be easy and would require a substantial programme of re-armament; the war was becoming effectively internationalized despite Franco-British efforts at non-intervention, and this was going to change the character of the fighting. Franco had continued to receive German and Italian equipment through the months from August to November and had used the planes, tanks and armoured cars against Madrid. The republic had received aircraft from France and, in and after October, when the communists had two portfolios in the Largo Caballero government, planes and tanks arrived from the Soviet Union. The planes took part in a great air battle over Madrid on 6 November and the tanks in the attempted counter-attacks at Seseña and Pinto, launched to halt the advance of Franco's columns.

From then onwards, foreign intervention escalated. In November, the Germans sent the Condor Legion of about a hundred planes piloted by Germans under German command, which joined the battle for Madrid as early as 18 November. Germany also put 5,000 advisers at Franco's disposal in the course of the war. The communists – albeit not entirely alone – raised the International Brigades, which would grow to number more than 60,000 men and which would also put their first recruits into action in the battle for Madrid. By the beginning of November 1936 there were already some 500 Soviet advisers in the republican zone – pilots, army officers, instructors, gunners and so on – and these would increase to a total of more than 2,000. Italian intervention on Franco's side would be even more extensive. It grew to number 70,000 men. Some 8,000 took part in the attack on Málaga in the second half of January 1937.

Germany and Italy had officially granted diplomatic recognition to Franco on 18 November 1936. France and Britain's efforts, in both 1937 and 1938, to achieve international non-intervention in Spain, and to localize the Spanish war by means of a naval blockade to prevent the supply of arms to either side, in order to promote a negotiated solution all failed. They could not possibly have succeeded at at a time when the western democracies' policy of appeasement merely served to stimulate the belligerent trend of Italian and German policy. Numerous episodes in Spain illustrated this fact. To cite only two examples, nothing was done when the Germans bombed Almería in May 1937 in reprisal for a republican air attack on a German ship, nor when Italian aircraft bombed Barcelona, from their base in Majorca, in March 1938. Franco sized up the international situation accurately and squeezed the maximum benefit from it for his own interests and those of his cause.

He did not abandon hope of seizing Madrid. When the frontal attack was halted, he devised a new strategy based on the envelopment of the capital on both flanks: by the north-west, cutting off the Madrid-Corunna road via villages close to the highway, such as Boadilla del Monte, Majadahonda, Las Rozas, Aravaca and Pozuelo; and by the south-east, crossing the river Jarama and blocking the Madrid-Valencia highway. The operation on the Corunna road, which roughly followed the *Blitzkrieg* principles recommended by the Germans, began in early December 1936, continued in extremely adverse weather of cold and fog and ended in the middle of January without a decisive result. Franco's troops had cut the road, without encircling the capital. The battle of the Jarama was fought during the following month. Like the preceding battle, it was particularly bloody. Franco won little territory; at times his forces came close to losing their own positions; and the battle ended indecisively, a failure for Franco: he had wanted to take Madrid and he had not been able to do it.

So he was unable to savour fully the satisfaction he must have felt at the capture of Málaga, which fell on 8 February (between the two battles in the environs of Madrid) to the army of the south under General Queipo de Llano, supported by the Italian troops that had recently arrived in Spain. Franco told the Italian ambassador, whom he saw in Salamanca a few days after the victory at Málaga, that the war would be a long one and would have to be fought to the finish. He was still planning a last manoeuvre with Madrid as the main objective: he gave the go-ahead for an ambitious Italian offensive with 35,000 men in four divisions supported by a further 15,000 under Moscardó to secure one flank, with 70 aircraft, 2,000 personnel carriers, 80 tanks and other advanced equipment. The attack started from Guadalajara, trying to reach Madrid directly from the north-east. This offensive, which began on 8 March, made greater tactical sense than those which had been attempted before, because the terrain was less unfavourable; but, after their spectacular initial advance, the Italians, were left almost on their own by Franco, who ought to have re-opened the Jarama front. In tough fighting, the republican forces under Líster and El Campesino were able to halt the attack, even obliging the Italians to retreat.

After that, Franco hesitated no longer. The Italian defeat was confirmed on 20 March and at the end of the month he took what was probably his best strategic decision, to carry the war to the north. He thus opted for a gradualist strategy, confronting the enemy region by region. His only departures from this plan would stem from his determination to counter immediately every attack launched by the republican army, wherever it might fall; and, as we shall see, republican offensives were numerous and remarkably wide-ranging. The fall of the north – the provinces of Vizcaya, Santander and Asturias – would bring Franco the main centres of iron and steel production and of mining; he would also be able to occupy the maritime cities of Bilbao, Santander and Gijón, which were of outstanding economic and strategic importance and of great international and, indeed, political significance.

First, from 31 March to 19 June 1937, came the offensive against Vizcaya. Franco's scepticism about a *Blitzkrieg* had increased after the Italians' failure at Guadalajara and he was unwilling to take risks. Against Vizcaya – since 1936 part of an autonomous region governed by the Basque Nationalist Party – he brought almost all the artillery and aircraft at his disposal, with highly mobile infantry units, consisting of the Navarrese brigades with Italians on the flanks under Mola's command. The tactics these forces were to employ were simple but effective: massive bombardments by aircraft and artillery, followed by infantry assault. The tactics worked, thanks chiefly to Franco's overwhelming air superiority on the northern front, but the scale of destruction inflicted had serious consequences for Franco's international standing. The bombing of Guernica by the Condor Legion on 26 April provoked an emotional response from around the world. Thanks to the genius of Picasso, the name of the Basque town came to symbolize the horrors of war and the barbarities of Fascism. To Franco, who seems to have had no prior notice of the likely extent of the bombing, the damage to his international image must have caused concern. There were no more operations of the same sort against civilian targets of small military or strategic significance for the duration of the war. Franco even accepted advice from the Church that he should behave generously on entering Bilbao, which was to fall, after fierce fighting on the heights of Sollube, Bizcargui, Peña Lemona and the hills that surround the chief city of the Basque country, on 19 June 1937. Mola was not there to see the triumph. He was killed in a plane crash near Burgos on the 3rd.

The republican government had tried to relieve pressure on Vizcaya by diversionary attacks at Alcubierre in April and Huesca in June and by an offensive against Valsaín and Segovia at the end of May. It was all in vain. Franco's political victory was substantial: the fall of Vizcaya implied the defeat of Basque nationalism, which was an affront to the concept of national unity espoused by the rebel generals of 18 July. Franco lost no time in abolishing Basque autonomy. Bilbao was, moreover, easily the biggest city so far conquered by the nationalists: its loss was a hammer-blow for the new republican administration, formed on 17 May under the socialist Dr Juan Negrín, in which no fewer than four ministers – Prieto, Zugazagoitia, Irujo and Uribe – had close links with the Basque Country. Franco's triumph was rounded off on 1 July when his cause was upheld in a collective letter from the Spanish episcopate, signed by 48 bishops in all, with only two notable absences – the Archbishop of Tarragona, Vida y Barraquer, and the Bishop of Vitoria, Mateo Múgica. This implied religious sanction for the military insurrection and spiritual legitimation of the war.

Yet Franco's joy was to be short-lived. On 6 June a formidable republican force of two army corps, with 90,000 men, 160 guns, 200 aircraft and 130 tanks, broke through the nationalist lines at Brunete, near Madrid, and penetrated ten kilometres into 'national' territory. 'They've knocked my Madrid front over,' Franco is supposed to have exclaimed. The republican attack, planned by a military genius, General Vicente Rojo, who had taken over as Chief of the Central General Staff, took him completely by surprise. Franco himself admitted that he had left precious few troops around Madrid and, moreover, that they were very poorly deployed. He might have added that the whole idea of leaving himself with a long line of defence half-encircling Madrid was, to say the least, strange. But Franco reacted brilliantly. He called a halt to his Santander offensive, sent a large force of reserves to Brunete and entrusted the command of this extemporized army to General Varela. By 11 July, the tide of battle had turned. On the 25th, St James's day, feast of the patron saint of Spain, Franco had won another victory over republican forces.

This enabled him to turn again to the north and launch his offensive against Santander. This operation, begun on 14 August 1937, was almost flawless in planning and execution. A republican counter-attack in Aragon at Belchite could do nothing to stop it. On 25 August the Navarrese and Italian brigades entered Santander; meanwhile, at Santoña, the remnants of the Basque army had surrendered to the Italians. Asturias was the next target. The most famous strongholds of that bastion of the republican working class fell one after another despite fierce resistance. On 1 October, now proclaimed Leader's Day (Día del Caudillo), Franco took Cova-donga, legendary birthplace of the Spanish Reconquest from the Moors. His propaganda made the most of the historical associa-tions, as had been done with the victory at Brunete on St James's Day, to emphasize the almost miraculous timeliness of Franco's triumphs, and he began to believe in his own messianic role. On 21 October, when Avilés and Gijón were taken, Franco became master of the entire Cantabrian coast.

Victory in the north greatly enhanced Franco's position in international politics. By April 1938, his government had been recognized by El Salvador, Guatemala, Nicaragua, Albania, Japan and Hungary, as well as Germany and Italy, and, more importantly for Franco's purposes, by the Holy See, represented at his court by the nuncio Antoniutti, and Portugal. Franco had begun to play the international game with skill. After the capture of Bilbao, specula-tion had begun about possible recognition by Britain, which had a long-standing interest in the fate of Basque iron ore. In fact, though recognition was withheld, Britain did appoint a Resident in Burgos, Franco's new capital, in November 1937, while the Duke of Alba acted from then on as Franco's representative in London. Franco was even able to resist pressure from his German allies to grant mineral exploitation rights, while preserving the excellent relations between his state and Nazi Germany from the effects of the ensuing friction, which continued throughout 1938. Nor was there any fall in the lavish aid Hitler was giving to nationalist Spain.

The process of constructing the new Francoist state had made considerable progress since the flight to the nationalist zone of Ramón Serrano Suñer; he was Franco's brother-in-law, a former CEDA member of the Cortes, and a close friend and executor of José Antonio Primo de Rivera, the founder of the Falange. Unlike earlier members of Franco's 'closet' circle, such as his brother Nicolás, the diplomat Sangróniz and the army lawyer Martínez Fuset, Serrano had a background in politics and law which gave him a real understanding of the sort of state he wanted. His vision of the state was developed from thoroughly totalitarian principles, but he had thought out the problems of how to provide it with all the administrative, political and judicial organs which it would need to function.

The top priority was to create a political structure. Serrano was the inspiration behind a proclamation of 19 April 1937, which combined all the forces that had contributed to the generals' rebellion in a new umbrella organization called the 'Spanish Phalanx of Traditionalists and of the National-Syndicalist Offensive Committees' (*Falange Española Tradicionalista y de las JONS*). Its leader was the head of state, assisted by a secretariat known as the 'Political Committee' (*Junta Política*) and a 'National Council' (*Consejo Nacional*).

Franco himself had summed up the ideology of the new movement in a speech on the 17 April at Salamanca. It was a mixture of patriotic, Catholic, traditionalist and national-sindicalist ideas. On 19 April Francoism was born. Nationalist Spain adopted a totalitarian profile: the unification decree said so explicitly; it was also to be Catholic and, in effect, a single-party state, though Franco preferred the word 'movement' to 'party'. The decree dissolved all other organizations and parties. The statutes of the new organization were published in August 1937, creating a structure of services parallel to those of the state, as in all totalitarian systems. Furthermore, Franco's personal power was extended. The statutes gave him the right to nominate members of the National Council, declared him accountable only to God and to History – which was as much as to say, *not* to the party, much less to the people of Spain – and gave him the right to appoint his own successor as head of state. A decree of 30 October 1937 defined the only permitted ritual acclamations of the new state: the cries of 'Franco! Franco! Franco!' and the 'Up with Spain!' (*¡Arriba España!*) of the Falange with the 'Long Live Spain!' (*¡Viva España!*) of the army.

Franco said in Salamanca that his state would offer 'effective democracy' as opposed to the democracy of liberal states, which he dismissed as merely 'terminological and formalistic'. He also claimed that in his system political participation would be organized on the basis of the family, the municipality and the trade union or syndicate. The form that the new state would take remained unresolved. Franco mentioned the possibility of a monarchy for the first time in a statement to *ABC* in Seville on 17 July 1937, but he made it clear that if a restoration were to occur, a new monarchy would have to be very different from that which fell on 14 April 1931. There was no room for doubt. 'The new state,' wrote Franco in an article for *La Revue Belge* on 15 August 1937, 'will not be based on democratic models which are obviously unsuitable for our people.' Again, he said in Saragossa on 19 April of the following year, 'We do not believe in the liberal democratic system.'[10] As Franco himself often repeated in 1937 and 1938, his regime was going to be totalitarian. It was not going to ape the German, Italian or Portuguese models, but would follow a formula of its own. Its distinctive character would be revealed in constant appeals to Spanish history – to the Spain of Ferdinand and Isabella and of the 'Golden Age' of the Spanish empire – mingled with the imperatives of the Catholic Church, to the immeasurable annoyance, for instance, of the first German ambassador, Von Faupel.

Thus a dual process was apparent. On the one hand, the apparatus of the state and the tone of political life in nationalist Spain were increasingly to resemble those of Fascism; yet simultaneously, religious life was to be restored. The rate of progress in both respects increased as victories in the field strengthened the nationalist movement and consolidated its position. Thus on 12 October 1937 in Burgos Franco made his first appearance in the Falangist blue shirt, which became part of the uniform of the new umbrella organization. Soon after in November, he was claiming that his new system was inspired by the teachings of the Church and that 'Spain has been, is and always will be Catholic' – a corrective to Azaña's famous declaration as republican prime minister in 1931, that Spain had 'ceased to be Catholic'.[11]

In October 1937 Franco had appointed the first National Council of his new organization. In January 1938, when a new law put omnicompetent legislative power in his hands as Head of State, he took a further step. He formed his first ministerial government in place of the technical 'council of government' which had been established in October 1936. This represented a decisive change, for the 'Council of Ministers' (*Consejo de Ministros*) was to remain, throughout the forty years of Francoism, the real power-centre of the regime and the only institution that truly counted with Franco himself. All the rest – the National Council, the *Cortes* (the assembly created in 1942), the Trades Union Organization of the official syndicates which was built up from 1940, the Councils of State and of the Realm – were, in effect, mere theatre, as Serrano Suñer himself said much later.

Serrano himself played a decisive part in forming the first ministerial government. As Interior Minister and Secretary of the Council of Ministers he was the real strong man of nationalist Spain, chiefly because he had all press and propaganda services in the palm of his hand. It was he who suggested the names of various possible ministers to Franco. At the same time, the government still had to reflect one of the constant features of Francoist cabinets: it was a coalition of all the forces that had contributed to the movement of 18 July: Falange, traditionalists (as the Carlists were called), army men, and orthodox monarchists.[12]

The government declared that the state would be organized on national syndicalist lines and at once launched an important package of laws and decrees. The most significant was the Labour Rights Law (*Fuero del Trabajo*) of 9 March 1938, a genuine attempt to define what was meant by 'national syndicalism'. This law reflected the regime's dual inspiration of Fascism and Catholicism: it declared that trade unions would be 'vertical', proclaimed the role of the state in welfare and in the defence of rights, recognized private property and acknowledged that the family was the basic unit of society.

Much more followed. Decrees were issued for the re-introduction of the crucifix to schools and courts of justice. The republican civil marriage law was rescinded, as was that on divorce. Catalan autonomy was revoked even before the territory was conquered. The state assumed total control of the press and established rigid censorship by the press law of 22 April 1938, which remained in force until the sixties. The Society of Jesus was made lawful again. Co-education was banned. Labour tribunals and the Maritime Social Institute were created. A system of family allowances was devised. In June 1938 the death penalty was re-introduced. In September of that year a new plan for secondary schooling, devised by the education minister, Sainz Rodríguez, was approved, with emphasis on religious education and the humanities. 'Vertical' trade unionism began to take shape and numerous measures were introduced covering pressing problems like public works, housing, health, the banking sector, culture – everything, in short, proper to a state under construction. On the 18 July 1938, Franco again described his state as 'totalitarian' and 'possessed of a mission'.

'The war has already been won,' Franco declared on 2 November 1937. He was wrong. What was more, his own military capacity was to be put to the test again a short time later in December 1937, when, after three long months of relative calm, a new operation by the republican army was to take him by surprise once more. This time, the republicans struck at Teruel, while Franco and his generals were in Medinaceli, preparing a further attack on Madrid from Guadalajara.

The republican army took Teruel on 7 January 1938. It was the first time the republicans had recaptured a provincial capital. As at Brunete, Franco chose to try to parry the enemy attack, prompted by the usual obsession with territorial control that dominated his strategic thinking. This time, however, the reflexes that had served him so well before failed him. His counter-attack was too hurried. He chose his objectives and methods badly and obvious tactical errors became apparent as his plans unfolded. Only at the end of January did he correct his initial mistakes, when he mounted an impressive operation to turn the enemy's flank well to the north of Teruel, in the Alfambra mountains. Some highly effective tactical manoeuvres involving artillery, aircraft, infantry and even cavalry were again carried out by Yagüe and by García Valiño, one of the officers who had fought with greatest distinction in the north, and on 22 February, Teruel was at last recaptured. The inadequacy of Franco's initial response however, was made clear in despatches from the German ambassador Von Stohrer, in the entries the Italian ambassador Ciano made in his diary and even in the analyses made by some of Franco's own officers, such as Carlos Martínez de Campos.

Soon after, on 7 March 1938, Franco launched his offensive towards the Mediterranean, spreading units led by Varela, Yagüe, Aranda, Moscardó, the Italian Berti, Solchaga (another of the leaders of the Navarrese brigades), García Valiño and Escámez through the valley of the Ebro. On 19 April, a nationalist column under his friend and colleague from his time at the Toledo Academy and future collaborator in government, Major Alonso Vega, reached the sea at Vinaroz and cut the republican zone in two.

Franco now took another of his controversial decisions: to march on Valencia, where the Negrín government and Azaña, the president of the Republic, were based, rather than attack Catalonia as almost all his confidantes seem to have advised. Franco must have been afraid of provoking a hostile reaction from France and thereby exacerbating an increasingly tense international situation since Hitler's annexation of Austria in March. The chance that events might take an unexpected turn – such as a European war or an agreement between Britain, France, Germany and Italy to impose some form of mediation on Spain – seemed to be looming throughout 1938, which was why Franco decided not to attack Catalonia. But the alternative – the march on Valencia – turned out badly for his troops. The nationalist advance was painfully slow over terrain which favoured the defence. At last, the offensive ground to a halt in the Espadán mountains to the north of the city of Valencia.

Franco's error was made apparent on 25 July, when Rojo caught him off guard for the third and last time. On that day, the republican army of the Ebro, under Lieutenant Colonel Modesto, crossed the river at various points on a front 75 kilometres long.

They made considerable inroads along an arc of territory around the town of Gandesa and threatened to penetrate as far as Alcañiz and break through Franco's lines. The Caudillo's obsession with territory came to the fore once more, with greater obstinacy than ever. He became committed to a combination of defensive tactics with frontal attack *à outrance* to dislodge the republican enemy from his territorial gains.

To the annoyance of his advisers – Mussolini actually came to believe that the war could be lost – Franco refused even to contemplate an enveloping manoeuvre, against a force lodged in a pocket of land 35 kilometres deep with a river at its back. From his headquarters in Alcañiz, Franco tried to prove to his advisers the destructive power of his chosen tactics. Time and again, between 11 August and 16 November he would fling his men against the enemy lines in a war of attrition waged mainly by the artillery. Some of the places along the front – Venta de Caposines, Gandesa, the Cavalls hills – would be remembered for the intense bitterness of the battles fought over them.

Franco himself reckoned that the Battle of the Ebro was the fiercest and 'ugliest' – his word – of the war. There were 50,000–60,000 casualties in all of which some 20,000 were fatal. According to *ABC* of 1 April 1964, these months were one of the worst periods of Franco's career, not just because of the battle, but chiefly because of the international situation. Hitler's determination to take over Czechoslovakia, which had been in the air since April, was a threat to the peace of Europe, for Germany's latest demands had been rejected by France (now under a Popular Front government, as in 1936) and Britain.

Faced with the threat of a European war, Franco assured Britain and France that *his* Spain would stay neutral. This angered the Germans and Italians. That, in turn, was why Franco was afraid that the meeting held in Münich on 29 September 1938 between Hitler, Mussolini, Chamberlain and Daladier, prime ministers reseptively of Britain and France, would sacrifice him in the course of achieving a general settlement. Nothing of the sort happened. In 1938 it had become apparent that Chamberlain, obsessed by the need to achieve some agreement that would guarantee peace, would be unwilling to risk war over Spain. France seemed to have a different attitude, and between March and June, the Popular Front government even renewed its aid to the Spanish republic in its anxiety over the Czechoslovak crisis. Münich, however, represented another act of appeasement of Hitler by the western democracies, as became all too clear in March 1939 when Hitler occupied Czechoslovakia.

What was more, even the Soviet Union was to put its own interest above the needs of the war in Spain. Afraid that the Münich agreement would enable Germany to start a new confrontation in the east, the Russians hurriedly began to slacken their support for the republic in the autumn of 1938 in an attempt to revive their old non-aggression agreements with Nazi Germany. All this was advantageous to Franco. The League of Nations had endorsed the Negrín government's call for the withdrawal of foreign volunteers: the International Brigades began to leave Spain on 22 November 1938. The Italians were supposed to have done the same on 16 November, when an earlier Anglo–Italian agreement came into force. Some 10,000 men were recalled, but a further 12,000, under the command of General Berti, remained to fight on in Spain until the end of the war. The Condor Legion did the same.

When the Battle of the Ebro was over, the republic still held on to Catalonia, Madrid, a large part of La Mancha, Valencia and the south-east of Spain. Negrín, the prime minister, agreed with the communists that resistance should continue. This was a mistake. The Battle of the Ebro, as Franco realized, had destroyed the morale and operational capability, albeit not the numerical strength, of the republican army. General Rojo no longer had the means to mount the last campaign which his genius for improvization had devised – offensives in Extremadura and the centre, combined with an amphibious operation against Montril on the Mediterranean coast.

Franco on the other hand had everything ready for an attack on Catalonia for 10 December, although it seems that he would still rather have favoured an advance on Valencia. Furthermore, he had recovered his gifts as a commander. In overall planning, in the identification of objectives, in the deployment of forces, in the suitability of the orders issued to the various army corps, in the interplay between units of different types and in the co-ordination of the entire effort, the offensive against Catalonia took its place with those against Santander and Alfambra as one of Franco's most brilliant operations in the whole war.

The only real fighting was confined to the early days of the offensive. Moreover Franco easily repulsed the counter-attack launched by the republicans on 5 January in Extremadura. Then followed the sudden collapse of Catalonia. Barcelona fell on 26 January 1939. On 10 February Franco's forces reached the frontier, while half a million people streamed across it into exile. The republic's president, Azaña, was among them. Ireland, Uruguay, Poland, Peru and Bolivia recognized Franco and at last, on 27 February, France and the United Kingdom followed.

Before the fall of Catalonia, Franco's agents had begun to take secret soundings for a negotiated settlement among republican army leaders in Madrid who were opposed to Negrín and the communists. After the French and British policies had changed, there was clearly no other practical course for the republic, even though it still had an army of 800,000 men in the heart of Spain. Lieutenant-Colonel Casado, the obvious leader of those republicans willing to abandon the government, seized the opportunity for a rising against Negrín. His insurrection took place on 4 March 1939 and between the 6th and the 12th Madrid was the scene of serious confrontations between pro-Casado forces and communist troops loyal to Negrín. Casado formed a Council of National Defence (*Consejo Nacional de Defensa*), in which well known figures of the Second Republic, like the socialist Julián Besteiro and General Miaja took part, with the aim of negotiating peace with Franco.

Franco had rejected, repeatedly and unequivocally, every proposal for a negotiated settlement, all through the war. His response now was in line with his essentially military understanding of the conflict and with his awareness of the undeniable superiority of his position. He demanded and exacted unconditional surrender. On 28 March 1939, Franco's forces, under the command of General Espinosa de los Monteros, entered Madrid. On 1 April, Franco – still in Burgos with a high fever caused by 'flu, brought the last phase of the war to a close – the phase which set the seal on victory.

'We army men,' Franco reminded his cousin on 5 July 1965, 'rose up to save the fatherland from chaos and to prevent a communist republic. There was a good deal of injustice and of inexactitude in that declaration – apart from the fact that it was not only the army men who wished to save Spain in 1936 and that rebellion was not the only way of doing it. But what matters is that Franco believed it with all his heart in 1936 and went on believing it all through his life. The cost of saving the fatherland included 300,000 dead (some 140,000 at the front, the rest in the rearguard of both zones), 250,000 homes and 183 towns and cities (these last two figures refer only to what was totally destroyed or rendered uninhabitable: what was merely damaged cannot be calculated). Half the rolling stock, a third of the livestock, a third of the merchant navy were lost. The total cost was some 30,000 million pesetas at 1935 prices or 2.6 billion pesetas in those of 1982.

3
The Third Man

'I have never been motivated by a desire for power,' said Franco, in front of the cameras of Spanish television on 12 December 1966. He was asking people to vote for the Organic Law of the State (*ley Orgánica del Estado* – LOE), which was about to be the subject of a plebiscite. 'Service to the fatherland,' he continued, 'has absorbed my time and occupied my life.' At that time he had spent thirty years 'at the helm of the ship of state' or 'by the cannon's breech', to use his own words, and he still had nine years more to go.

So it would not be unfair to Franco to attribute to him something, at least, of that desire for power which he disclaimed. He was first and foremost a man deeply and genuinely imbued with an almost messianic sense of his own mission; and whatever one thinks of it,[1] this self-perception convinced him of the legitimacy of his own authority. In a letter of 6 January 1944, to Don Juan de Borbón, son of the ex-king Alfonso XIII, Count of Barcelona, and heir to the monarchy that fell in 1931, Franco listed the reasons in favour of his own unquestionable right to rule: first, because he had saved the Spanish people; next, because of his 'own merits, manifest in a lifetime of unremitting service'; then, his 'prestige and esteem throughout all ranks of society' and 'popular recognition'. All these are Franco's own words. Next came his acclamation as head of state by the army and by all the forces that rose up on 18 July 1936 and finally 'victory, won by God's grace, time and again bestowed'.[2]

That was how Franco saw himself. From 1 April 1939 to the day of his death on 20 November 1975, Franco's life fused with the life of his regime. He himself said on one occasion that he could hardly be thought of as an individual. From 18 October 1939 he lived at the palace of El Pardo, some 10 kilometres from Madrid, on a large estate in hilly, wooded country. He used few of the rooms – only those his family needed – and decorated them with restraint in a style appropriate for a middle class household. He had two studies. One was large, for use as an official reception room; meetings of the Council of Ministers took place in what had been the banqueting room of the palace. In summer, Franco divided his time between San Sebastián and a traditional Galician country house at Meirás, near Corunna, whose town council presented it to him in 1938.

There were changes in the family circle, as was only to be expected over a period of forty years. His brother Ramón, the famous aviator and political chameleon, who oscillated between various extremist positions before settling down to co-operate with Franco in the Civil War, died in a flying accident in 1938. He was Franco's favourite brother, despite the irritation caused by his political peccadillos, and his death was deeply felt. In February, 1942, their father died, though ever since his abandonment of the family, Franco had had nothing to do with him. In 1950, Franco's only daughter married: Carmen was the idol of her father's affections; born in 1926, she was universally admired for her good nature and faultless behaviour. Her husband was a physician of noble birth, Cristóbal Martínez Bordiú, Marquess of Villaverde, who, on the other hand, was soon condemned by public opinion for his arrogance, worldliness and abuse of his privileged family position. Between 1951 and 1964 the couple had seven children who Franco loved deeply. The stifling atmosphere of adulation with which the head of state was surrounded induced the Francoist *Cortes*, to propose that one of them, Francisco, born in 1954, should have the order of his surnames reversed so that, according to the custom by which Spanish patronyms descend through the generations, his grandfather's name should be made perpetual in his line.

Franco was a man of simple tastes and methodical habits. His only trips outside Spanish territory were in 1941, when he visited Mussolini in Bordighera and Pétain in Montpellier; the previous year when he saw Hitler just over the border in Hendaye; and 1949, when, at Oliveira Salazar's invitation, he paid a visit to Portugal from 25 to 27 October (the following year, he escorted the Portuguese dictator, on a reciprocal visit, back to Oporto but returned to Spain at once). His official day, which began at ten o'clock each morning, was spent in giving audiences to soldiers and civilians on Tuesdays and Wednesdays, or in meetings with his ministers, whom he received every Monday and Thursday, one at a time, for short working sessions of half an hour each in the afternoon. On Thursday mornings he conferred at length with the man who was to serve as Secretary of the Presidency – effectively, the equivalent of Cabinet Secretary – from May 1941, and who was soon to become Franco's authentic alter ego, Admiral Luis Carrero Blanco (1903–1973). On Fridays the Council of Ministers met at El Pardo.

At weekends and on holiday, Franco gave much of his time to his favourite pastimes of shooting and fishing, the latter both at sea, where he fished in summer aboard another of his great loves, his yacht *Azor*, and on the salmon rivers of Asturias. He kept up his sporting life until 1973, when he was eighty years old, still making great catches in which he took a childish delight. As long as his health permitted he began his day – he got up at eight o'clock – on horseback or on the tennis court. Later in life, he would play golf instead. He loved films, which he could watch at private viewings at El Pardo, as well as television and soccer: in 1967 he won nearly a million pesetas on the football pools which he filled in regularly.

He liked to paint, albeit with tenacity rather than talent. Though Carmen Polo claimed in 1927 that Valle-Inclán, a bizarre novelist, was her husband's favourite author, and though it was often said that he loved books and learning, he had no intellectual tastes. He distrusted cleverness and despised intellectuals. In 1940 he wrote a novel called *Lineage* (*Raza*), a melodrama of army life which told the story of the Churruca dynasty – an ennobled version of Franco's own family – between 1898 and the Civil War. The book was an unsophisticated eulogy of patriotism and heroism on a par, for quality, with a penny dreadful. Because he was by nature reserved and remote – though not, as we have seen, without qualities of charm and moments of talkativeness – Franco had only a small circle of friends. To his shooting and fishing companions and comrades in arms can be added his private doctor of 1940–1974, Vicente Gil and Gil's brother Federico, Franco's confessor Father Bulart, and a few individuals from among the family and his civil and military households. Franco liked to talk with them in the evenings around the dessert table or play rummy, ombre or dominies.

Franco did not smoke and drank sparingly. Nor was he demanding about food. Other than at official meals he was served with small portions of simple dishes. But his favourite food was foie-gras and from his sixties his doctors put him on a diet to control his tendency to put on weight. He kept his own household accounts. He bought first one estate, called Valdefuente, at Navalcarnero near Madrid, where he built a house, and then another known as Canto del Pico at Torrelodones. He seems to have left his grandchildren a total of 20 million pesetas (about £200,000).[3]

As head of state, Franco adopted a style and tone which combined the sumptuous etiquette one might expect in a royal household with the mass demagogy typical of totalitarian states and personal dictatorships. The sumptuous style was demonstrated by portentous ceremonial at, for instance, the presentation of ambassadorial credentials in the old royal palace in Madrid, or by the annual commemoration of 18 July at the Royal Country Seat of St Ildefonso at La Granja. These were status symbols, as were the annual summer progresses to San Sebastián and the Moorish Life Guards who formed the leader's retinue, replaced in 1956 by the 'Franco Guard' (*Guardia de Franco*), as well as the occasional investitures at which Franco would grant titles of nobility – some thirty of them by 1969, mostly to old comrades in arms. Franco also attended events appropriate for a head of state, such as the state opening of sessions of the *Cortes*, meetings of the executive of the National Movement (as the umbrella organization of Francoism came to be called), Army Day on 6 January, the 'Victory Parades' which were held, at first, every 1 April but later became moveable springtime occasions. He was also to be seen at important funerals and at religious festivals of traditional national significance, after appearing beneath the canopy historically reserved for the king. Not for nothing did Franco claim in Seville on 1 May 1956 that his regime was quite unlike a republic and showed no trace of a presidential system. 'We are, in fact,' he said, 'a monarchy. We have no king, but we are still a monarchy.'

It was, however, a monarchy unable to escape from its origins in national syndicalism, which survived in populist rituals that co-existed with the quasi-royal style. To the end of his days, Franco went on travelling around Spain. The usual routine was for him to make a speech, from the balcony of a town hall or some other public platform, addressed to a great crowd gathered in homage and loyalty to the leader. The huge concentrations of thousands of people in the Plaza de Oriente in Madrid became legendary. The biggest were in 1946 to express defiance at Spain's condemnation in the UN, in 1970 in reply to international protests at the death sentence passed in Burgos against members of the Basque terrorist organization ETA, in 1971 'to say Yes' in an undifferentiated affirmation of support and in 1975 again in response to international condemnation of Franco's regime for executing five terrorists belonging to FRAP (the 'Revolutionary Anti-Fascist Patriotic Front') and ETA.

Franco regularly took the chair at important popular sporting events or celebrations: the Spanish equivalent of the Charity Shield, the soccer Cup Final and the annual northern small ships regatta. At the end of every year he presented a message to the Spanish people, first on the radio, then on television. From 1958 onwards, he presided at an annual Festival of Trade Unions – an extravaganza of sport and folklore mounted by the state trade unions to celebrate May Day. It was all part of a considered policy, a kind of triumphant populism by implied plebiscite, a form of 'direct democracy' which linked Franco, as leader, directly with his people in a state that had no genuine representative institutions. Franco came to believe in his own propaganda. He saw the huge popular demonstrations – many of which were organized by the state services – as a genuine expression of popular approval of his person and his policy by the Spanish people.

On one occasion – in 1959 – Franco himself defined his regime as government by personal fiat. He always regarded his position as head of state as lifelong. He spoke of his 'magistracy for life' for the first time in a statement to the daily paper *Arriba* on 27 February 1955 and later repeated the same words many times over. He never contemplated resignation or thought of yielding power to a system different from his own. As he said to his cousin Franco Salgado-Araujo in 1960, 'I have stated before, many times and in public, that while I have health and retain my mental faculties and physical strength, I shall not leave the office of head of state.'[4]

The Council of Ministers was the effective instrument of government. Franco had 19 governments in all – though technically speaking there were only 12 – with an average life of about two years. He was served by some 120 ministers. Franco seemed to think it advisable to discard them after about four or five years though around fifty of them served longer terms. Carrero Blanco was a minister for twenty-five years and José Antonio Girón de Velasco for more than fifteen. Franco allowed his ministers considerable latitude in the performance of their duties. It annoyed him to hear them challenged behind their backs and he always rose to their defence. Few of them were dismissed in anger, though one such example was that of Yagüe, Aviation Minister in 1940, who had been a focus of intrigue against the leader. A later example occurred in 1956 with Ruiz-Giménez, at the Department of Education, and Fernández Cuesta, Minister for the Movement, as a result of the violence between students and young Falangists which broke out in February of that year.

When he was aware of serious rifts in the cabinet, Franco's methods were those of a Solomon. In 1942 he sacked ministers suspected of responsibility for a Falangist outrage against a traditionalist ceremony: Galarza (Minister of the Interior), Varela (Army Minister) and his own brother-in-law Serrano Suñer

(Foreign Minister) were all dismissed. In 1969 he did the same with a number of ministers who belonged to Opus Dei and who were implicated in financial irregularities revealed by the Matesa scandal (see p. 135 below); but he also sacked the ministers Solís Ruiz and Fraga Iribarne who tried to take advantage of the opportunity to purge Opus Dei from the government.

Save in these cases, and one or two others, Franco's sackings were carried out with a sort of suave autocratic disdain. Notice of dismissal was served in a letter delivered by a despatch rider. At meetings of the Council of Ministers, which Franco chaired without a break, no matter how long they lasted, smoking was banned and there was no room for argument, much less insubordination. Nor would Franco ever say anything out of place: he observed the highest standards of courtesy and one of his ministers, Girón, went so far as to characterize his technique in the chair as 'astonishingly impersonal'. The only jokes he allowed himself were made at the expense of his good friend Alonso Vega, Minister of the Interior between 1957 and 1969. The occasions when he had a harsh word for a minister were few and far between: Fraga Iribarne was a victim on one such occasion in 1965 when he questioned something Franco had said about the relative merits of a republic and a monarchy. 'Do you think I'm not aware of that?' Franco interjected, 'Do you take me for some sort of circus clown?'[5]

The composition of his governments always stuck to the same formula. They were Francoist coalitions in which the several groups that had played a part in the rising of 18 July were all included. Franco himself, in a statement to *ABC* on 2 April 1957, defined his governments as 'teams of men who accept the principles and share the sense of history which underlies our Movement.' Between 1939 and 1945, it is true that there was a certain Falangist preponderance, followed by a period of Catholic ascendancy between 1945 and 1947, with a strong contingent from Opus Dei and from among the ranks of the technocrats between 1957 and 1973. The 1974 and 1975 governments were formed by Arias Navarro as prime minister in Franco's place, while continuing to follow a formula based on Franco's.

Franco took little interest in what he called 'politics' – democratic politics, as we should say – which he regarded with contempt. In a sense he did regard what he was doing as 'politics' too – though of a different, authoritarian kind. As we have seen, he thought of his own work rather as 'service' and 'duty'. Furthermore he had no political philosophy in the strict sense of the term. His policies, whether economic, social or foreign, derived neither from any overall plan of state action nor from any political ideology or doctrine. He was a pragmatist, free of doctrinaire or ideological influence. As we shall see, he simply adapted his policies as circumstances required. One might almost say of him what Wellington said of Lord Liverpool, British prime minister from 1812 to 1827; the secret of his policy was that he had none.

Obviously, Franco had a number of basic tenets in which he believed. Tomás Garicano Goñi, his Minister of Administration between 1969 and 1973, correctly identified some of these as patriotism, religion, unity and order. Franco's thinking was a tissue of vague and unsophisticated notions about authority, spirituality and paternalistic social responsibility. It all seemed to stem from his years in the army. 'Without firmly established authority,' he told the *Cortes* on 17 November 1967, 'there can be no peace, no order, no justice.' Again he stressed in his end-of-year message for 1968, 'Without authority, men cannot live together in society. Without rule and without government, a harmonious society cannot exist.' Franco ill understood the complexities of modern life. He thought that industrial, political and social conflict and the existence of competing systems of thought were all the fault of small groups of agitators and subversives, such as communists and freemasons, with whom the leader was morbidly obsessed. He felt that above all else Spain needed unity and order. Liberty could only be included 'within a framework of order', as he said on 9 March 1963 and repeated so often that the words became a monotonous catch-phrase. The same thing happened with other favourite phrases of his, like 'Unity among the lands and peoples of Spain', 'Sewn up and well sewn up' (*'Atado y bien atado'* – used to sum up what he had done to the reputed instability of Spain), 'Spaniards All' (as a term of address), etc.

His most virulent dislike was reserved for political parties and liberal democracies. 'We abominate political parties,' he went so far as to say on 4 December 1952. He saw them not as means of expressing differences of opinion and viewpoint in a complex and mature society, but as weapons of class conflict and national disintegration. He was incapable of seeing them as making any useful contribution – particularly in a country like Spain of whose political maturity his opinion was unreservedly low. He admonished the Francoist *Cortes* on 22 November 1966 with these words: 'Let the people of Spain never forget that every nation has its own familiar demons, peculiar to each one. Spain's are: the spirit of anarchy; carping mutual criticism; lack of fellow-feeling; extremism; and internecine hatred.' His own umbrella organization he regarded resolutely as a 'national movement', not a party.

He even characterized it as a 'great anti-party', in another speech to the *Cortes* on 27 November 1967.

Innocent of all political doctrine and ideology, with nothing of a politician by vocation about him, deeply hostile to the very idea of party, Franco was no Fascist. The first ambassadors from the German Führer and Italian Duce at the court of the Spanish Caudillo realized this at once: Wilhelm von Faupel summed up Franco as a 'clerical' and 'reactionary', which indeed he was. Franco realized it, too, and commented to his cousin on 6 March 1965, 'As you well know, I have never been a Fascist.'[6]

Franco could not come to an understanding with José Antonio Primo de Rivera, leader of the Falange, the party of the 'national-syndicalist revolution' that was Spain's nearest equivalent to Fascism. Franco came to respect the Falange – he said as much in 1942 – but this was only in recognition of the loyalty with which the Falangist rank and file had supported him. He did not, however, want a state cast on Falangist lines, nor, as we shall see, would he allow the Falange to run Spain. Franco's ideals were closer to those of Victor Pradera, the traditionalist leader murdered during the Civil War, who had formed the ultra-right 'National Block' under the Second Republic. The key words 'religion, state, property and family' summed up Pradera's scale of values and his book *The New State* (*El nuevo Estado*), published in 1935, presented the 'traditional and social' monarchy of Ferdinand and Isabella as a model. All these ideas were close to Franco's own. In 1945 Franco supplied a foreword to Pradera's collected works, and a note he left in his personal archive records the friendship he felt for the Navarrese statesman.[7] At some points, Franco's thought exactly co-incided with Pradera's. There were almost no other ideas in which he did believe, except, of course, for the legitimacy of his own regime founded on the rising of 18 July.

After the victory of 1 April 1939, Franco's regime was bound to gravitate towards the Fascist powers that had given their decisive support to the military rising. The trend could be detected in the following respects:

I. Spanish foreign policy favoured Italy and Germany. On 27 March 1939 Spain joined the Anti-Comintern Pact and confirmed her adhesion for five years in 1941. On 31 March 1939 a friendship treaty with Germany was signed. On 8 May Spain withdrew from the League of Nations. On 31 May, Spanish delegations, one led by Serrano Suñer and the other composed of a number of high army personnel (Aranda, Alonso Vega, Solchaga, García Valiño, Yagüe), visited Italy and Germany respectively. The Italian Foreign Minister, Ciano, went to Spain in July 1939 and the following year, in October, Spain received a visit from Himmler.

II. The influence of the Falange was strengthened in political institutions and social life. Membership rose spectacularly from the closing days of the War: soon there were 650,000 members. The Women's Section, the Youth Front and the University Students' Union – all of them Falangist groups – helped to bring diverse social groups into the framework of the movement. From the outset, the Falange formed the backbone of the Syndicalist Movement founded in 1940. The press, radio and organs of official propaganda were in Falangist hands. Falangist rituals were given official standing – among them the wearing of the blue shirt, the use of the Fascist salute, the cry of '*¡Arriba España!*', the term 'comrade', the red and black flag, the yoke-and-arrows motif and the anthem *Face to the Sun* (*Cara al sol*). Between 20 and 30 November 1939, the state sponsored a massive spectacle to mark the translation of José Antonio's remains from Alicante, where he had been shot by the republicans, to an official resting-place in Philip II's Escorial, where many kings of Spain were buried. On 10 August 1939, when Franco appointed a new government, his brother-in-law Serrano Suñer, known as the 'man of Italy', who had made the post-Civil War Falange the base of his rapidly expanding political power, became the strong man of the new regime. (The cabinet did, however, follow Franco's usual formula of a carefully balanced coalition and also contained ministers opposed to Serrano Suñer, especially among the soldiers, none more so than the Army Minister General José Enrique Varela.) On 17 October 1940, when Serrano already held the Interior Ministry and chairmanship of the central committee of Franco's umbrella organization, he added the foreign affairs portfolio to his empire. Between 1940 and 1945, Falangist representation on the National Council of the Movement was progressively strengthened.

III. The principles of a command economy, with self-sufficiency, nationalization and corporatism were allowed to dominate economic and social policies. Franco's elementary notions of economics were satisfied by the ideals of self-sufficiency – the 'autarchy' espoused by Falangist ideologues. In a speech to the National Council of his umbrella organization on 5 June 1939, Franco had said that the national syndicalist revolution would mark the 'triumph of economic principles which are in conflict with the old liberal theories'. The watchword he proposed on that occasion – 'Production, more production, more production still' – left no room for doubt. Franco wanted to increase production and limit imports in order to stimulate employment and reduce the foreign debt.[8] In February 1940 he paid a visit to Puertollano in the province of Ciudad Real, where a coal pit had become the centre of a big industrial complex which was one of the first symbols of the government's drive for self-sufficiency. On 24 January 1941 the railways were nationalized and the Spanish National Railway Network (RENFE) came into being. On 30 September of that year, the National Industrial Institute (*Instituto Nacional de Industria*) was formed along Italian lines with Franco's friend and nominee Juan Antonio Suances at its head, to front the state's industrialization programme. It soon grew into a costly giant. From August 1937, a National Grain Directorate (*Servicio Nacional del Trigo*) regulated cereal production. In 1939 the General Commission on Provisions and Prices (*Comisaría General de Abastecimientos y Tasas*) came into being, and the following year the Prices Tribunal (*Fiscalía de Tasas*). The state was taking on the task of controlling the supply and prices of consumer goods. A law of 26 January 1940 integrated the trade unions in a single organization and in December the 'vertical' syndicates inspired by Fascism were set up. Franco probably saw these as no more than devices to conciliate the working classes and avoid the kinds of class conflict he had seen in strife-torn Asturias in 1917–20 and 1934. In fact, there was much more to them: they were intended as means of re-deploying the working class and the entrepreneurial sector in the service of the totalitarian state. Economic interests had been made subject to political aims, following the examples of the axis powers.

IV. Repression became institutionalized. Legislation such as the Law of Political Responsibility (1939), Law in Suppression of Freemasonry and Communism (1 May 1940), Law of State Security (1941) and others created the basis of a tough and repressive police system on which the stability and survival of Franco's dictatorship would come to depend. In addition to the 300,000 war exiles, a further 300,000 people were imprisoned between 1939 and 1945. It is hard to be sure of the numbers of those shot in the same period, but estimates vary between 28,000 and 200,000. The disparity of the figures comes from the variety of methods of reckoning historians have used. The figure of 28,000, the lowest of those suggested, calculated by Ramón Salas Larrazábal – would mean that 10 individuals, on average, were shot each and every day throughout the seven years of the period 1939–1945.[9] Franco, who was not a violent man by temperament, applied the policy of repression dispassionately and implacably, as if fulfilling a duty. He introduced the system of remission for hard labour. Hundreds of political prisoners worked on the construction of the *Valle de los Caídos* – the Valley of the Fallen – begun in 1940 and completed in 1959, a sort of gigantic mausoleum erected by Franco in the mountains to the north of Madrid as a memorial to the dead of the winning side and in emulation of Philip II's basilica of El Escorial. Some individuals received pardons, too, before 1945, but there was no general and generous amnesty such as might have set the seal on national reconciliation and dispelled the lingering atmosphere of civil war. From a total of 270,719 in 1940, the prison population had dropped to 39,527 by 1945, of which political prisoners accounted for some 17,000. Normal prison levels were only recovered in 1950.

V. The emphasis on Franco's personal leadership (*caudillaje*) was strengthened. The power Franco exercised, which was to receive theoretical treatment in writings such as those on the doctrine of leadership (*doctrina del caudillaje*) which Professor Javier Conde published in 1942, comprised the headship of state, the prime ministership, leadership of the Movement, command of the armed forces and sovereign legislative authority, as confirmed by the new Law on the Office of Head of State of 8 August 1939. The introduction neither of a Council of State (*Consejo de Estado*) as an advisory body in 1940 nor of the Francoist *Cortes* in 1942 changed the position. The law which set up the *Cortes* on 17 July 1942 stated that the head of state would retain the right to promulgate all general legal 'norms' – laws, decrees, etc. – with statutory force. Franco called the assembly into being to collaborate with him in the exercise of his powers, but not to be a legislature that could impair his authority.

Thus Don Juan de Borbón was not far from the truth when, in his *Rome Manifesto* of 19 March 1945 – probably the document that caused Franco most annoyance in all his forty years of power – the pretender declared that the regime imposed by General Franco was 'inspired from its inception by the totalitarian systems of the Axis powers' – that is, Germany and Italy.[10] So it was. In particular, when the Second World War broke out on 4 September 1939, Franco's Spain sympathized with Germany, and when, on 10 June 1940, Italy entered the war, Spain stood unmistakeably by the side of the two totalitarian powers.

Yet Spain did not enter the war – a decision which Franco's regime always emphasized as one of the leader's great historic acts of sagacity. Spain declared her neutrality on 4 September 1939. She opted for non-belligerence – a step away from straightforward neutrality – on 12 June 1940, and reverted to neutrality in October 1943.

Spain's non-intervention in the war was the result of a combination of factors – strategic, diplomatic and economic –

many of which had nothing to do with the wills or wishes of Spanish decision-makers, including Franco. Franco had wanted a long period of peace and stability to give himself time to re-build the country; despite his alignment with the Axis he was looking for opportunities to co-operate with the international community and in 1940 signed twin commercial agreements with France and the United Kingdom. The World War was therefore a serious setback for him. Probably neither he nor the most closely involved of his advisers, including above all Serrano Suñer, who, with Franco, was the architect of foreign policy until August 1942, wanted Spain to take part in the war. That was why Spain declared for neutrality in 1939. Franco even called on the great powers to prevent the destruction of Poland.

But between April and June 1940, when the Germans attacked on the western front and forced the capitulation of France, the Spanish decision-makers must have believed that it was either expedient or inevitable for Spain to enter the fray. Spain made no declaration of war against France or Britain, as Italy did, nor did she attack the French in North Africa, though the possibility was considered. Spanish action was limited to the seizure of Tangier on 14 June 1940 and to the declaration of non-belligerence. At the same time – that very June – Franco initiated an exploratory approach to Hitler, entrusted to General Vigón, to see what response might be forthcoming if he offered to enter the war in exchange for substantial military and economic aid, Gibraltar and a large extension of Spain's possessions in Africa.

It was Germany's lack of interest in the Spanish offer that changed the thinking behind Franco's diplomacy. The Germans did not believe that Spain was in any condition to make an effective contribution to the war. The only thing they wanted from Spain was the prospect of free passage for German troops in the event of a decision to attack Gibraltar. Germany also regarded Spanish demands in Morocco as exorbitant and agreed with the Italians in preferring to maintain the existing balance between Spain and France in north Africa, so as not to prejudice relations with the collaborationist French government set up in Vichy in June 1940 by Marshal Pétain.

From then on, Franco adopted a policy which, indeed, closely resembled Pétain's own *attentisme* – the policy of 'wait and see'. He opted to combine clear affirmations of friendship for Germany, voiced by Serrano Suñer, the Falange and the official press, with indefinite postponement of any decision to join the fighting, at any rate until the Germans should accede in return to Spain's demands. This was the posture Serrano Suñer adopted with Hitler and Ribbentrop on his German visit of September 1940 – when he was not yet a minister – and which Franco maintained at his meeting with Hitler at Hendaye on 23 October 1940; Serrano would re-iterate the same position in later discussions with leading Nazis.[11]

In the story of Franco's life, that interview with Hitler at Hendaye was a turning-point. Stripped of all the legend with which his eulogists surrounded it, and which Franco himself declined to countenance, preserving scrupulous discretion about the whole affair, the basic truth of the meeting was that Hitler and Franco did not get on with one another. Hitler formed a very unfavourable impression of the Spaniard. Franco explained to the Führer Spain's aspirations in north Africa and her need for supplies and arms; and on the same night of 23 October, in San Sebastián, Franco and Serrano drew up a protocol under which Spain would join the armed alliance of Germany, Italy and Japan and would be committed to joining the war, but reserving the right to decide on the date of commencement of hostilities. At Hendaye, Hitler did not try to force Spain to a decision and it is idle to speculate about what Franco would have done if the Führer had agreed to his demands. Hitler still preferred to be sure of the collaboration of Pétain's France. He was content with Spanish neutrality as long as Spain was loyal and friendly, and that loyalty and friendship had been emphasized by Franco and repeated at Hendaye. The possibility of a German move against Gibraltar remained in the air; Hitler had thought about it many times since the beginning of the Battle of Britain in August 1940 and if he had resolved upon it, Spain would have been forced into an extremely difficult decision. In December, however, the German plan was shelved and soon after, in the spring of 1941, the opening of the offensive on the Russian front shifted the focus of the war far from Spain, as, indeed, Italy's attack on Greece had begun to do only five days after the Hendaye meeting.

It is therefore incorrect to say that Franco – and Serrano – had preserved Spanish neutrality at Hendaye.[12] They had, at least, avoided any irreversible commitment. From then onwards, Spain's neutral status became firmer; the cautious Carrero Blanco had some influence on this trend. And there was a further, decisive factor: the policy of conditional support for Spain in the form of food and oil supplies, from the outbreak of the war, followed first by the United Kingdom and later by the United States. The British, who had set up an international maritime blockade of German trade, used 'navycerts' – safeconducts to grain and oil shipments bound for Spain – to put pressure on the Spaniards and force them to maintain their neutrality. The Americans used the oil weapon in the same way.

Spanish survival depended on those supplies. Spain was in no position to go to war. That was why, as a delaying tactic, Spanish demands were progressively augmented as German pressure increased. The Germans were at their most persistent at the beginning of 1941, though German anger at Spain's equivocal behaviour, reflected for instance in Hitler's letter to Franco of 6 February 1941, never got to the point of being expressed in a real ultimatum. The Germans asked Italy to intercede. Franco saw the Italian leader at Bordighera on 12 February 1941. The interview was extremely cordial. Mussolini understood Spain's arguments and emerged convinced that Franco neither could nor would go to war. Franco's arguments had re-affirmed his position.[13] He would state it again in a letter to Hitler on 26 February, adding a further reflection: that Gibraltar would be worthless to Hitler unless the other end of the Mediterranean, at Suez, was sealed in advance.

'The three of us – the Duce, yourself and me –' wrote Hitler to Franco in the letter of 6 February 1941, 'we are drawn together by the irresistible force of destiny.' Franco probably thought the same thing. He always remembered Mussolini with admiration and always felt that he and Hitler had raised up their countries with energy, authority and patriotism: he said so twenty years later to Franco Salgadfo-Araujo. Clearly, however, Franco did not believe that the 'irresistible force of destiny' obliged Spain to enter the war. That may have been Hitler's understanding, but he would no longer continue to insist on it. He was sure of Spanish constancy. Spanish ports provided bases for the supply of German submarines in 1940 and 1941. The two countries' friendship was reflected in a substantial German presence in Spain.

Franco did even more. On 28 June 1941, just six days after the German invasion of Russia, and a violent campaign in the Spanish press, the Blue Division was created. Some 18,000 Spanish volunteers, commanded at first by General Muñoz Grandes, who had been a minister in the 1939 government, were to fight on the Russian front alongside the German forces until 1944. The decision angered the western allies, who restricted supplies to Spain, especially in view of the ill-considered speech to the National Council of the Movement on 17 June in which Franco blustered about the allies being finished and hinted darkly at the 'debt of blood' Spain owed to her 'Axis comrades'.

Pressure from the Anglo-Saxon powers, applied in Madrid with great finesse by ambassadors Hoare and Weddell, had the desired effect.[14] Spain was to do no more than send the Blue Division. To mollify the western democracies, Spanish diplomacy developed the 'two wars theory'; this sophisticated but improbable piece of casuistry – Russia was, after all, an ally of the west – stated that Spain was at war against communism, as she had been since the Civil War, but neutral in the struggle between the Axis and the western powers. In December 1941, with the Japanese attack on Pearl Harbour and the intervention of the United States in the world conflict – the two wars became three. In two of them – in Europe and the Pacific – Spain declined to meddle. On 18 December Spain re-stated her non-belligerent status.

Spanish sophistry was blatant. Franco provoked another indignant shudder across the western world on 14 February 1942, when, speaking in Seville, he offered a million Spanish volunteers to defend Berlin should the communists win on the Russian front. Yet he had probably just used the opportunity of discussions in Seville with Oliveira Salazar to invoke the good offices of the Portuguese, as traditional friends of England, in building bridges to the allies.

This ambiguity arose from the obvious and increasingly acute dilemma facing the Franco regime in 1942, because of a series of events influenced not only by the progress of the war but also by the rival tendencies within the Francoist camp. In brief, these events were: the emergence of dissatisfaction among the monarchists; the fall of Serrano Suñer; and the beginnings of a switchback to strict neutrality in foreign policy, which would gradually develop – though not fully until 1944 – into a form of neutrality *benevolent* to the allied cause. None of this would affect the nature of Franco's regime nor his position of personal power at its head. But new problems were opened up which naturally helped to shape the leader's decisions.

Discontent among the monarchists was caused – simply – by disillusionment at Franco's failure to restore the monarchy. In December 1939 Franco had criticized the 'two-headed' system which, in his opinion, had crippled the regime of Primo de Rivera. He sent only a short telegram when Alfonso XIII died in Rome in February 1941, though he did declare three days of official mourning. In Barcelona on 28 January 1942, in the course of one of his triumphal progresses, he had left scant room for doubt about his own point of view: 'We never said,' he pointed out, 'that we would restore the Spain that brought us the republic and lost some of the greatest fragments of our fatherland'. That was quite clear. Franco was not thinking in terms of a restoration of the liberal monarchy over which Alfonso XIII presided till 1931 and which had descended by hereditary right to his son Don Juan.

A showdown seemed inevitable. Franco knew that in 1941 and 1942 there had been contacts between the British embassy and leading monarchist generals, like Aranda, Kindelán, Orgaz and others. It was taken for granted that if the Germans occupied the Iberian peninsula, Britain would support the creation of a junta under Aranda with a view to restoring Don Juan and forming a new liberal and neutral regime. In 1942, the ex-minister Sainz Rodríguez and Eugenio Vegas Latapie, the two leading monarchists in the plot – or rather, the tentative speculations – were forced into exile. On 12 May, Franco had taken the initiative in writing to Don Juan, who had settled in Lausanne, to tell him candidly that the 'revolution' he favoured jointly with the Falange was incompatible with the restoration of the monarch, and to assure him that there was absolutely no monarchist feeling in Spain – which was probably true.

Don Juan made no immediate reply. He did so only on 11 November, some days after the allied landings in north Africa, in statements to a Geneva newspaper. His words were brief but to the point and included an unmistakable challenge to Franco. Don Juan affirmed that the role of the monarchy was to be open to all and to promote reconciliation; he declared himself in favour of 'absolute neutrality' in the war. And he went further still in a private letter to Franco dated 8 March 1943, when he wrote of the 'ominous risk' to Spain in a situation where power was 'concentrated exclusively in a single person, unsanctioned by any statute enacted in a lawfully constituted institution'. This, of course, was merely another way of referring to Franco's personal dictatorship. He urged Franco to restore the monarchy and firmly rejected any idea that he could align himself with the programme of the Francoist movement, as Franco had suggested in his original letter. Don Juan re-affirmed the two main themes of his argument: the monarchy as a government of reconciliation for the Spanish people, and the monarchy as guarantor of genuine Spanish neutrality, which was what the international context required.

Franco must have been indignant at Don Juan's letter. His reply on 27 May 1943 was sharp, unambiguous and occasionally irate. Franco pointed out to Don Juan that he, Franco, was head of state and his correspondent a mere pretender to the throne. He warned him against the collaborators he had gathered around him, among whom José María Gil Robles the former CEDA leader was now prominent. He reminded him that the monarchy had presided over a century and a half of decline and of civil wars and political divisions; he condemned the way Alfonso XIII, Don Juan's father, had treated Primo de Rivera in 1930. He made it clear that his regime was in no sense provisional, nor dependent on party but a movement of national salvation. And finally he informed Don Juan that the policy of neutrality in western Europe, non-belligerence in the Mediterranean and intervention on the Russian front was what Spain's interests demanded.

Useful dialogue beteen Franco and the representative of the monarchy therefore seemed impossible. Franco probably eliminated Don Juan from further consideration as a possible candidate for the throne in the event of a future restoration. From 1942–1943 Franco came to see Don Juan as symbolizing the liberal constitutional monarchy which he had utterly rejected. He had probably not discounted a monarchical future altogether. But, if he had anything of the sort in mind, it was more likely to have been a 'Catholic social monarchy', inspired by the ideals of 18 July, such as Carrero Blanco had sketched out for the first time in a memorandum dated 28 September 1942. In the event, there would be no final decision until 1969. In the short term what Franco did – apart from sending his tough reply to Don Juan – was to keep up the doses of caution and astuteness that had already become familiar features of his practice of government. Of the monarchist officers only Aranda was sacked from his post as director of the Army staff college, to be replaced by another prominent monarchist general, Kindelán. Well-known monarchist sympathizers were appointed as members of the *Cortes* announced in 1942 and operative from 20 March 1943.

The tactic of drawing the monarchists more closely into the fold was to have mixed effects. 'The murky waters of political life' – to use an expressive and revealing phrase coined by Franco on 17 July 1943 – were experiencing a storm. On 5 June, twenty-seven members of the *Cortes*, with the Duke of Alba at their head, had proposed, in exquisitely reticent language, that the monarchy be restored. On 15 September, after the fall of Mussolini, the allied landings in Calabria and the surrender of Italy, Franco was handed a note by General Varela, who had been his Army Minister only a year previously. The note was signed by Varela and seven other generals of irreproachable reputation and prestige: Orgaz, Dávila, Kindelán, Solchaga, Saliquet, Monasterio and Ponte. Aranda's name was missing, but he had broken with the regime completely and was in touch with elements on the left. The signatories asked in the note, 'with loyalty, respect and affection', whether Franco agreed with their view that the time had come 'to endow Spain with a system of state' in accordance with 'the pattern of a monarchy'. Franco, however, did not agree. He paid no heed, but he took no action against the generals. He merely called them in one by one and, mixing the language of command with gestures of comradeship and affection, he subdued their potentially defiant mood.

Without determined military action, a restoration was out of the question. For Franco's position on the home front – apart from the problems posed by the war – was becoming even stronger. Franco handled the two political crises which arose in 1941 and 1942 with undeniable dexterity. Both brought noticeable new strength to his power base and increased the means of control from above, from Franco's own person, of the various institutions of state that functioned in Spain.

Two distinct stages underlay the crisis of 1941. On 5 May, Franco had appointed General Valentí Galarza as Minister of the Interior. The appointment seemed logical, since at that time Serrano Suñer was doing the job in addition to being Foreign Minister. But it provoked a certain restlessness in Falangist circles, expressed in a sarcastic article criticizing the new minister in the Falangist daily *Arriba* on 18 May. Franco therefore proceeded to re-shuffle his cabinet, bringing in, by way of compensation, three well-known Falangists, José Antonio Girón de Velasco, José Luis de Arrese and Miguel Primo de Rivera. He did not, however, stop there. In response to the views published in *Arriba*, he sacked the men responsible for controlling the press and state propaganda, Dionisio Ridruejo and Antonio Tovar, the two young intellectuals identified with Serrano's brand of Falangism. Galarza's appointment had pleased the army, which resented the formidable power accumulated by Serrano since 1937. The arrival of the three new ministers seemed to favour the Falange – but only those sectors not controlled by Serrano, whose only focus of identity was total allegiance to Franco. Serrano, moreover, lost control of the press and propaganda. In August 1941 Franco gave these portfolios to men who were Francoists pure and simple, Gabriel Arias Salgado and Juan Aparicio. The previous month he had sacked the independent-minded Gerardo Salvador Merino as trade union chief and replaced him with another of the Falangist 'old shirts' Manuel Valdés. In November he abolished the 'national services' of the Falange – a kind of parallel administrative system – and absorbed them into three civil service departments.

Serrano was isolated: ranged against him were the army and the 'Francoist' Falange headed by Arrese, the new General Secretary of the Movement. His isolation grew worse during 1942 until the point was reached where it was said that he was making overtures to the monarchists, having been one of the fiercest opponents of a restoration. On 15 August came the worst case of disorder the regime had yet experienced. Young Falangists hurled two bombs at the end of a religious service held by Traditionalists in Bilbao in the basilica of Our Lady of the Begoña, patroness of the city. Presiding at the ceremony was the Army Minister, General Varela, who was regarded as an Anglophile and a monarchist opposed to Serrano and who was linked to Carlism through his wife's family. Varela condemned the incident as an attack on the army. He demanded – successfully – the death penalty for a young Falangist who was arrested.

Franco was unruffled by events which threatened to produce dangerous rifts between the army and the Falange or between the Falangist and the Carlists. He appeared in public in Galicia, where he was spending his summer holiday, accompanied by Arrese. He telephoned Varela to admonish him for having given matters an unhelpful twist and did nothing more for the next fortnight. On 3 September, however, he made a spectacular move. He sacked both Varela, whom he replaced with another of his closest war-time colleagues General Asensio Cabanillas, and Galarza, who as Interior Minister was to blame for having failed to prevent the incident: he was replaced by a 'strong man' of no political affiliations, Blas Pérez, who would remain in charge of home affairs until 1957. Thus, so far, Franco had dismissed two army men. Now, at Carrero Blanco's suggestion, and as a balancing act, he also sacked Serrano Suñer, who had previously seemed indispensable to Franco; his replacement was General Gómez Jordana, a man of moderation and discretion, who had shown himself to be a neutralist and who would change the emphasis of foreign policy. It was the first time Serrano had been out of the government since 1938. The new government, which would remain unchanged until 1945 except for the addition of José Félix de Lequerica when Jordana died in 1944, was more cohesive than its predecessor and – what was most important – was a serviceable, reliable tool of the leader. Franco did not find dynamic, unbiddable men like Serrano Suñer congenial.[16]

Serrano's departure had been caused by problems on the home front; his foreign policy had been Franco's, too, although it later suited the regime to make him the scapegoat for the blatant pro-German stance of the years 1939–1942.

When Jordana took office, Spain's policy of friendship with Italy and Germany continued. In any case, after Mussolini's fall in July 1943 Italy tended to vanish from Spain's diplomatic horizon; Franco did not recognize the 'Social Republic' of Saló, the puppet regime set up by Mussolini with German help in northern Italy. The Blue Division remained at the front and high ranking Spanish military personnel kept making fairly frequent visits to Germany. Trading relations between the two countries continued to be close and active. Tungsten exports alone, which had been worth 2.1 million pesetas in gold in 1940 rose to 200 million in 1944. But Jordana's term of office, from 1942 to 1944, would be stamped by the minister's concern to make approaches to the western allies and to the United States in particular. The rapprochement was all the more necessary from the summer of 1942 when allied plans for a landing in north Africa began to take shape. The danger, for instance, that the Canary Islands might become a secondary objective in allied plans could not be discounted until late September.

Because of Gibraltar's significance in any north African offensive, the western allies attached particular importance to the maintenance of strict Spanish neutrality. The American ambassador, Carlton J. Hayes, arrived in June 1942 with the job of ensuring this,[17] and once again leverage over seaborne supplies proved decisive. Officially, Spain's non-belligerent status was not revoked in favour of neutrality until October 1943. But in the meantime, the desire for rapprochement on both sides began to have some effect. On 2 November 1942 Hayes informed Jordana that the United States would respect the territory of Spain and her colonies. On the 8th of that month he delivered a letter to Franco in which the American president, Roosevelt, in extremely cordial terms, guaranteed that Spanish sovereignty would be unimpaired by the imminent allied landing in north Africa.

In fact, the landings took place that day. Three days later, German occupation was extended to the whole of France, though there was no serious thought of doing the same to Spain and seizing Gibraltar. Both sides, for different reasons, had an equal interest in Spanish neutrality. In the final analysis, that was what saved Spain, rather than the merits – or otherwise – of Spain's diplomats and policy-makers. Franco must have realized this. At least, he was aware that the final decision on Spain's fate did not rest with him: he spent the night of 7 November 1942, when Roosevelt's letter had not yet reached him, in prayer.[18]

Franco thought he could see a possible role for himself as a mediator opening up in the international arena as a result of his new circumstances. He was still dubious about the military outcome of the war: not until 1944 did he feel certain that the Germans must lose. In the early months of 1943, therefore, he tried to mount a peace-making initiative among the neutrals. His plan was based on one of his favourite arguments: Stalinist Russia represented the real danger to the western world and a strong Germany was needed as a buffer against communism.

Contrary to what one might suppose in the light of events after 1945, Franco's proposal was a non-starter. Nobody – especially not the British – could classify as an enemy the country which was bearing the brunt of the fighting and which at that very moment – at the beginning of February 1943 – was winning at Stalingrad a victory which would help turn the tide of the war. Franco's initiative, which Jordana pressed in a speech at Barcelona on 17 April 1943, aroused allied suspicison. It seemed tantamount to a guarantee of the survival of Nazi Germany. Events such as the arms sales agreement which Spain signed with Germany in February and the new commercial accord between the two countries in December 1942 tended to confirm these suspicions.

What the allies wanted from Spain was stated clearly by Hayes in an interview with Franco on 29 July 1943, a few days after the fall of Mussolini: a return to strict neutrality and the recall of the Blue Division. On 19 August, the British ambassador, Hoare, added two further points: the German consulate in Tangier would have to be closed and tungsten exports to Germany stopped.

Franco seemed unwilling to give in too readily to allied demands. But as their advance in Italy continued, with Italy herself now turning against Germany, and in view of plans for further allied landings in Europe, he did not have much choice. On 1 October 1943, the Spanish government reverted to neutrality. On 17 November the Blue Division was dissolved, though a small contingent of volunteers stayed on to form a minuscule 'Blue Legion'.

Yet Franco's problems, far from being over, had only just begun. As Franco himself later admitted, on 18 May 1949, the worst period of the war for him was in the first few weeks of 1944. There were three main reasons for this.

I. Pressure from Britain and the United States got to the point where oil supplies were completely cut off. Ostensibly this was in response to Spain's refusal to suspend tungsten exports to Germany, but it may have been a mere pretext for keeping tension alive in order to justify, if necessary, the invasion of Spain in support of the planned landings in Normandy.

II. The government was afraid that Spain might become the scene of a partisan resistance movement, like those at work in Yugoslavia, Greece and France.

III. Tension between Franco and Don Juan had entered a new phase.

This background makes it evident that Franco's regime must have been particularly apprehensive about allied pressure. Spain could do nothing but submit. On 3 February her neutrality was re-affirmed. On the 11th the Germans were asked to disband the Blue Legion. On 2 May, Spain promised the British and Americans that tungsten exports would be restricted, the German consulate in Tangier closed and German espionage curtailed. The allies allowed oil shipments to start again. There was no new invasion in Europe, apart from Operation Overlord in Normandy in June 1944.

Nor was there to be any guerilla movement inside Spain, until after the liberation of southern France when suitable units could be prepared and equipped. That did not happen until the autumn of 1944, when the communists mustered a force of 12,000 guerrillas who entered Spain through the Arán valley.

As for Don Juan, on 6 January 1944 Franco wrote to him again, in effect repeating the arguments he had already expounded on 27 May 1943 but this time pressing them to the point of definitive rupture. At least, he made his own account of the recent past quite clear: in 1931 the monarchy had abandoned power; the army rose against the republic; their movement was not monarchist in character but simply 'Spanish and Catholic'; the pro-monarchists had formed a tiny minority among the million men who joined the 'crusade'. 'Thus,' Franco wrote, 'this regime did not bring about the fall of the monarchy and is under no obligation to recognize it.' Bereft of any support that went beyond mere sympathy, in the Spanish army and the allied camp alike, there was little Don Juan could do. He did the only thing open to him, admitting as much to Franco in a letter of 25 January 1944: he declared the monarchy's 'total antipathy' to the 'national-syndicalist regime' of Franco and thus fortified the monarchy's moral credentials with an eye to Spain's future. The various plans for conspiracies which Generals Aranda, Kindelán and Beigbeder thought up between 1944 and 1946 in the hope of restoring the monarchy elicited sympathy from the British and American ambassadors but never took concrete form.

Franco, meanwhile, having got over the bad times of 1944, had taken another step along the road towards long-term security for his regime. For several months, Francoism was going to have to co-exist with the allies in what Ambassador Hayes called 'benevolent neutrality'. This came about as the result of a rapprochement impelled by circumstances. It did not mean that the new state of affairs would last, nor that the allies would necessarily go on tolerating the existence of a regime which had set up its 'Caudillo' as a third edition of the German Führer and Italian Duce.

That was why in the autumn of 1944 Franco started a cosmetic operation to give his regime an acceptable image. On 8 October he sent a letter to Churchill, who had recently made some generous remarks about the Spanish regime; Franco's proposal was for an alliance on a basis of opposition to communism – a theme which always interested the British statesman. On 3 November 1944 he issued a statement to the United Press News Agency in which, among other matters, he denied that Spain had ever been Nazi or Fascist and argued that in any event Spain's domestic politics were no obstacle to co-operation with the allies. Shortly after, Arrese announced that a '*Fuero de los Españoles*' was being prepared. *Fuero* was an archaic term for a grant of liberties. It would be a sort of Declaration of Rights which would define Spaniards' civil liberties.

Franco, however, was about to be made aware of his regime's fundamental problem, which would dog him for the next forty years: its lack of genuine moral legitimacy by democractic standards. This could already be seen in the terms of Churchill's reply to the letter of January 1945: Germany's influence in Spain was recalled, as were the many occasions on which Franco himself had forecast allied defeat, and the 'relationship of intimacy' which he had maintained with Germany and Italy. A little later, on 19 March, Don Juan published his *Rome Manifesto*, in which, as has been mentioned, he claimed that Franco's regime was 'inspired from its inception by the totalitarian models of the Axis.' On 25 March, Franco was to hear what President Roosevelt thought of him. In his instructions to his new ambassador to Spain, Norman Armour, the president declared that there was no room in the United Nations for a government established on Fascist foundations. Indeed there was not. On 19 June, by which time Hitler and Mussolini were dead and Germany had capitulated, Spain's admission was rejected by the United Nations, whose opening session had begun in San Francisco on 25 April 1945.

This showed how Franco's regime would be received in the new international order that emerged from the Second World War: Spain's condemnation and isolation would culminate in the resolution of censure passed by the United Nations on 12 December 1946 and the ensuing recall of ambassadors. Before that date Franco had been working intently at improving his image. On 13 July the *Fuero de los Españoles* had been promulgated; on the 17th he issued a selective amnesty; on 11 September he banned the Fascist salute; on the 18th Spain withdrew from Tangier; on 22 October Franco signed a law on national referendums, which for the first time envisaged that certain laws might be put to the Spanish people for them to vote on.

The most significant step was the formation of a new government on 20 July 1945. This was because Alberto Martín Artajo joined the cabinet as Foreign Minister while Arrese was removed as Minister and General Secretary of the Movement. The job was left vacant until 1951. The changes, suggested by Admiral Carrero Blanco, marked an obvious shift in the identity and content of Francoism: a period of adjustment to the demands of distinctively Catholic political principles began, in the course of which the regime was to come to be defined as a 'Catholic state'.[19]

This was not only because of Artajo. Franco wanted the Church's blessing and received it willingly and with pleasure. The Church had stood by Franco, as we have seen, from 1936 onwards, in spite of certain problems – over the integration of trade unions which harmed Catholic syndicates, relations with Nazism and provisions to bishoprics, for instance – and the friction and discord that sometimes ensued. In 1945 Franco played the Catholic card from the top of the deck. He did so simply to safeguard the survival of his regime. He was following the watchword which Carrero Blanco crudely and cynically coined for him: 'Order, unity and – above all – endurance'.

The signals were clear enough. On 9 May, before the new government took office, Cardinal Pla y Deniel broke his long silence and issued a pastoral letter in defence of the regime. Next, on 28 August, he endorsed the *Fuero de los Españoles*. On 17 July a new primary education law had been approved, firmly hinging on Catholic doctrine. The new government put Catholic politicians in control of censorship and the press. On 18 November 1945 Pope Pius XII addressed a fulsome message to the Spanish people. In December Joaquín Ruiz-Giménez, the president of the Catholic institution Pax Romana, went to London and New York virtually as a roving amabssador for Franco: he found Cardinal Spellman was an influential advocate of the Spanish regime and its leader.

On 14 May 1946 Franco made an important speech in the *Cortes*. Its significance lay in the new way he defined what he wanted his regime to be. The key phrase was: 'Against conventional democracy we set our Catholic and organic democracy . . .'. His thesis, in other words, was that Spain was a democracy too, albeit an 'organic' one, a term Franco had employed in statements to United Press on 7 November 1944. According to Franco, democratic credentials were demonstrated by the Council of State, the *Fuero de los Españoles*, the representative assembly and the law on referendums. What he wanted to stress was that the Spanish regime was not a dictatorship: rather, as Franco had said once before, on 9 February, 'an original solution – social, Catholic and Spanish'.

Not without cynicism, Franco called it 'dressing up in democratic clothes'. The wardrobe, however, was too threadbare to attract the sort of international acceptance Franco was seeking. The *Fuero de los Españoles* did not even recognize the basic democratic rights of freedom of expression, political association, meetings and demonstrations. Nor was the Spanish *Cortes* a democratic parliament, because its members were not elected but appointed. Nor did the referendum law install a democratic electoral system.

International opinion continued to see the Franco regime for what it really was: a personal autocracy, a dictatorship – however much Franco might recoil from the term – based on ideas alien to the spirit of liberal democracy. On 1 March 1946, the French government sealed the frontier. On the 4th, the United States, France and Britain issued a joint communiqué expressing the hope that Spaniards would come to find a way of achieving Franco's peaceful retirement and the formation of an interim government that would call free elections. In April the eastern bloc countries that had diplomatic relations with Spain severed them unilaterally.

Poland, in particular, took the Spanish case to the United Nations. The debate was postponed until the autumn and winter of 1946 but the outcome was predictable. The communiqué issued by the United States, Britain and the Soviet Union in Potsdam on 2 August left no room for doubt. And so, on 12 December 1946, the UN General Assembly passed, by 34 votes to 6 with 13 abstentions, a motion condemning the Spanish regime and recommending severance of diplomatic relations.

The resolution began to be applied with immediate effect. One after another, ambassadors were recalled from Madrid. All left, save the Portuguese representative, the papal nuncio and the Irish and Swiss ambassadors. Only one country issued a direct challenge to the UN accord: Argentina, where what General Perón called his 'justicialist' regime, so reminiscent of the totalitarian systems of the Axis, had been in power since 24 February, appointed Dr Radio as ambassador to Franco.

Thus occurred Franco's first big defeat since 18 July 1936. The UN resolution declared that 'in origin, nature, structure and general conduct' Franco's regime was 'a Fascist regime, organized and installed in large part with the aid of Nazi Germany and Mussolini's Fascist Italy'. This was extremely tough language. The resolution expressed the conviction that the Franco regime had been imposed on the Spanish people by force of arms and, in addition to recommending Franco's exclusion from all international bodies, called on the United Nations to take steps to restore a free government to Spain if the course of time failed to bring about such a change.

Still, Franco was not yet beaten, not by a long way. 'No one,' he said when presiding at a military parade on 16 February of that year, 'can take our victory away from us.' He had not remained idle while international pressure built up against his rule. His reaction, apart from his bid for the Catholics and the Church, was to try to rally opinion inside the country in support of his leadership, appealing to Spain's resources of national pride and civic prowess while depicting what was really a rejection of his regime as a conspiracy against Spain. The method worked. More than half a million people turned out to cheer Franco in the Plaza de Oriente in Madrid on 9 December, three days before the UN vote of censure. It was not a plebiscite; but it did show the breadth of popular support for Franco in Spain. It was enough to relieve Franco of serious anxiety about the UN vote. He was later to claim that he spent the 12th – the day of the vote – painting.[21]

The claim was probably no more than bravado. Franco can hardly have failed to feel hurt by the terms of the UN's condemnation. On 1 January 1939, speaking to the journalist Manuel Aznar, he had said this: 'I simply want to say that my aim is not only to beat foes but also to win friends. Let me go further: victory means little or nothing to me unless it helps to influence people's convictions.'[22] As far as international opinion was concerned, it was obvious in December 1946 that Franco was very far from realizing that aim.

4

The Sentry of the Western World

'We are proud of being the first people to rise up and defend western civilization against the threat posed by the east,' declared the document in which Franco proclaimed the army's insurrection against the republic on 18 July 1936.[1] As we have seen, ten years on, western civilization had still not got round to thanking him. It never did so nor did it ever come to understand what seemed the rather fatuous argument of a self-important soldier. But the west did one thing which, for Franco, was enough – it put up with him as a member of the international community. This did not amount to any moral recognition of Francoism's legitimacy. It was, rather, a practical acceptance conferring some of the advantages of legitimacy on the regime.

This acceptance was no small matter. In 1955, the same Franco who had been declared 'guilty of conspiring' with Hitler and Mussolini to unleash the war was admitted to the United Nations. This was the very organization which had condemned him and which had said that, as long as his regime survived, Spain could not be allowed to join. This great victory for Franco, was the result of a number of factors. Decisive among them was, no doubt, the support of two great pillars of 'western civilization': the United States and the Holy See.

Franco did not have to do much to bring this change of heart about. The international situation and the Cold War were enough in themselves. Once the need to contain Soviet ambitions had become the top priority of the west, Franco had only to display his pedigree. There were few contenders better qualified for the post of 'sentry of the western world'. Franco's propaganda machine was well aware of the fact, as it showed in 1956 by publishing a sketch of the leader's life under that title. The piece was written by Luis de

Galinsoga with the assistance of Francisco Franco Salgado-Araujo.

Franco had survived the challenge of isolation abroad coinciding with the chance that some democratic alternative might arise within Spain. From the mid-fifties the regime seemed solidly established, despite apparent failures in economic and social policy. What was more, Franco had hardly had to make any concessions. On the contrary, his regime had developed just as he chose. By 1 October 1953 he felt able to declare, 'The time has come for our foreign policy to be fulfilled.' The same was true for his domestic policy.

His response to the events of 1946 had a great deal to do with it when Franco and his advisers, especially Carrero Blanco, saw both the need and the opportunity to launch a political offensive. They needed, on the one hand, to close ranks against international rejection and, on the other, to cut short the hopes of the various centres of opposition at home. The key device was the law of 1947 regulating succession to the headship of state. This was a further step – after the labour rights law (*Fuero de Trabajo*), the creation of the *Cortes*, the civil rights law (*Fuero de los Españoles*) and the law on referendums – in the long and laborious process of building up the 'original solution' which, according to Franco, was the essence of Francoism.

The succession law was of the highest importance. The first clause at last defined the nature of the state that had emerged from 18 July. 'Spain,' it stated, 'considered as a political entity, is a Catholic, social and representative state, which, following Spanish tradition, is declared to be a monarchy.' So Franco had opted for a monarchical formula. But at the same time the law re-stated the fact that Franco's personal power was permanent. Clause Two declared that the office of head of state was vested in Franco. Clause Six gave him the right to nominate his own successor, to be either king or regent. Any idea of a restoration as such was still discarded. As Franco explained to *The Sunday Times* on 27 April 1947, the aim was the creation of a monarchy of a new stamp, not the restoration of the pre-1931 monarchy.

For this reason, Don Juan could not accept the succession law. Franco tried hard to obtain his approval, sending the faithful Carrero Blanco to the Count of Barcelona's new residence in Estoril, but to no avail. On 7 April, a few days after Franco had laid the text of the law before the *Cortes* and had announced over Spanish radio that a referendum on the subject would soon take place, Don Juan made his dissent public in the ringing terms of his Estoril Manifesto. He rejected the succession law in favour of indefeasible hereditary right. 'What is now being done,' he said, 'is purely and simply an attempt to prolong a personal dictatorship for life.'

Don Juan was right. Nonetheless, his efforts and those of other opposition groups proved fruitless. Franco had total power in his hands and he used it to carry out his plans. A press campaign was orchestrated to discredit Don Juan, repression was tightened, no whisper of disagreement with the law was allowed, and public opinion was manipulated. Franco went on a tour through various provinces in May. The date when the law was passed in the *Cortes* was chosen to coincide with the visit of Eva Duarte de Perón, who was greeted with a wealth of demonstrations. On 4 July Franco went on the radio to ask for approval in the referendum. When it was held on the 6th, every opportunity to manipulate or falsify the result was exploited. The result was scandalous. Of a roll of 16,187,992 voters, 14,054,026 had turned out, and of those 12,628,983 had 'voted' in favour, according to the result revealed to Franco. As if this were not enough, the press was made to announce that the turn-out had been 15,219,563 and the yes-votes 14,145,153.[2]

Not that it made any difference. What mattered was not the statistics but the belief that the outcome was a manifest triumph for Franco's policies. It was not only Franco who interpreted it as such. (He went so far as to say that it was the most significant event in Spain's recent history and, as late as November 1966, still spoke of it as a democratic mandate for his regime.) Even the opposition accepted it as a victory for Franco. Philip Bonsal was the first to understand this. He had been looking after American interests since the recall of ambassadors and had worked harder than anyone with Generals Aranda and Beigbeder to bring together the monarchists and the member-groups of the 'National Alliance of Democratic Movements' (*Alianza Nacional de Fuerzas Democraticas*). Indeed, he pointed out that throughout the difficulties over the succession law, Franco had shown undeniable political sagacity.

So he had. At one blow, the succession law felled Don Juan's monarchist alternative and shattered whatever importance the republican government in exile might still have had. (It had never had very much, anyway, especially since the UN refused to recognize the republic.)

Don Juan and the exiled socialists both realized the force of the law from their different perspectives. Among the socialists, Indalecio Prieto, who had been one of the leading politicians and ministers of the Second Republic, now began to urge a policy of co-operation with the monarchists. He proposed that the republican formula should be gradually abandoned as the only way back to a democratic system. In Estoril, the same policy was followed by José Maria Gil Robles, the old chief of the Catholic right. He had been Minister of War in 1935, with Franco as his Chief of General Staff. Exiled in 1936, he had joined Don Juan's camp in 1942. Prieto and Gil Robles held discussions in London under the auspices of Britain's Labour government and on 30 August 1948 at St Jean de Luz they signed a pact which committed them to the common principles that would lead to democracy. The most important principle was that an impartial interim government would be formed and would call a plebiscite as to whether Spain should be a republic or a monarchy.

The pact was stillborn. Don Juan was probably convinced, since the referendum of 6 July 1947, that outright confrontation with Franco (as advocated by Gil Robles) was bound to fail because the Franco regime was so solidly entrenched.

At almost the same time that Gil Robles and Prieto were signing their agreement in St Jean de Luz, Don Juan had his first meeting with Franco. The encounter had been fixed up by some of Don Juan's other advisers. It took place on 25 August 1948 aboard the yacht *Azor* off San Sebastian. Franco and Don Juan found they disliked each other. But they were able to agree that Prince Juan Carlos, Don Juan's eldest son and the dynasty's would-be heir, should be educated in Spain. Thus Don Juan opted for restoration by a roundabout route.

It was a route that needed Franco's co-operation even though he had little enthusiasm for the idea and many reservations about it. Its supporters included the many followers of Don Juan who were willing to collaborate with Franco – among others Julio Danvila who had arranged the meeting, the Count of Ruiseñada, José María Pemán and, from among the Catholic triumphalists of Opus Dei, Rafael Calvo Serer, Florentino Perez Embid and others.

The occasional monarchist conspirator could still be found. General Aranda, for instance, did not give up until 1949. Monarchists still sometimes voiced opposition, as in January 1950 when 300 leading monarchists wrote to the new American ambassador, Paul Culbertson. They were protesting at some remarks in support of Franco made by the US Secretary of State, Dean Acheson. There were some new liberal utterances from Don Juan as, for example, in a letter he wrote to Franco on 10 July 1951. In the local 'elections' of November 1954 there were even monarchist candidates, to the annoyance of the Francoist authorities. But from 1948

Franco could rest assured that the monarchist cause – as Gerald Brenan suggested in 1950 – was just 'a feeble affair of café politicians and malcontents'.[3]

The 1947 referendum probably marked the beginning of the end for another anti-Franco front. At least it was soon afterwards, in 1948, that the communists decided to disband their guerrilla partisans. The cost of their effort had been far higher than the Spanish people suspected at the time. Since 1944, the Civil Guard had suffered 500 casualties and the partisans about 4,500, of which about half were fatal. The guerrilla war had failed. The partisans, isolated in remote areas, cut off from a population that was cowed and tired of violence, could do nothing better than try to dodge the Civil Guard.

Franco's referendum had been an almost flawless manoeuvre, which committed him to nothing. The succession question had not been settled in favour of the descendants of Alfonso XIII, which would have provoked unrest among the traditionalist Carlists, who favoured a rival line. The Falange, presumably anti-monarchist, had been offered the prospect of a regency, and they continued to favour this option thereafter. They could take comfort from the fact that the future monarchy would not be in the liberal or democratic mould. Catholic political feeling had been reassured by the official definition of the state as a Catholic realm, as well as a 'social and representative' one. This must have been particularly satisfying to the Foreign Minister, Artajo, the leading figure in the Catholic tendency. The personal 'programme' he had put forward when he joined the government had included the introduction of a traditionalist monarchy.[4]

The impressive dexterity which Franco had shown – only possible, of course, because of his autocratic power – had both a complement and a counterpoint. Its complement was prudence, a quality which Franco had amply demonstrated under the republic, during the Civil War and again throughout the World War. Caution was clearly second nature to Franco and could hardly fail to affect his political conduct. Franco told Dr Soriano (who treated him for the paralysis of his left hand in 1961) that is, 'a long-term, patient way of looking at things'. 'In my life in government,' he said, 'I've found it a great help to be patient and unflappable and to try to get a clear view of whatever is on the horizon.'[5]

Franco always proceeded with 'the prudence required by the circumstances' as he told the *Cortes* on 8 July 1964. His prudence suggested that the institutions of his regime should develop as slowly as possible. 22 years were to pass by before Franco rounded off the succession law of 1947 by choosing an heir. Until 1966 his regime did not have its 'Organic Law' – in other words, there was no legal framework to regulate and strengthen its administrative machinery. This lack of regulation was what Franco described as an 'open constitution', on 31 December 1955, and it formed the basis of his famous 'masterly inactivity'.

Franco deliberately delayed the development of the institutions partly because of his natural prudence, of course, but also for tactical reasons. It was a means of eluding or outfacing some of his most intractable problems. Restoration of the monarchy, for example, would have impaired his relations with Carlism and the Falange. To leave the state in Falangist hands, as Serrano wanted in 1939–1942 and as Arrese would try to contrive in 1957, would have brought him up against monarchists, Catholics (for another idea in Artajo's programme was the purging of the Falange from the regime), traditionalists, many of the army officers and even Carrero Blanco. Franco's policy of inactivity, which became blatant after the referendum of 1947, was undeniably serviceable. It strengthened his hand as the internal broker, the ultimate and essential arbiter of the power-system of the regime. On the other hand, it provided evidence for those who thought Franco had no political aims except to cling to power. The longer his caution and inactivity lasted, the more it seemed that Franco was incapable of institutionalizing his regime in time. And there would be no shortage of those who thought and said that he had not known how to retire in time.

In some respects, too, his long-range, patient 'shepherd's' outlook failed to see what was on the horizon. Here was the counterpoint of the undeniable political skill he showed. On 14 December 1946, two days after the UN note of censure, Franco published a piece in *Arriba* under the pseudonym Jakim Boor. It was the first of a series of 49 articles that would continue to appear until 3 May 1951 and which would be collected in Franco's third book, *Masonería* (*Freemasonry*) in 1952. *Freemasonry* was a strange, unbelievable book. What was unbelievable was that the head of state of a modern country, who was a gifted soldier and prudent political figure, should have a vision of the world and of international affairs based on a gigantic and obsessive fantasy: the delusion that all modern history was nothing more than the result of an enormous conspiracy by the masons, and that Spain was its principal target.

The theme of *Freemasonry* was the same throughout: masonry and communism; the history of masonic conspiracies; the origins, number and rites of the lodges; masonry and Spain; the masonic international, and so on. Franco claimed in his prologue to have unearthed one of the least studied of history's secrets – 'an obnoxious mystery', he called it. He must have spent many hours on the task, and his articles displayed no mean erudition. His purported discovery was that almost all the politicians who, at one time or another, had said or done anything against his regime, were freemasons: Roosevelt, Churchill, Truman, Blum and above all the Norwegian UN Secretary General Trygve Lie, who was the main target of Franco's invective. Moreover he claimed that the entire policy of Britain and France since the eighteenth century had been dictated by masonry. Masonry had worked to exacerbate the decline of Spain ever since it had been introduced in 1728 by Philip Wharton, who was the author's other bugbear. Everything that had happened in Spain since then could be attributed to the influence of freemasonry: the expulsion of the Jesuits, the loss of the empire, the revolutions, the civil wars, the anticlerical riots of 1909, the fall of the conservative prime minister Maura, the political crimes and so on.

It is probable that Franco actually believed this farrago of wasted effort. However, it also had a serious political purpose: to explain away the international rejection of his regime. 'The entire secret of the campaigns which have been unleashed against Spain,' he wrote, 'can be found in these two words: masonry and communism.'[6] To Franco, the reason behind it all seemed plain. Spain had beaten communism, in the Civil War, and now Spanish Catholicism and loyalty to the Church had begun to excise the 'cancer of masonry'. Nor was this all. On 19 August 1949 he wrote that the plots against Spain were just one example (the creation of the state of Israel was another) of how the world suffered under 'the dictatorship of masonry'. Franco's arguments sometimes overspilled into delirium. He claimed that a masonic conspiracy had begun during the First World War as a reaction against the rise of the popular masses in the modern world. This had taken over the League of Nations in the twenties but was checked by Hitler and Mussolini, as Franco repeated in the book on more than one occasion. When they fell, and the UN was founded in 1945, the conspiracy recovered its lost ground. At that moment what Franco called 'the most serious and sensitive point in the history of international politics' was reached, and he alone had known its secret. 'The prominent masons Roosevelt and Churchill,' he wrote on 2 July 1950, 'formed a pact with Russia at Yalta, Teheran and Potsdam.' The conclusion seemed obvious. Masonry and communism, of which Franco considered the former, if anything, to be the more dangerous, constituted the great menace of the contemporary world.

This wild interpretation not only verged on the morbid but sometimes strayed into defamation, as when Eleanor Roosevelt was stigmatized as a 'mason-ess' who was also 'a case of what would here be called a dyke'.[7] Fortunately, the book was intended for domestic consumption only and did not have any effect on Franco's diplomacy. Indeed it seems likely that apart from a few devotees and Carrero Blanco no one took the theories of 'J. Boor' seriously.

The objective of Franco's diplomacy after 1946 was to break out of Spain's international isolation. This need arose in response to a particular series of events rather than as part of a planned programme of action in the international sphere. It was to lead to a transformation of Spanish foreign policy. Franco himself enumerated the new pillars of his policy in the *Cortes* on 17 May 1952. They were the Iberian Pact with Portugal, links with Latin America, friendship with the Arab world and the security agreements with the United States which were then being negotiated. This all added up to a considerable change. Franco no longer mentioned Spain's 'right to territorial renewal' – the wild scheme for constructing a north African empire mooted by the regime in 1940. Nor did he even speak of Gibraltar, an objective he did not altogether renounce but which would not have much of a role in his policy until the sixties: indeed, it was something on which he personally declined to dwell, believing that Gibraltar would only be recovered with time and patience.

Some of these new foreign policy priorities were entirely logical. Francoism had enjoyed a very high level of mutual understanding with the Portuguese dictatorship from its inception. With the Latin American states obvious ties existed and some of them – Perón's Argentina in particular – had not fallen in with the UN resolution of 1946.

The relationship with the Arab world, however, made less sense. Franco and his spokesmen always spoke of Spain's friendship with the Arabs, but it remained somewhat paradoxical. Spanish history had been characterized in part by the struggles of the Christian kingdoms against Islam in the Middle Ages. The modern Spanish army, and Franco himself, had been forged in a war against Muslim insurgents in Morocco. On the other hand, Franco's Spain had been unwilling to recognize Israel in 1948 (partly so as to keep in line with Vatican diplomacy) and had supported the Arabs in the ensuing Middle East war. In September 1949 Franco welcomed King Abdullah of Jordan to Meirás – the first foreign head of state to visit Spain since 1939. Franco got his reward. International isolation began to crumble.[8]

The initiative in building a relationship with the United States, probably of all countries the most hostile to Franco in 1945 and 1946, came not from Spain but from America. The post-war international situation induced the United States to favour an approach to the Spanish regime. Franco soon arrived at a fairly acute appraisal of the new world order born of the Second World War. 'Before the last war,' he told *Le Figaro* on 14 June 1948, 'we had the era of national rivalries . . . Now the mindless egoism of nation-states has been succeeded by the equally mindless egoism of groups of nation-states. The era of national rivalries has been replaced by the era of rivalry between groups of nations – the "blocs".'

Franco found a place in one of the blocs through bilateral arrangements with the United States in 1953. To do so, he did not have to undergo a change of course, conversion or adaptation of any sort. 'The key to our policy is anti-communism,' he said to the National Council of his Movement on 17 July 1943. And he was quite right. The struggle against communism always featured prominently among the arguments justifying the rising of 1936. What was more, it was one of the arguments in which Franco believed – and believed to the core – without considering the facts. In July 1936 the communist party was insignificant in Spain and rebels were making false allegations when they claimed that extremists in the Popular Front were planning a communist takeover. On the contrary, it was a popular revolution reacting to the military rising of 18 July that triggered off the class war suffered by the republic after 18 July and that enabled the communist party to gain power. Nor did Franco limit his argument to Spain. He presented the rising of 1939 as an act in defence of western civilization and of Europe. 'In our struggle against communism,' he told *Le Journal de Genève* in December 1938, 'we believe we are doing all Europe a service.' The argument of *The Sentry of the Western World* was thus pre-figured in the theory of the nationalist 'crusade'.

This was why Franco was at last admitted to the western bloc, even though his new partners had condemned him unreservedly in December 1946 and would always keep him in quarantine. Franco's anti-communism was in tune with the west's policy of 'containing' communism. It was a policy formulated by the new US president Truman in May 1947, and totally supported by a Europe anxious to have American leadership and protection of the free world. In view of the redoubtable growth in Soviet power between 1945 and 1950, Franco could even claim that events had proved that he had been right all along.

Franco did not subscribe to cold war anti-communism merely out of opportunism or in order to survive. He had been a man of the Cold War ahead of schedule. In his end-of-year message for 1954 he was able to claim, with reason, that he spent twenty years arguing in the face of Soviet communism for the absolute need to be forewarned and forearmed. He would endorse neither the peaceful co-existence of the fifties nor the subsequent détente. Far from diminishing, his anti-communism hardened over the years. The anxiety he evinced seemed particularly intense, for instance, in speeches made in the sixties. He never dropped his guard. He would frequently complain that prosperity and secularization – or, to use his words, materialism and loss of faith – had sapped the western world's capacity to resist the Soviet threat.

Thus in the Cold War years from 1947 Franco played a card – anti-communism – which suited his mentality and fitted his deepest convictions. He had an exceptional stroke of good fortune when the international tension made the United States value the strategic defence of the west above all ideological or political preferences. He was lucky that America attached more significance to Spain's strategic usefulness than to its anti-democratic regime.

Franco was right to realize this and wise to put recognition for his regime above other considerations, and to make the concessions which clinched agreement with the US in 1953.

The Spanish-US thaw began in 1947. One of the first signs was a document drawn up in October 1947 for the Department of State in Washington, in which the American diplomat George F. Kennan, one of the originators of the 'Truman doctrine', recommended that his country's anti-Franco policy ought to be modified. Another indication, in February 1948, was a private visit to Madrid made by Admiral Forrest Sherman, chief of the US Mediterranean fleet. This visit led to a clearly important relationship between Sherman and Carrero Blanco. Between these two events, on 17 November 1947, the United States had voted for Spain for the first time at the UN, when a Polish motion against the Spanish regime was rejected by 29 votes to 16 with a number of abstentions.

Not until 1950, however, did relations between the two countries enter a phase that led directly to an understanding. Spain, therefore, was left out of the Marshall Plan in 1948 (the American plan for aid to free Europe in post-war reconstruction) precisely because of the Franco regime's undemocratic character. Some benefits were denied to Spain because Franco rejected Truman's stipulation that there should be no further obstacles to the practice of non-Catholic religions.

The thaw quickened in 1950 after a letter from Dean Acheson to

Senator Tom Connally appeared in *The New York Times* on 18 January. The Secretary General stated that the US ambassador would soon return to Madrid – the UN had not yet revoked the 1946 resolution – and that there was no alternative to Franco. In the course of the year various State Department and Pentagon personnel spoke up in favour of granting credits and aid to Spain, or emphasized her strategic importance in the defence of the west, though Spain did not yet belong to NATO, which had been created in April 1949.

The change which had come about was apparent in the decision of the US Congress, made on 1 August 1950, to authorize President Truman to give Spain $62.5 million on credit through the Import-Export Bank. It was less than the 100 million asked for by the supporters of Senator Patrick Mac Carran's amendment, in which the idea was promoted but it was the first time the US government gave economic aid to Franco. At Mac Carran's initiative, aid was often renewed thereafter.[9]

So the wind seemed to have changed – and not only from the United States. In February 1948 the French government had agreed to re-open the frontier which had been closed since 1946. At the UN meeting in Paris in September of that year, 15 Latin American countries had presented the first motion – which did not get put to the vote – in favour of admitting Spain. In May 1949 the General Assembly approved a motion proposed by Brazil, Bolivia, Colombia and Peru which would have restored to UN members the right to pursue independent policies towards Spain, though the resolution did not receive the two thirds majority required to put it into effect.

From then on Franco's recognition seemed inevitable. King Abdullah's visit, already mentioned, was a typical indication. Costa Rica and Colombia, breaking ranks with the UN, sent ambassadors early in 1950. When the Spanish case was again put to the UN in the autumn of that year, the result was a foregone conclusion. A resolution favouring Spain was approved in advance by all the various committees and sub-committees before being debated in the General Assembly. On 4 November 1950 the latter officially revoked the resolution passed in condemnation of Spain. Votes were cast in Spain's favour by the Latin American countries, apart from Mexico, Uruguay and Guatemala (and Cuba, which abstained), the Arab countries, the United States and some European countries, though France and the United Kingdom abstained. The votes against came from the eastern bloc states, Israel and the three Latin American countries already mentioned.[10]

Franco was able to declare to a journalist from an American

radio and TV network that he felt entitled to expect the mistakes which had damaged Spain to be put right. The ambassadors returned with surprising haste. Spain was not yet a member of the UN – and did not become one until 1955 – but she automatically became a member of the various dependent organizations.

Once the international condemnation of Franco's regime had been revoked, the Spanish-US agreement could go ahead. After all, the question had been in the air at least since the creation of NATO in 1949. It had been said then – and even earlier – that Spain was undeniably important in western strategic planning. In the United States, there had been talk of bringing Spain into the Atlantic alliance or of having a bilateral alliance with her. It was soon apparent, however, that some European countries would veto the first of these options.

Franco himself made it clear that he would prefer a bilateral arrangement. He said so several times during this period. He and his advisers, particularly Carrero, always thought that such a formula would offer greater material advantages and fewer political complexities than would NATO membership. What mattered was that America wanted Spain in the allied camp.

That was decisive. Franco did no more than to capitalize on American initiatives, and he did so without undue haste in negotiation and without displaying excessive initial enthusiasm. His overriding concern was to achieve international recognition of his regime. The moment of decision – there were previous exploratory contacts, of course – came on 16 July 1951, when Franco met Admiral Sherman and Ambassador Griffis. The question of planting American bases in Spanish soil was now openly raised.

A few ripples were still to come – as in February 1952 when President Truman said publicly that he did not like General Franco. But the November election of that year brought General Eisenhower to the White House. He had shown an interest in Spain as NATO Commander-in-chief in 1951 and the negotiations conducted by Generals Kissner and Jorge Vigón now made rapid progress. They reached agreement in April 1953. The signing, however, was delayed until September. Spain wanted to sign the new concordat with the Holy See first.[11]

The concordat was signed in Rome on 27 August 1953 by the Spanish minister Artajo and the Vatican Secretary of State Monsignore Tardini. As has been said, it represented the second pillar supporting Franco's final victory in the quest for international recognition. The concordat arose almost naturally, between the Church and a state born of a 'crusade for God and Spain' which defined itself as a 'Catholic monarchy' and based its social and educational laws on the teachings of the Church. Franco had the facts on his side when he claimed in his end of year message for 1954 that Spain had created a 'Catholic' state. He added the words 'social and representative', but these were more open to question.

Since 1936 an intensive programme had been going on to restore religion. From 1945, as has been seen, it was reinforced by the Church's leading role in keeping Spain safe while the critical international situation lasted. What Gerald Brenan saw in Spain in Holy Week in 1950 – women decked out in penitential finery, with long satin robes and the traditional veils of intricate lace over an elaborate coiffure, and rosaries and prayer books in their hands – was just a symptom. Franco had put education under the control of the Church, with extraordinary power to censor books and entertainments and to influence behaviour. Franco's first act after the Victory Parade of 1939 was to preside at a solemn *Te Deum* at the Church of St Barbara in Madrid. There Franco and Cardinal Gomá, primate of Spain, dedicated the nation to the Catholic cause.

Franco bestowed his presence on every sort of religious gathering – Holy Week processions, coronations of statues of the Virgin, significant anniversaries of shrines, and presentations of offerings to the apostle St James. The picture of Franco in uniform, kneeling before the cross during the translation of relics to the Santa Camara (the treasury of relics of Oviedo Cathedral) on 5 September 1942, can stand for all of them. Major events in the religious calendar – Holy Week, Christmas, Corpus Christi, Ascension Day and so on – came to be celebrated in Spain with unwonted intensity. The crucifix was solemnly restored to places of honour in university buildings. In 1950 Spain marked Holy Year with official celebrations and commemorated the proclamation of the dogma of the Assumption. In 1952, Franco took the chair at an impressive Congress on eucharistic doctrine at Barcelona. In 1954, Spain was solemnly dedicated to the Immaculate Heart of Mary. Since the end of the war, the number of vocations to the priesthood had soared. In the years 1950–55 Catholic culture established the kind of hegemony over intellectual life which it had not enjoyed for almost a century, encompassing a diverse range of work and thought, including that of Bishop Angel Herrera Oria and the Catholic publishing house Editorial Catolica, as well as Opus Dei, the cultural periodical *Arbor*, and the integrist school of Rafael Calvo Serer.

In these circumstances, Church-State relations achieved perfect harmony, as Monsignore Eijo Garay said in the daily *Ya* on 12

February 1950. Of course, there had been some clashes. In 1939, a pastoral letter from Cardinal Gomá calling for reconciliation among Spaniards had actually been banned. And there would be further differences in future. The intemperate integrist sympathies of the excitable Archbishop of Seville Cardinal Segura provoked a series of incidents between the heirarchy and the regime in the course of the fifties. Franco said that he bore them like a cross. There were, indeed, times when the perfect harmony claimed by Bishop Eijo in 1950 was far from apparent. In particular, between 1945 and 1948, although the heirarchy and the Spanish Church were clearly throwing in their lot with Francoism, it was apparent that there were some cross-currents beneath the surface.

The convenience of a concordat was needed. Spain's ambassador to the Holy See, Joaquín Ruiz-Giménez, took the initiative (with the rather sceptical consent of Franco and Artajo) in October 1949. He saw it as a mutual benefit, which would consolidate the position of the Spanish Church on the one hand, while on the other, it would definitely secure the Vatican's full confidence in Spain.

The Holy See adopted the idea in February 1950. Negotiations took a long time. They were conducted with top security and were fraught with difficulties, as a result of the misgivings with which the Vatican still viewed some aspects of the Franco regime. In the end, however, agreement was reached. The concordat was drawn up with decisive help, on the Spanish side, from Fernando Mariá Castiella, ambassador to the Holy See since 1951, and it was signed on 27 August 1953.

Franco evinced deep satisfaction with the concordat in his end of year message that year. This was only to be expected. The concordat from his point of view, was neither essential nor effective, for it merely enshrined the good relations with the Church which he already enjoyed, and Spain had broken out of international isolation in 1950–51. Nor did the concordat serve to resolve all possible future differences between Church and State. In 1955, to cite only one instance, the Information Minister, Arias Salgado, became involved in a controversy (of a rather formal but revealing kind) with Bishop Herrera on the question of press freedom, which the Church wanted to see established. Despite all this the concordat was of inestimable value to Franco and his government. It represented the final and unambiguous acceptance by the Church of the Catholic motives claimed for the uprising of 1939 and of the Catholic nature claimed for Franco's regime and movement.

Franco's concessions to the Church were numerous. The

Franco with Hitler at Hendaye, 23 October 1940.

Franco with Mussolini in Bordighera, 12 February 1941.

An early photograph of Francisco Franco during the Legion's campaign in Africa,
October 1920–25.

ABOVE: General Franco, flanked by Generals Varela (left) and Moscardo (right) at the liberation of Toledo, 27 September 1936. BELOW: Franco's installation as head of state at Burgos, 1 October 1936. To his immediate right is General Cabanellas; behind and to his right is General Queipo de Llano; behind and to his right is General Mola; and further to his left, General Saliquet.

Juan Carlos nominates as Franco's successor in the *Cortes*, 22 July 1969. Below the platform, Carrero Blanco is seated nearest the prince.

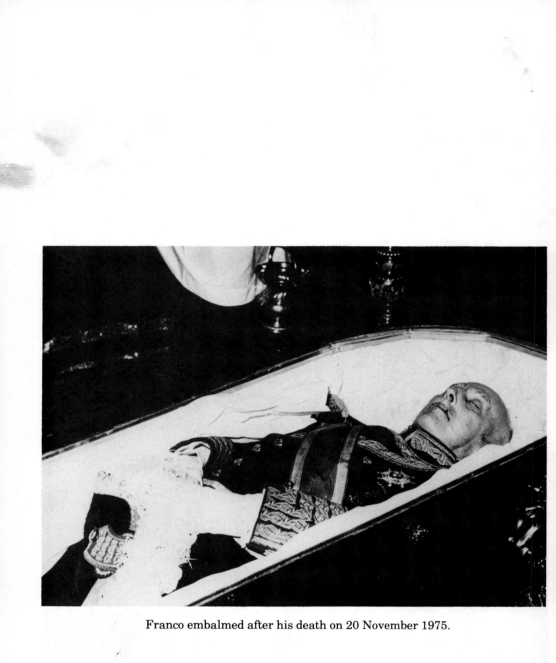

Franco embalmed after his death on 20 November 1975.

Franco receives the King of Morocco, Mohamed V, in 1956.

Franco receiving General Eisenhower on his official visit to Spain, 21 December 1959.

A portrait photograph of Franco with his wife Carmen Polo, taken in later life.

concordat in fact changed Spanish society and the state by embodying Catholic precepts in the law. It was true that Franco retained the right to make and to veto episcopal appointments, but this was a right he had enjoyed since the accord of June 1941. The Church could anyway circumvent it by leaving the sees vacant indefinitely and appointing auxiliary bishops directly from Rome, as was to happen in the sixties. This was not, therefore, a concession by the Church. It was the Spanish state that made the bigger concessions. Franco made them happily, not only because the concordat was his greatest diplomatic success to date – far more valuable to him than the UN vote of 4 November 1950 – but also because of his own deep religious convictions. His faith was uncompromisingly integrist, as could be seen in his *Freemasonry*, published in 1952. Moreover, the concordat brought him some of his most gratifying personal rewards. Pius XII restored to Franco the privileges enjoyed by Philip IV – giving him, among other equally quaint dignities, the title of Canon of St Liberatus. Later, the Pope made him a Knight of the Order of Christ, the highest distinction the Vatican could confer.[12]

A month later, on 26 September 1953, when Foreign Minister Artajo and Ambassador James Dunn signed the accords (not explicitly a 'treaty' or 'alliance') between Spain and the United States, Franco's foreign policy was, as he said himself, fulfilled. The agreement was threefold, and comprised a defence pact, a commitment to mutual defence and a convention on economic aid. It was obvious what mattered: for a period of ten years, subject to renewal, the United States could use the bases which were to be established – jointly, be it noted – in Torrejón, Saragossa, Morón and Rota, while America was to grant substantial economic aid to Spain, fixed initially at 226 million dollars but eventually rising to 1,183 million dollars.

Obviously, these agreements were of immense importance. They shattered the tradition of political isolationism maintained by Spain – with occasionally disastrous consequences – since the last third of the nineteenth century. They tied the defence of Spain to that of the western world, the area to which she belonged by virtue of geographical and historical factors. In doing so, they gave Spain and the army a defence and a foreign policy.

The political character of Franco's regime, however, had meant that Spain had to negotiate from a position of evident weakness and that, in order to be sure of American recognition, some sacrifice of Spanish sovereignty had to be made. Still, this was not how the accords were perceived at the time. There were, after all, US bases in most western democracies and no one saw them as neo-colonial in nature, but rather as bulwarks of national defence and international peace. Four foreign bases were created on Spanish soil. They may have been nominally 'joint' bases but the epithet was dubiously applied. A secret clause allowed the Americans to use the bases unilaterally in the event of 'a communist attack threatening western security' with no more than prior communication – not consultation – with the Spanish government.

It seems likely that Franco, who had refused to grant bases to Nazi Germany in 1940, was less than fully satisfied with this. He certainly devoted a great deal of diplomatic effort to trying to improve these conditions during the negotiations over successive renewal. His aim was to replace them with a fully fledged alliance between equals – something which the 1953 pacts did not remotely resemble. Franco received no mark of honour from the Americans to accompany the accords. Some time later, however, in December 1959, a visit from President Eisenhower more than compensated. For the first time, a democratic head of state paid an official visit to the man with whom Hitler had claimed to be joined by the irreversible course of history.[13]

By 1959 Franco was a fully fledged member of the international community. His diplomatic successes – for such they were, despite the cost which we have mentioned – were to have further, cumulative consequences. In January 1955 the UN invited Spain to send an observer. In August, Franco's Spain joined the Inter-parliamentary Union. On 1 November, the US Secretary of State Foster Dulles called on Franco at the Pardo. On 15 December 1955, the US General Assembly definitively authorized Spain's entry into the organization by 55 votes in favour, with Mexico and Belgium abstaining. 'At last I have won the Spanish Civil War,' Franco is said to have declared after the signing of the US accords on 26 September 1953.[14] The UN acknowledged as much in their decision of December 1955, which Franco seems to have received with indifference, showing the same impassivity he always displayed in the face of important news.

Franco could rest secure. He was already confident enough before the 1953 accords or UN membership in 1955. So confident was he that in 1951, during a cabinet re-shuffle, he had allowed cabinet rank to be attached to the post of Secretary-General of the Movement which had obvious Falangist leanings. He also appointed one of the leading figures of the Falangist past, Raimundo Fernández-Cuesta, to head the new ministry. Furthermore, in 1953 the Falange was allowed to hold its first congress for 20 years, and in September 1955, in a speech in Corruna,

Franco stated that the Falange was 'the authentic medium for expressing nationwide concerns'.

None of this implied that the Falange would be allowed to return to take up the role of the single party. Moreover, the Falange was now 'tamed' and willing to be absorbed in the Movement. Indeed, the 1951 government was based on Franco's understanding of what the Movement ought to be – 'a cluster of brilliant men undimmed by faint-heartedness', as Franco called it in his end-of-year message for 1954. Franco brought the Falange back in order to assert the legitimacy of state of 18 July. He did so in the face of a world which had condemned this legitimacy in 1946 but in 1950, was coming to accept it. 1950, then, was the year of the return of the Falange. As well as the Ministry for the Movement, it controlled the Ministry of Labour in the person of Girón and could count on the sympathy of the ministers of the Army (Munoz Grandes), Agriculture (Cabestany) and even commerce (Arbarua). At the same time, the representation of the Catholic faction was increased: Artajo continued at the Foreign Ministry, while Ruiz-Giménez took over national education. Traditionalism (Iturmendi at the Justice Ministry) and monarchism (Vallellano at Public Works) continued to be represented. Technocrats and straightforward Francoists, from whose ranks Carrero Blanco was now put in charge of the cabinet office, remained in the government. In this cabinet, of all the elements in the 'Movement', the Falangists and Catholics seemed preponderant. This was why in 1953 the Opus Dei theorist Rafael Calvo Serer proposed a 'third way': starting from the triumphalist assumptions of Catholic integrism, he advocated a 'social and representative' monarchy – that is, a monarchy neither liberal nor parliamentary.

In a number of speeches of 1952 Franco re-launched the theory of 'organic democracy'. He did so, for instance, when opening a session of the *Cortes* on 17 May and he returned to the same theme in Valencia on the 27 and again in Pamplona on 4 December. His 'democracy' was, at the end of the day, an antidote to the Second Republic, which Franco described in Seville on 17 April 1953 as 'a fraud practised on the Spanish people' and 'a well-to-do men's swindle'. It was a 'democracy' which, rain or shine, had no place for parties. 'We abhor parties,' said Franco at Pamplona in December 1952. Later in his end-of-year message for 1955 he spoke of parties as a 'lamentable and unnatural abortion' and he blamed them yet again for the misfortunes of Spanish history.

National Movement, organic democracy and Catholic, social, representative state – these were the formulas most often repeated by Franco in the fifties. Uncertainty about the succession remained. Carlism – or at least the Bourbon-Parma family whose head, Don Javier, was the Carlist pretender from 1936 onwards – had been showing public restlessness since the beginning of the decade. A markedly liberal monarchist group, which tellingly included Joaquín Satrustegui, had taken part in the local 'elections' of November 1954.

A month later, on 29 December, Franco had a further meeting with Don Juan in a country house at Navalmoral de la Mata, in the province of Cáceres. The house was owned by the Count of Ruiseñada, a leading figure among monarchists allied to Don Juan who also maintained loyalty to Franco. The subject was again the question of how Prince Juan Carlos should be brought up. They agreed that the prince should study in Spain and enter the Saragossa Military Academy. This was highly gratifying to Franco who was probably already thinking of Juan Carlos as his eventual successor. The prince was, after all, of a suitable age. He was sixteen years old in 1955, which meant that, according to the terms of the Law of Succession, Franco still had fourteen years to go – until 1969 – before nominating him as heir, should he choose to. Franco was 62 years old in 1955 and his health was splendid. In view of his 'magistracy for life' – to paraphrase his own statements to the paper *Arriba* of 27 February 1955 – it was hoped that many years still lay ahead for him. But lest anyone should see his meeting with Don Juan as a step towards restoring the liberal monarchy, Franco defined his own expectations of the succession in a significant formula in his end-of-year message for 1954: 'The future of the National Movement is the continuation of the National Movement.' Spain was not in any sort of transitional phase. Franco was more convinced of this than ever, and with good reason. 'He wants nothing save perpetual power for himself. He is arrogant and self-besotted. He thinks he knows it all and he's playing for rash stakes in the international game.' That is what the Duke of Alba, his representative in London, thought about Franco in May 1945.[15] It was a harsh judgement and it is impossible to say whether it was fair, or whether it was merely the expression of some temporary displeasure of the duke's. Ten years later, however, in 1955, one thing seemed certain. Franco had been right to play the international game with confidence. The enduring solidity of his regime had been his winnings.

5
A Change of Spots

'I am the sentinel who is never relieved, who receives the thankless telegrams, who prescribes solutions, who keeps watch while others are asleep.' With these words of Franco's, uttered in the Army Museum on 7 March 1949, Luis de Galinsoga and General Franco Salgado-Araujo prefaced a biographical sketch of the leader which they published in 1956.

This may have been all very well, but there were times when the vigilant, alert sentinel seemed to drop his guard. For instance, in 1956, precisely when Franco was claiming that his policy had reached fulfilment, the whole complex edifice which he had erected amid so many difficulties threatened to collapse beneath him. Disorder returned to the streets, after repeated claims that social peace had been Franco's great achievement. In the same year, independence had to be given to Morocco, where the 'African' identity of Spain's leader had been forged in war. Over the next two years, fear of strikes haunted Spain again, under a regime that had claimed to have the formula – vertical syndicalism – that would abolish the class struggle. In 1957–58 the regime was on the brink of bankruptcy and suspension of international payments when its leader had recently said that he had done more in ten years than other Spanish regimes in half a century.

The sentry, moreover, seemed to have fallen out of step. In the eleven years from 1945 to 1956 Franco had only two governments. Now, in only two years from 1956 to 1957, he would find himself obliged to appoint two more. And he was showing signs of uncertainty. In 1956 he seemed about to back the Falange as the basis for building the future institutions of his regime and gave the go-ahead for Arrese's plans along these lines; the following year, 1957, he allowed the Falange to organize independently – something which, in defiance of all logic, he had refused to countenance in 1945. Yet in 1958 he introduced the Law of

'Principles of the Movement' (*Ley de Principios del Movimiento*) which effectively destroyed the Falangist preponderance by defining the Movement as a 'communion' of all political forces.

Nor was this all. In 1957–59, Franco accepted that his economic policies had to be radically changed. Thanks to this change, the crisis would soon be overcome and the ground would be laid for the spectacular economic progress of the sixties. But first, though Franco obstinately refused to admit it, the national-syndicalist ideas on which the economic and social policies of his regime had been founded since 1939 had to be discarded.

The national-syndicalist state of 18 July 1936 had opted for an economic and social policy clearly derived from the model of Fascist Italy. Its watchword was self-sufficiency. Franco had no economic training or knowledge. When he came to power in 1936 he was probably thinking simply of pursuing a policy similar to that followed by Primo de Rivera in 1923–30, which embodied nationalist ideas of stimulating production by huge state investment in public works. On 1 January 1939 he told the journalist Manuel Aznar that his economic and trading policies would be based on 'patriotism' – begging him not to ask for enlargement on this point – and that he was absolutely confident about economic prospects.[1] However he gave no reason for his optimism, which may perhaps have derived from the fact that the nationalist zone had experienced no serious economic problems during the war.

The problems – lack of foreign exchange, heavy external debt, shortage of raw materials and foodstuffs, adverse trade balance – only came to Franco's notice when the war was over. His economic and trading policies 'based on patriotism' probably meant, to him, a few straightforward and elementary ideas: import substitution, a strong currency, increase of industrial and agricultural production, co-operation between owners and workers in the task of national economic recovery, investment in large-scale work on the infrastructure, rebuilding of areas and assets destroyed by the war and so on. Such aims were in tune with the opinions of advisers who, in the months after the end of the war, were already talking in terms of 'autarchy' – that is, self-sufficiency.

Self-sufficiency was not solely or chiefly the result of circumstances imposed by the World War or, later, by international isolation. It was at root an ideologically-inspired programme, uncompromisingly consistent, for the creation of a new economic, social and industrial order that would replace the old liberal system.

Self-sufficiency and state direction went together. With these as his aims, Franco set about the construction of an economic system which the Labour Rights law (*Fuero del Trabajo*) of 1938 defined as 'totalitarian' and which opposed 'liberal capitalism' and 'Marxist materialism' alike; its principles were economic self-sufficiency, vertical syndicalism and the command economy.[2]

Franco always showed a concern for social issues which must be accepted as sincere. He was a man of the middle classes who never felt at ease with the traditional aristocracy, though he would respect their privileges. He shared the Falange's populist outlook, though always from a more cautious and conservative point of view. In a speech setting out his programme on 1 October 1936 he promised to maintain guaranteed wages and respect all the gains previously made by the working classes. From the first he insisted that the army men had not been leading a class movement. As he told Manuel Aznar in January 1939, 'I want my policies to have the same deeply popular character that has always marked policies of the greatness of Spain.' In a chapter of an unpublished book of Franco's, which appeared in *Il Corriere della Sera* in December 1938, he rejected the notion that only the privileged classes supported him and reminded readers that the Navarrese peasants who joined his rising belonged to the people. 'We shall take special care,' he said on another occasion early in the war, 'to improve the lot of the working classes and of all who have suffered through no fault of their own.'

In the year the war ended, he recalled how he had already introduced such measures as unemployment relief, remission of rent and of electricity and running water charges for the unemployed, saving schemes designed to promote the idea of a family wage, state aid for public housing – which was one of Franco's abiding concerns – the fighting fund against tuberculosis, and many other projects. When he made the *Fuero del Trabajo* the first of his 'fundamental laws' he was trying precisely to emphasize the presumed *social* character of his Movement.

Franco, however, combined his Catholic social paternalism with an authoritarian view of social peace. In the first important interview he gave to the press, to *ABC* in Seville on 19 July 1937, he was asked about the social programme of the new state. He replied, 'First, total elimination of the class struggle; liquidation of strikes and lock-outs; reliance on arbitration.' He never believed in a right to strike. 'Strikes,' he said on 12 May 1951, are crimes.' They were treated as such under his regime until the end of his days. Franco's social system would be a combination of abundant legislation favouring and protecting the working classes with the denial of trade union freedoms and suppression of all unauthorized collective action.

The results were the creation of a large number of state institutions and the introduction of some important social and economic measures. Some of these have already been mentioned. In October 1939 the National Land Settlement Institute (*Instituto Nacional de Colonización*) was set up with the object of increasing land let to peasant farmers, cultivating under-exploited lands, increasing yields and stimulating production of crops and livestock without a major agrarian reform. In December 1940 the trade union organization of official syndicates started up. In September 1941 the Institute of National Industry (*Instituto Nacional de Industria* – INI) was created through which the state would play a large and direct part in the process of autarchic industrialization.

The state took rigid control of supply, prices and wages, the latter fixed by the Ministry of Labour. It also assumed control of creation of new industries and expansion of old ones. Tight restrictions on imports and foreign trade, and so on, were imposed, with quotas and threshholds and a complex system of multiple exchange rates. In the social sphere, the Labour Tribunal (*Magistratura de Trabajo*) was founded to arbitrate in labour disputes – a role which Franco extolled. Strikes were proscribed but security of employment was guaranteed. Compulsory old age and disability insurance was introduced, with family allowances, compulsory sickness insurance, the family bonus scheme (the 'points', as it was called in the forties), the industrial friendly societies (introduced in the same decade to regulate pensions and other benefits) and many other similar devices.[4]

Yet the results were conspiculously ineffective and inadequate. Agrarian policy was a disaster. From 1939 total production declined sharply. On 17 July 1944 Franco said that there had not been a good harvest since the war, and from that year until 1949 'chronic drought' would make matters even worse. From the first year of peace there was black market activity on a large scale because farmers were forced to produce and sell at official prices and the state was obliged to import cereals on a large sale, chiefly from Argentina. In 1950 production was still below 1936 levels.

The same thing happened in the industrial sector. Franco – who like Primo de Rivera and the socialist Prieto, had a fixation about public works – was able to announce in his end-of-year message for 1950 that in ten years his regime had built great hydro-electric dams, some 30 reservoirs, about 40 large generating stations and thanks to INI had set up factories for aluminium nitrates, chemical industries, pharmaceuticals, engineering, motor-lorries (the Pegaso plant), shipbuilding (the Bazán yard), oil refining (the Escombreras refinery) and much else besides. The facts were beyond dispute, as was the claim that by 1944–45 the repair of war damage was complete. But it had all been done at exorbitant cost, with minimal returns, low productivity and severe inflationary consequences. Monopolistic tendencies were favoured. Import restrictions led to the use of low-quality materials and inadequate industrial equipment. Only the increase in the output of electricity proved to be a real and lasting achievement.

The years from 1940 to 1951 were marked by economic stagnation and scarcity, admittedly exacerbated by problems of oil and food supplies during the Second World War, although in this connection, the sad contrast with the enormous increase in prosperity brought by neutrality in the First World War could hardly have been more flagrant. State control of new industry and of import quotas favoured corruption and personal patronage. Wages were always behind prices. 1939–42 were truly years of hunger. School books issued in May 1939 could not be replaced until 1951. Payments 'over the odds' and the black market flourished over the same period. Not until 1951 did the GNP exceed the 1936 level and it was another two years before income per capita climbed to overtake the pre-war rate. In 1951 the first large-scale social disturbances of the post-war era occurred when the Barcelona tram system was boycotted from 1–6 March; strikes followed shortly afterwards against the cost of living, again in Barcelona and in the Basque Country and Madrid.

Franco could not ignore what was happening. The change of government of 1951, according to a note from Carrero Blanco to Franco of 4 April, was the result of the need to make changes in economic policy, with the aim of liberalizing foreign trade and relaxing price controls. Franco accepted this. From 1951 to 1955 his speeches would put much more stress on economic matters, especially in connection with industrialization policy.

Indeed, the 1951 government, and especially the Minister of Commerce, Manuel Arburúa, did begin to liberalize and deregulate the market. Exchange rates were simplified; imports were made easier; private sector lending was expanded; capital investment was encouraged; and INI was switched to a role that complemented that of the private sector instead of competing with it.

The overall picture was almost immediately transformed. At least until 1954, almost all indicators became and remained positive. In the fifties the regime registered some of its most important achievements. In Asturias, the great Ensidesa steelworks began production. In Barcelona, Seat was created, launching its first cars in 1953. In 1952 the Badajoz Plan went into operation for the irrigation of 100,000 hectares, the building of dams and generating stations and the introduction of cotton and tobacco farming and of new agro-industries.

The changes of 1951, however, did not go far enough. 1954 was a year of catastrophe for agriculture and the state had to import more than a million tonnes of wheat. Public spending, in a country with a fiscal base that was actually shrinking and which had no monetary policy or serious budgetary discipline, continued at excessive and inflationary levels. Investment declined compared with 1953. Inflation shot up again in 1954. The Minister of Labour – José Antonio Girón de Velasco, the Falangist boss whose activity since 1941 had been synonymous with the regime's welfare policy – put up wages by decree in December of that year. All his efforts merely succeeded in making inflation worse. Imports proved much higher than expected. The balance of payments deficit and the loss of foreign exchange reached, as we shall see, levels that were unbearable.[5]

In sum, with a per capita income of less than $300, Spain in 1960, twenty years after the end of the Civil War, jointly with neighbouring Portugal, was the poorest country in Europe. She continued to occupy that position despite the evident industrial progress which had been made, despite the increase in the standard of living achieved since 1950, and despite the fact that, low income levels apart, Spanish society showed undeniable vitality. When Ortega y Gasset returned from exile in 1946, he was surprised, even at that early date, by the 'indecent healthiness' which could apparently be observed in Spain.[6]

It was clear that the regime had made great efforts. Franco, in particular, was full of enthusiasm for the work of INI. But it was equally obvious that levels of welfare and consumption in Spanish society, industrial capacity and the quality of the industrial output, to say nothing of agricultural productivity, were, relatively speaking, seriously disappointing. Spain in the forties and fifties was still an under-developed country. In 1950, for example, only 33.7% of dwellings had running water, though 79.5% had electricity. Only 1.4% of the population of 18 to 25 year olds went to university.[7]

Franco himself, to his own annoyance, could confirm on his frequent journeys around the country that there were still large pockets of poverty and misery to be found in Spain in the sixties and that the shanty towns, which he characterized as a source of shame to be rooted out, still existed.[8]

Spain's under-development, moreover, persisted amid tremendous sacrifices of hard work and saving on the part of the middle, lower and working classes. As he told his cousin Franco Salgado-Araujo in 1961, Franco thought his own labour laws were the most progressive in the world.[9] Not only was this a palpable error; but it also seems likely that he was unaware of the only three consequences that the 'national-syndicalist revolution' had yielded by 1960: (1) a definitive shift of economic power from the aristocratic and landowning oligarchy to financial, industrial and entrepreneurial circles; (2) the integration into the bureaucratic machinery of the state of a large sector of the middle class: 'the Falange', said Gerald Brenan, 'is simply the party of the Spanish lower middle class';[10] (3) a certain amount of social mobility, effected with great effort and hardship, between the middle and lower ranks of the middle class. In any case, Franco's social paternalism could do little for the rural workers who, after the crisis of 1957–59, were faced with a choice between the grinding misery of a form of agriculture that was obsolete and under-capitalized and despairing migration to the poor quarters of the big cities.

Spain changed in the sixties, as we shall see. It took Franco twenty years to realize that his system did not work and that the way out lay through the economic liberalism which he had criticized so emphatically. A great deal had to happen before he could be convinced. It was only the build-up of social conflicts from 1956 onwards that, eventually, induced him to change his mind.

Chronologically speaking, the first warning bell sounded on 9 February 1956 with a grave incident in the middle of Madrid. A clash between students and young Falangists led to the death of one of the latter, Miguel Álvarez, from a shot in the head. The problem was not limited to the events of 9 Februry, serious as these were: it lay rather in the growth of political agitation apparent in the University of Madrid since 1954–55 and took a number of different forms. The most significant had been demonstrations at the time of the death of Ortega y Gasset in October 1955 and attempts to organize a young writers' congress and a free students' conference.

This was politically significant because it implied a challenge to the representative role and even the very existence of the University Students' Union (*Sindicato de Estudiantes Universitarios* – SEU) which had started in the Falange and to which all university students were obliged to belong. What was more, the hard men of the regime saw the student unrest as the outcome of liberalization timidly initiated by Ruiz-Giménez and his friends in 1951 and severely criticized ever since. Franco had let the process go on because of his practice of giving his ministers their head; but he now found it deeply disquieting.

The events of 9 February were the culmination of several days of incidents. Public opinion received the news with stupefaction: it was the first time any information – albeit scandalously distorted in this case – had been released about public disorder. Falangist circles were outraged, to the point where it was feared that if the wounded boy died, the Falange would decree a night of long knives. The fact that the wound had been caused by a stray police shot was concealed from the public.

Franco's reaction was decisive and dramatic. On 10 February the government declared a state of emergency throughout the country; on the 11th, Dionisio Ridruejo was arrested. (He was the long-serving Falangist who had collaborated closely with Serrano Suñer, volunteered for the Blue Division and then broken, some years previously, with the regime.) Various writers and young intellectuals were taken into custody, all to be charged with organizing the student riots. They included Tamames, Sánchez Mazas, Enrique Múgica, Javier Pradera, and Ruiz Gallardón. A few days later Sánchez Dragó, José Luis Abellán, López Pacheco and others were also taken in. The University was closed for several days.

Never for a moment did Franco's nerve waver, though this could not be said of other members of his government. The meeting of the Council of Ministers on the 10th was tense. Only Artajo stood up for the Minister of Education. Franco resorted to a characteristic ploy, the judgement of Solomon – punishing both sides even-handedly. On the 16th he suspended the Minister for the Movement, Raimundo Fernández Cuesta, who had been out of Spain when the incident occurred, and the deputy Secretary General, Tomás Ramojaro; the Education Minister, Ruiz-Giménez and collaborators of his such as Laín Entralgo, Rector of Madrid University, and Antonio Tovar, who held the same post at Salamanca were sacked at the same time.[11]

That proved to be enough. Franco attached little importance to student agitation, probably rightly. The cause of the tension had not been the student unrest, which was confined to a small minority, but the Falangists' ferocious reaction to what happened to Miguel Álvarez, who, contrary to early reports, did not die.

Franco, however, failed to grasp the full significance of the incident. He thought it was an adolescent dust-up manipulated by the communists. It was much more than that. On the one hand, it showed the growing distance between young people and the regime: a cultural rebellion was afoot against the 'boredom of idleness' of which Serrano Suñer had spoken in 1949 and which the 18 July formula, combining national syndicalism and religious revival, had brought about. On the other hand, the birth of a new kind of opposition was being witnessed, still rather protean and without any distinct ideology. This new opposition arose inside Spain and had nothing to do with either the legacy of the exiled republic or the monarchism of the court of Don Juan at Estoril.

The second warning sounded from Morocco and, like the first, it caught Franco and his regime off guard. It was not that they were unaware of what was happening in Morocco. They knew that in the French zone of the protectorate, since the end of the Second World War, an important independence movement had arisen which Sultan Mohammed v himself would eventually lead. The situation had even been debated at the UN in 1952. But Franco, who appointed prestigious generals to run the Moroccan High Commission (Asensio, Orgaz, Varela, García Valiño, the last of them gazetted on 31 March 1951) thought that he could avoid problems by adopting a benign policy in the protectorate. He encouraged the development of the Moroccan economy to some extent and maintained friendship with the Arab world by, for example, refraining from recognizing Israel. To judge from his conversations with Franco Salgado-Araujo, Franco believed that Moroccan independence was inevitable in the long term but favoured gradual progress towards it – over a period of 25 years.[12] He wanted to undertake a thorough programme of action against communism first, and he was thinking, as he told the director of the press agency *EFE* on 15 December 1955, in terms of a future for Morocco without political parties.

In any event, since nationalist agitation began in 1952–53, the regime had followed a clearly anti-French policy, even to the extent of tolerating Moroccan nationalism. Franco, ever cautious, would have preferred a more guarded attitude to the nationalists than that evinced by High Commissioner García Valiño, but he upheld the latter's policy. When the French deposed Mohammed v on 20 August 1953, Spain declined to recognize the new authorities set up by France. Franco himself called the new sultan, Mulay Arafa, the 'Quisling sultan', using the name of the Norwegian Nazi leader who had become synonymous in political jargon with treachery and 'collaboration'. In October 1955, when the French army tried to take action against the berbers of the Spanish zone, Spain risked a certain degree of military tension by closing the frontier of her protectorate.

Even if the motive behind this was only to gain Arab support, which Franco indeed received, for his efforts to break out of isolation, it was, if not a particularly intelligent policy, at least better than any other available option. What it lacked was foresight. Franco expected that Moroccan nationalism would take some time to turn against Spain. Thus when, suddenly and unilaterally, the French granted independence to Morocco on 2 March 1956, shortly after restoring Mohammed v to his throne, Spain was left with no choice. Franco, taken by surprise by the French U-turn, called for 'peaceful concord'. In less than a month he dismantled the protectorate and on 7 April 1956, despite some resentment within the army, the protocol recognizing Moroccan independence was signed, to be confirmed by a treaty signed by Franco and Mohammed v at the Pardo on 12 February 1957.

Spain's lack of foresight – and, what was more, the consequences of the inconsistencies of her policy – now became apparent. Not only was there no 'peaceful concord'; at the end of November 1957 war returned to northern Africa. Moroccan irregulars mounted surprise attacks on the remaining Spanish posts in Africa: Ifni and the northern Spanish Sahara. The action again took the Spanish authorities by surprise; a contingent of 8,000 troops had to be rushed over and French help summoned to contain the offensive. Normal conditions were not restored until after a fierce counter-attack by the Legion in January 1958. Spain had then to cede northern Ifni to Morocco.

The entire situation had been turned on its head. Deceived by Moroccan proceedings, Franco watched as Spain became the target of Moroccan irredentism, behind which, as usual, he saw the hand of Russia. As he watched, relations between the two countries became irremediably soured. From that time onwards, he was convinced that the Moroccans would demand all Spain's African territories without allowing any concessions. Franco was determined to resist Moroccan claims but not at the cost of war. On 4 January 1969 he was to surrender Ifni. The Saharan question remained in abeyance until the very last days of Franco's life.

The irony was twofold. Not only did one of the most conspicuous African veterans of the Spanish army hurriedly surrender a protectorate zone which had been Spanish since 1912; more than that, a regime which had made Arab friendship one of the pillars of its diplomacy now found that an Arab state, Morocco, had become the major stumbling block in its foreign policy.

Franco's problems did not even stop there. In 1956, the twentieth anniversary of his elevation as head of state, an economic crisis and social problems were glaringly obvious. Girón, the Minister of Labour, wanted to allay discontent by another rise in wages. On 3 March, 1956, he obtained government agreement for a new increase: 20% immediately followed by another 10% in the autumn. The result was an almost intolerable situation: in the next two years the cost of living would rise by almost 40%. Foreign exchange reserves fell, moreover, from $220 million in 1955 to $57 million in 1958. In 1957, the foreign debt rose to the record level of $387 million. In January 1957 there were strikes in Barcelona – against increases in fares – and Madrid.

It was obvious that the 1951 government had outlived its term. During 1956 a political crisis developed alongside the economic crisis. Franco had not wanted to make a fresh start with a new government in February in order to avoid giving the impression that he was paying any attention to student unrest. Far from it, he instructed the new Minister for the Movement, José Luis Arrese, to draw up a programme of 'fundamental laws' which would give the regime the 'constitution' it still lacked, and so supply a widely felt need. For a moment it looked as if Franco had decided to rely wholeheartedly on the Falange and there was even talk of a thoroughly Falangist cabinet.

Arrese prepared three drafts: one on the principles of the Movement, one on the organization of government and finally a so-called 'Organic law of the Movement'. They raised two basic problems: nowhere within them was any reference made to the institution of the monarchy or to the future king; and the drafts envisaged a state in which real power remained in the hands of the Movement and its supreme organ, the National Council, in both of which the Falangists were dominant. As Martín Artajo, the Foreign Minister who was totally opposed to the plans, said, they would have aligned the regime with totalitarianism and would have presented the Falange with the means of indefinite control of the government.

It was the reaction the drafts inspired that decided Franco against them. The president of the *Cortes* (Esteban Bilbao), the Ministers of Justice, Foreign Affairs, Public Works, Finance and Education (Iturmendi, Artajo, Vallellano, Gómez de Llano and Jesús Rubio, who had replaced Ruiz-Giménez), Carrero Blanco and Cardinals Quiroga, Arriba y Castro and Pla y Deniel not to mention others, all told Franco of their total opposition to Arrese.

Franco therefore decided to embark on a change of government and shelve the plans of the Minister for the Movement in February 1957.[13] Some changes were spectacular, like the dismissal of Alberto Martín Artajo, who was replaced by Fernando María Castiella at the Foreign Ministry, after twelve years in the job. His record included Spain's gradual recovery from diplomatic isolation and the definition of the key principles of foreign policy. Blas

Pérez, too, was removed from the Ministry of the Interior, also after twelve years' service. He was replaced by the energetic General Camilo Alonso Vega, a friend of Franco's from their time together in the Military Academy, who had commanded the paramilitary Civil Guard for many years.

The most important change, however, was the withdrawal of the Falange and the arrival of prominent members of Opus Dei to take charge of the economic ministries. Girón retired as Minister of Labour after 16 years and Arrese was demoted to the Ministry of Housing: Franco was unwilling to dispense with him altogether, saying that he wanted him to 'cool off' first in a new job; he was to resign in 1960. His replacement, José Solís Ruiz, would lay more stress on the notion that the Movement was an extension of the trade union structure rather than the Falangist tradition. It was at the Treasury and Ministry of Commerce that the two new Opus Dei ministers entered the government: Mariano Navarro Rubio and Alberto Ullastres – the 'technocrats', as they would be called because of their strictly professional credentials. These new ministers were closely connected with a third Opus member, Laureano López Rodó, Carrero Blanco's éminence grise since his appointment in 1956 as 'Secretary of the Presidency' – in effect, Cabinet Secretary.[14]

Arrese's plans were jettisoned for good. In their place the political project of Carrero Blanco and López Rodó would eventually win out: a traditional monarchy, deriving its claim to legitimacy from 18 July, with reform of the state administration and with Prince Juan Carlos as heir. This was probably the plan which Franco, ever more inscrutable, privately favoured, but the slow pace of his decision-making spread its implementation over twelve more years.

In any event the crisis of 1956–57 revealed some inconsistencies in Franco's behaviour. Franco consented to certain projects – those of Arrese – in which he had little confidence. He even went so far as to tell Arrese himself that he would govern with the liberal constitution of 1876; soon after, he told his ambassador Garrigues that he saw the Movement as nothing more than a claque, good only for applause.[15] And what was more, Franco stifled Arrese's plans, not because he thought them bad or disliked their totalitarian assumptions – on the contrary, he defended them to Cardinal Pla y Deniel – but because they aroused hostility from almost all the non-Falangist elements in the regime.

Be that as it may, Franco seemed to feel comfortable and optimistic with his new government. That the crisis had been serious and the change significant was made apparent by the unusually large number of explanations Franco felt obliged to offer. In 1957 he gave long interviews to some important media (*The New York Times*, *ABC*, the *EFE* Press Agency and others) to publicize a twofold message: his regime was as stable and firmly rooted as ever; and its continuity would be assured by the laws of the Movement itself.

As time went on, Franco discounted the importance of the crisis of 1957: he had done the same with former crises and would do so with later ones. He shrugged off the change of ministers as 'natural wastage' produced by the wear and tear of the work of government or as a routine changing of the guard which did not alter the direction the regime was taking. He would deny, as he always did, that the change of ministers implied any change in policy. His obsession with the legitimacy of 18 July, his insistence on the coherence of his system and his emphasis on the justifiability of his regime, forced him to represent every ministerial change and political decision, however internally inconsistent, as a logical, intelligible step in the development of a perfect system, fully thought out in advance from 1936.

Within a few months the new government stumbled into the Ifni war and then in March 1958 faced serious strikes in the mines of Asturias. Meanwhile, three questions were broached at once: how to develop state institutions (the 'institutional process' as it was termed), how to meet the economic crisis and how to normalize relations with the outside world.

On 19 May 1958 Franco laid before the *Cortes* a law on 'Principles of the Movement' prepared by Carrero Blanco and López Rodó. Franco explained what the law was about in a long speech which combined an epic account of the past with a definition of what Franco understood his regime to be. The main ingredients of the analysis were: (a) superiority of the 'national revolution' of Franco's 'National Movement' over democratic systems by virtue of its political, religious, national and social coherence; (b) historical vindication of the Movement, manifest in the economic achievements won over twenty years and the country's agrarian and industrial growth; (c) the just basis of the regime's foreign policy and of its anti-communist stand; (d) definition of the regime as a 'traditional Catholic, social and representative monarchy'.

This last point was fundamental. Amid the applause of the deputies, Franco exclaimed, 'Our state lives on its own political resources. We want nothing from outside. Our state is its own heir and we look to no other successor. We are not a transitional phase and we are not an interim dictatorship . . .'. He ruled out any mode of succession that was not a monarchy identified with the principles of 18 July. The future king would have to swear to the principles of the Movement, which were then awaiting the approval of the *Cortes* and which were defined as 'enduring and unalterable'; so would anyone holding any public office have to swear to abide by them.

These principles, which replaced the precepts of the Falange as the key points of Francoist ideology, were twelve in number. In clear and unadorned language, they encapsulated everything that official propaganda had been saying since 1936: the reality and single destiny of Spain ('Unity of Destiny in the Universal' as the Falange put it); the supremacy of the law of God; the unquestionable unity that bound all the people and territories of Spain; the family, municipality and trade union as the basic building-blocks of the community and as the channels of political participation; the rights to justice and to work; and the new formula, already mentioned: 'traditional, Catholic, social and representative monarchy.'

Franco had brought the process of defining the nature of his regime to its conclusion. Other complementary projects, which Carrero Blanco and López Rodó – and not only they – considered vital, would be left in cold storage for many years: the Organic Law on the organization of the state, for instance, and the nomination of his successor. The essential groundwork, however, had been laid. As we shall see, Franco would make no changes to the principles of the Movement. All he did, at least in the short term, was to repeat them and expound them. He took the opportunity of doing so at the numerous public events between 1958 and 1961 – speeches, tours, openings, press statements, end-of-year messages. The ideas he expressed were always the same: the legitimate origin and rightful conduct of his regime; the communist campaign against Spain since 1934; the breakdown of the rule of law in 1936; the criticisms directed at liberalism and at political parties; the defence of his own regime as a just social and political system; the key importance of unity in his policy of reviving Spain's fortunes and for Spain's future; the crusade, interpreted in a social sense, and so on. In short, what he offered was always a justification for the military uprising, and an almost unceasing eulogy of the work of his regime and of his nationalist and Catholic, anti-democratic and obsessively anti-communist ideals.

His life was still marked by an intense and varied official programme, rich in ritual. On 30 October 1958 he presided at the anniversary celebrations of the Falange and on 18 February 1959 at the National Conference on the Family in Spain. On 1 April of the same year he opened the monument to the war dead at the Valley of the Fallen, where the remains of José Antonio were translated. On 1 May 1960 he reviewed a trade union parade in Barcelona. On 13 July he was in Madrid for the unveiling of the monument to Calvo Sotelo. In March of the following year he presided at the first Trade Union Congress. On 17 July 1961 he was at a march past, in which 25,000 veterans took part, to celebrate the 25th anniversary of his victory in the Civil War. In September he opened the Eucharistic Conference at Saragossa and on 1 October, at Burgos, he solemnly celebrated his 'jubilee', again on the occasion of the 25th anniversary of his 'exaltation' – such was the preferred term – as head of state. There were, of course, many other engagements. Franco's diplomatic appearances, for instance, multiplied as Foreign Minister Castiella, continuing Artajo's work, made increasing progress in his appointed task of normalizing foreign relations. The number of foreign ministers and heads of state who visited Madrid and the Pardo grew perceptibly from the end of the fifties and in the early sixties. No visit can have given Franco more satisfaction than that of President Eisenhower on 21 December 1959, which was a triumph for Francoist diplomacy. A million people turned out on the streets of Madrid to demonstrate the approval with which public opinion greeted the end of isolation. To Franco, it seemed like a plebiscite in favour of his policies.

The 1957 government had also taken the economic situation in hand. Its response can be divided into two phases. In the first, between 1957 and 1959, Ullastres and Navarro Rubio tried to sort out the muddle and to begin preparing the Spanish economy for possible membership of the European Economic Community which was due to come into force on 1 January 1959. The multiple exchange rates were abandoned, interest rates were raised and after tax reforms in December 1957 which greatly increased the revenue, Navarro Rubio reduced public spending and ended up with a surplus. At the same time he provided export incentives and cautiously opened the door to foreign investment. In the second stage, on 20 July 1959 Ullastres presented his Stabilization Plan, which had been agreed with the Organization for European Economic Co-operation. The plan proposed control of inflation as the first priority and the immediate liberalization and rationalization of the economy as a basis for restoring its health. The peseta was devalued, the availability of credit was checked, interest rates were raised, import controls were relaxed and public spending was again frozen in the budget.[16]

The results were dazzling. Despite the devaluation of the peseta, prices were virtually stable for the next four years. Spain was allowed to join the great international financial institutions early in 1958 and already in 1959 was getting foreign credit worth 400 million pesetas. Foreign investment rose spectacularly from $12 million dollars in 1958 to $82.6 million in 1960. By the end of the summer of 1959, Spain had a balance of payments surplus of $81 million. In May 1960 reserves rose to $300 million. Devaluation stimulated a spectacular increase in tourism: 6 million tourists arrived in 1960, twice as many as in 1958.

Admittedly, the social cost of the plan was high. For a year and a half, most sectors of the economy were in recession. Wages were virtually static from 1957 to 1961: hence the strikes of 1958, mentioned above, which Alonso Vega suppressed with a severity and an implacability which Franco thought excessive. There were reckoned to be between 150,000 and 200,000 unemployed. In 1960 the mass exodus of workers to other European countries began. But by the middle of that year the economy was showing unmistakeable signs of recovery. The operation had been a remarkable success, probably the best economic move in the history of Francoism.

Technically speaking, the plan had followed an orthodox model of stablilization and control of inflation and represented a commitment to a neo-capitalist programme of de-regulating the Spanish economy. What was historically significant about it was that these very models had previously been utterly unacceptable to the Francoist authorities, to Spain's great disadvantage. Even in 1957, elements representing the Movement and the trade union system continued to view them with distaste. In 1957–59, the national-syndicalist tradition was wiped out.

It could not have been easy for Franco to see things this way, given his characteristic unwillingness to admit that his policies ever changed and his insistence that everything that had happened had been foreshadowed in a sort of master-plan conceived at the inception of his regime. He said as much at his jubilee in Burgos on 2 October 1961.

He disliked the word 'liberalization' even in a strictly economic context. 'I seem to be turning communist,' he told his ministers on one of the many occasions when they urged further liberalization. Yet he accepted the picture his ministers presented and, as usual, trusted them with considerable freedom to take appropriate action. In the end, he became convinced of the need for deflation. In his end of year message for 1959 he spoke of being ready to launch an ambitious development plan. On 11 June 1960 he told his cousin Franco Salgado that without price stability 'we would have gone on until we were broke, with our economy in the hands of the speculators, who drove up the cost of living and who started up businesses of all sorts without having the necessary capital.'[17]

At about that time he began to defend in public the measures devised by Ullastres and Navarro Rubio. In particular in Barcelona on 7 May 1960 he referred to control of inflation as 'our first goal'. Soon after, on 18 July in Madrid, he described it as a prerequisite 'of our joining the international world and of our giving our business men a solid basis of support for their enterprise.' Smug and self-congratulatory, he announced at the end of the same year that the Stabilization Plan – which, he insisted, had been made possible only by the preparatory work of the previous twenty years – had yielded and exceeded its expected results.

Franco's speeches of 1960 and 1961 show his growing interest in economic matters. From the twin themes of stabilization and recovery, the emphasis moved increasingly towards development and growth. Franco thoroughly blinded viewers with statistics when he went on television with his end-of-year message for 1961 and on innumerable subsequent occasions. It must be said, however, that he was very sceptical about how much attention he actually received: once, when he made a mistake in giving a figure during the recording of an end-of-year message, the Information Minister Arias Salgado insisted on a re-take. 'Don't worry,' Franco replied, 'it doesn't matter: nobody listens to these broadcasts anyway.'[18]

From the sixties onwards, the political vocabulary of Franco and Francoism underwent a thorough transformation. The Fascist-sounding rhetoric of national syndicalism was abandoned – save in the conspicuous case of one minister, Solís – in favour of a dry and colourless style, packed with economic jargon and technical terms. The new key terms used to vindicate Francoism were development and its rewards of prosperity and peace. Growth and development became the official ideals of the regime. On 26 January 1962 Laureano López Rodó was appointed Commissioner for Economic Development. Soon after a World Bank report was published, having been compiled in the course of the previous year, endorsing the view that a major drive for growth could be launched on the basis of the foreign reserves accumulated by Spain thanks to tourism and the policy of stabilization.

Franco felt very much at home with the new ideology of development. He saw it as yet another product – indeed, as the culmination – of the struggle for national revival on which he had insisted since 1936. He always denied – as, for instance, in his speech to the National Council on 9 September 1963 – that there had been a dramatic change from a policy of autarchy and self-sufficiency to one of 'competition' and participation in the world market. 'The Development Plan,' he said in his end-of-year message at the end of that same year, 'represents nothing new for this nation.' But it did, even though Franco may have believed, as he claimed, that what had been done between 1939 and 1957 amounted to an 'emergency development plan'. He showed intelligence in exploiting the political potential of development. Another argument of his which became familiar was that economic development was simply the result of political development and that without his Movement, as he said in an interview in *ABC* on 1 April 1964, the basis for growth would never have been achieved.

The truth, as we know, was almost the exact opposite. Development only became possible when the regime adopted the conventional wisdom of modern liberal economists, which the Movement, for doctrinaire and ideological reasons, had rejected until 1957. In effect, however, it did not matter. Success in development became an almost invincible argument for Francoism.

On 1 October 1961 Franco celebrated 25 years as head of state. He was 68 years old. His health was still superb. He was at the pinnacle of his power. There was every indication that Spain was about to enjoy a long period of growth. 'It is going to be the great achievement of our time,' was Franco's later comment on the Development Plan.

The strikes in Asturias in 1958 had been significant, but the energetic response of Alonso Vega, who declared a state of emergency in the region, was enough to keep them under control. In 1960 some nationalist agitation had broken out in Catalonia just when Franco was visiting the area: tough prison sentences had been passed on Jordi Pujol, Francesco Pizón and other detainees. In the Basque country in 1959, ETA (Euskadi ta Askatasuna or Basque Homeland and Liberty) had been founded as a revolutionary separatist force that soon launched an 'armed struggle' of violence and terrorism. The following year, 339 Basque priests published a letter denouncing torture and repression and demanding democratic rights for Spain and for the Basques.

Still, in the Basque Country and Catalonia alike all that had happened so far amounted to no more than the first tiny sparks – sporadic and isolated – of a conflagration which would not break out for many years. In neither area, nor in Asturias, was there wide-scale disillusionment with Francoism. Occasional conflicts apart, all three regions were comfortably ensconced in the system. The 'peaceful' 24-hour general strike against the economic situation and against the regime called by the Communist Party for 18 June 1959 was a total failure. When the intelligent Italian Communist Party militant, Rossana Rossanda, paid a secret visit to Spain in 1962, she could see none of the expected signs of the breakdown of Francoism nor any evidence of a revolutionary situation. On the contrary, she found a society indifferent to politics and a clandestine opposition nourished only by its own fantasies. 'This was not a society where the voice of politics had been silenced,' she later recalled, 'but apparently an apolitical society; not muzzled but mute, or speaking with other tongues.'[19]

In spite of this, the Franco regime still suffered from a kind of chronic sickness of conscience about the legitimacy of its origins, however much the legitimacy bestowed upon it by its achievements was emphasized: the Spanish phrase was 'legitimacy of exercise'. On 7 and 8 June 1962 a meeting in Munich attracted no less than 118 leading figures of the opposition. These included representatives of Christian Democratic tendencies (Gil Robles, Álvarez de Miranda, Cavero), liberal monarchists (Satrústegui, Senillosa), social democrats (Ridruejo), Socialists, Basque Nationalists, Republicans and independents like Salvador de Madariaga. They agreed on a joint resolution which implictly exposed to Eurpoean eyes the anti-democratic and repressive nature of Francoism. The government responded with an over-reaction verging on hysteria. The *Fuero de los Españoles* was suspended; some of the participants were condemned to banishment, while others went into voluntary exile, and the press, on the orders of the Information Minister Arias Salgado, unleashed a campaign of vilification against what was called 'the unholy alliance of Munich'.[20]

The irony was that it was all quite uncalled-for and counterproductive from the regime's own point of view. No sooner had Rossana Rossanda arrived in Barcelona than she heard the same message from all the opposition members she met: 'that Francoism and economic development are incompatible.'[21] Franco believed the exact opposite and here, as we shall see, he was absolutely right.

It was, however, false to claim that his masterly foresight had anticipated everything. On the contrary, by around 1960, his dilatory methods had left serious gaps in the institutional equipment of his regime, which genuinely threatened its future stability. On 24 December 1961 a hunting accident demonstrated how precarious the situation was. A shotgun blew up in Franco's hands, wounding his left hand. He had to be operated on at once, by Dr Garaizábal in a military hospital in Madrid. The accident was not serious, though till June 1962 Franco had to have several sessions of therapy every day. But the very fact that an accident had happened was enough to throw into stark relief the fact that the state lacked institutions capable of coping with a contingency for which it had been inadequately prepared. In short, the 1961 accident exposed the fact that no one knew what would happen if Franco died.

6
What Happens After Franco?

What Happens after Franco? (*Después de Franco, ¿qué?*) was the
title of a pamphlet published in the mid-sixties by the exiled
Communist Party leader Santiago Carrillo. It was hardly an original
title. The same question had come to be asked by everyone
connected with Spanish politics, both inside and outside the
regime, especially at the time of the Caudillo's hunting accident in
December 1961. As far as Franco personally was concerned, the
question had to be formulated differently, replacing the 'What?'
with a 'Who?' For Franco had made at least three things quite clear:
that Spain was already a kingdom; that the monarchy which would
succeed him would not be identifiable with the liberal parliamentary monarchy (that was why he spoke of 'instauration', implying a
distinction from the abhorred term restoration) and that the king
would have to be absolutely identified with the Movement in
order to be fit to succeed.[1]

Therefore, one way or another, the naming of a successor was
inseparable from the question of the nature of the monarchy that
was going to follow on after Franco's death. Franco's idea of
monarchy was almost entirely abstract. He favoured it because he
thought that the monarchy had been the essential element in the
history of Spain. The dynastic question for its own sake was of
slight importance to him. He did not miss the courtly, palace-
bound and aristocratic monarchy: he had never been part of it,
though Alfonso XIII had conferred various honours upon him. He
thought Spain had only one royal dynasty, the Bourbon family. But
the 'instauration' theory, which he favoured because it implied the
creation of a monarchy of a new kind, meant almost by definition
that the hereditary rights of that line – or of any other – would be
irrelevant.

For this reason, Franco's main problem in this connection was posed by Don Juan's indefeasible claims. Other possible pretenders probably never seriously entered his plans. Although the traditional, Catholic social and representative monarchy of which he spoke had obvious echoes of Carlism about it, and despite the zealous support the Carlists gave to the rising of 1936 – Franco conferred battle honours on the Carlist heartlands of Navarre – as well as Franco's unfailing inclusion of traditionalist representatives in all his governments up to 1973, the Generalissimo never took any account of the Carlist pretender Javier de Bourbon-Parma, much less of his son Prince Hugo (later Carlos-Hugo).

Franco regarded the traditionalist dynasty as lacking genuine historic rights. He took Don Javier and Don Carlos-Hugo, moreover, for 'foreign princes', as he said in a statement for *Arriba* in February 1955. He refused to grant them Spanish nationality when they asked for it in the sixties. He was deeply offended by Carlos-Hugo's political activities from the moment they began in 1957, especially as they had an obvious anti-Francoist slant and a surprising leftist content. On 26 November 1964 Franco assembled four of his ministers – Iturmendi, Alonso Vega, Solís and Fraga Iribarne – and left them in no doubt about his opinion of the Carlist prince. 'I am not yet in a position to make the final decision,' he told them, 'but I ought to make clear what I have decided so far. That gentleman [Carlos-Hugo] is heading for nowhere. I ask you to note this and do all you can, each in his own sphere, to make this clear to others.'[2] In 1968, as we shall see, he expelled the entire Bourbon-Parma family from Spain. Other pretenders had even less standing. In the fifties, though, Alfonso de Borbón-Dampierre returned to Spain. Like Juan Carlos, he was a grandson of Alfonso XIII. His rights were problematical, because his father, the infante Don Jaime, brother of Don Juan, had renounced them. Franco regarded him only as a fall-back candidate, to be kept in reserve in case no solution could be achieved in the line of Don Juan and his son Don Juan Carlos. And this remained true even after 1972, when Don Alfonso married Franco's eldest grand-daughter, María del Carmen Martínez-Bordiú.

Don Juan was the problem. Once he and Franco had agreed on the education of Prince Juan Carlos at their meetings in 1948 and 1954, it became increasingly clear, though Franco never said so, that the young prince represented the leader's choice of a solution to the problem. In Juan Carlos, the theory of the 'instauration' of a new monarchy could be made to coincide with the principles of hereditary succession. This, however, implied either that Don Juan should first renounce his own rights, as Franco often said in private – at an interview at Estoril on 17 September 1957 López Rodó went so far as to tell Don Juan to his face that Franco was toying with this idea[3] – or else that Franco should simply disregard them.

Franco, of course, had counted Don Juan out at an early stage. He never forgot or forgave the *Rome Manifesto* of 1945. He said again and again that from that moment Don Juan had set himself up as an enemy of the regime. He would not relent even when in 1957 Don Juan accepted the principles of the Communion of Traditionalists – the biggest step he ever took towards Francoism. Franco thought he was weak and poorly advised and that some of his entourage were freemasons, such as Pedro Sainz Rodríguez whom Franco had known since the twenties and who had been his own Minister of Education in 1938–39.[4]

There were two fundamental reasons for Franco's rejection of Don Juan. First, his accession would imply that the monarchy was being restored – an option Franco had excluded as far back as his statement to *ABC* in Seville in July 1937. Secondly, Don Juan's liberal profile – one of Franco's morbid obsessions – led to the presumption that any monarchy which he headed would be a constitutional and parliamentary regime, profoundly at odds with the 'monarchy of 18 July' which Franco wanted and which was specified in his laws.

Hence full understanding between Franco and Don Juan was never possible, not even after 1954 when Don Juan seemed to accept the 'collaborationist' arguments of the Count of Ruiseñada. These first appeared in an article which Ruiseñada published in *ABC* on 11 June 1957 under the title 'Loyalty, Continuty and the Shape of the Future'. The result was a third meeting between Franco and Don Juan, held in the same place as before, at the La Cabeza estate near Cáceres in Extremadura. From this emerged a new agreement on the education of Don Juan Carlos, who had now finished at the Military Academy. The agreement, moreover, was very much to Franco's taste. The prince would attend various university courses in Madrid – not in Salamanca, as Don Juan proposed – under the guidance of a team of professors (Torcuato Fernández Miranda, Antonio Fontán and others) who were supporters of the regime. At the same time, the official communiqué of the meeting pointed out that the future presence of Juan Carlos in Madrid, where he took up residence at the Zarzuela Palace from October 1960, was not intended to prejudice the question of the succession – which seemed to imply an affirmation of the claims of Don Juan.[5]

Yet though the meeting was agreeable and relations were good

– 'of perfect cordiality' Don Juan would say in November 1961 –
Franco was still not satisfied. He believed he had not got much
further forward and that Don Juan's policies would lead to
communism or something like it. Doubtless, he was disgusted by
Don Juan Carlos's marriage to Princess Sophia of Greece, arranged
behind his back and contracted without the courtesy of referral to
the Spanish *Cortes*; he reacted, however, with impeccable proprie-
ty and sent a representative of his regime to the wedding in Athens
on 14 May 1962. Moreover, he was driven even further from Don
Juan by the presence of a number of members of the pretender's
entourage (Gil Robles, Joaquin Satrústegui) at the Munich meeting
of 1962, even though Don Juan publicly distanced himself from the
event and Gil Robles resigned in protest from the pretender's
privy council a few days later on 20 June.[6]

In fact, the succession question was at a dead-end. Franco
refrained from settling it and Don Juan, in spite of his working
relationship with Franco, declined to accept the formula of the
'monarchy of the National Movement'. Juan Carlos was beginning
to find himself in an almost impossible position. As Franco
bestowed more and more signs of favour upon him, he would
gradually be forced to choose between upholding his father's
rights – and thereby probably foregoing all hope of reviving the
monarchy – or accepting 'instauration', with himself as king, on
terms dictated by Franco. That was the way things were going.
Franco himself clearly told him so on 1 March 1962. 'Your
Highness,' he informed him, 'has a better chance of becoming king
than your father.'[7] From as early as 1960 Franco had assigned him a
special place in official protocol. In 1964 he made the prince join
him on the podium at the Victory Parade in Madrid – and would
have done so in 1963 had the march not been cancelled because of
mourning for Pope John XXIII.

Yet Franco would delay for five more years before naming his
successor, despite repeated pressure from various quarters and
especially from Carrero Blanco, López Rodó and the ministers
Iturmendi – Minister of Justice from 1955 to 1965 – and Alonso
Vega, all of whom were committed to the adoption of Juan Carlos.
The only provision Franco made, at the time of the change of
government of July 1962, was to appoint a deputy prime minister –
Captain General Muñoz Grandes – to take over should a situation
like that caused by the hunting accident in 1961 recur.

It was not only the succession question that was held up by
Franco's dilatory methods in the period from 1960–65. Every sort
of institutional development was frozen. Franco was bombarded
with even more suggestions in this connection than over the suc-

cession. When the Archbishop of Madrid, Monsignore Morcillo, paid the head of state a visit in May 1965 on behalf of the Spanish hierarchy to convey the bishops' view that the regime should be given an institutional framework as a matter of urgency, Franco told him that he had 'a suitcase full of projects and memoranda'.[8]

Indeed, he must have had. By that date, he had received draft 'constitutions' or Organic Laws as they were termed at least from such ministers as Solís (whose effort was drawn up jointly with Herrero Tejedor, one of the most prestigious figures in the 'Movement'), Fraga Iribarne and Carrero Blanco (drafted by López Rodó). Carrero, Alonso Vega, Ambassador Garrigues, Oriol (Minister of Justice from 1965 to 1973), Lora Tamayo (Minister of Education from 1962 to 1968) and other personalities had pressed him one way or another to make a concerted drive on the institutional front. Fraga almost shouted it at a meeting of the Council of Ministers on 2 April 1965, which was the occasion, already mentioned, when Franco cut the minister short with some asperity, asking whether he took him for a circus clown who was unaware of such matters.[9]

Not until 1966, did Franco tell any of his collaborators – and in the event it was Carrero whom he chose to tell first – that he had arrived at a decision. This was not solely – perhaps not even chiefly – because of his cautious decision-making. He was in genuine doubt. He was anxious about the future, certainly, but, as he said to Lora Tamayo in March 1965, he found it difficult to come up with a solution.[10] The difficulties he experienced were not the result only of his greater or lesser competence in the field of constitutional law; above all, they arose from the contradictions and limitations inherent in the political system he had built up.

The task which faced Franco was to give a constitutional form and representative parliamentary institutions to a state which was neither constitutional, nor genuinely representative, nor parliamentary and to a regime which, as he had indicated himself, was based on personal power. It was an impossible task. The problems which gave him most trouble show this: he wondered, for example, whether to make the succession subject to a plebiscite, but this would have put the regime under intolerable stress with every change of ruler. As he refused to countenance a real system of political parties and free elections, he experimented with the novel idea that the premiership should be elective, but by a form of restricted election from among a list of three names put forward by the Council of the Realm.

In other words, Franco was up against the insoluble problem of how to create the structure of a modern state compatible with contemporary notions of legitimacy out of the 'organic democracy' based on the family, the municipality and the syndicates of the Movement. 'We are on the road towards modern politics,' declared Franco in León on 18 September 1962. It was precisely because Spain was on no such path that she was faced with problems of this type, resolved in modern states. 'We have not gone from being totalitarians to being liberals,' he said in Madrid on 9 March 1963, 'because we have nothing in common with either'. Liberals, to be sure, he and his men were not; nor, at least after 1945, were they totalitarians pure and simple. No one knew quite what Francoism was, not because it was an 'original solution', as Franco claimed, but because it was no solution at all. There was no room, despite all he may have said to the contrary, for radically differing kinds of democracy. 'Organic' democracy was not democracy at all. That was why Franco found it impossible to square his circle of institutions.

On 13 August 1965 he decided to lay before the *Cortes* a draft law on press freedom which his Minister of Information and Tourism, Fraga Iribarne, who served in that post from 1962 to 1969, had been working for ever since he took office. 'I do not believe in this sort of freedom,' Franco told the minister on that occasion, 'but this is a step which we have to take for many important reasons.'[11] This attitude probably explains much of Franco's hesitancy during the sixties. He was bright enough to realize that practical necessity impelled him towards changes which would tend to the liberalization of his regime. But he neither believed, nor could he bring himself to believe, in the freedoms which circumstances required.

Age, moreover, had only confirmed him in his convictions, fears and anxieties. He might formerly have felt disquiet, even alarm, at what he saw as the weakness of the western world in the face of Soviet communism, which he blamed for every international problem, and at what he thought was a crisis for the Christian values of the west. But by the sixties, this had become an almost monomaniac obsession. Communist expansion, to cover more than half the population of the world, seemed to him, as he told the National Council on 9 April 1964, the most significant fact of his lifetime. He saw communism as a permanent state of war against society and against all religion, as he said a little later, on 8 July, in the *Cortes*. As he explained things to the *Cortes* on the same occasion, the entire world was being subjected to incessant subversive propaganda, which the Soviet Union had launched as soon as communists realized that the main obstacle to their advance was religious faith.

From then on, the connection between the communist threat and freedom of thought and behaviour became fixed in Franco's mind. 'Religious indifference', 'the erosion of disciplined behaviour', 'whoring after evil', 'the shipwreck of all the virtues', 'intensive de-christianization' – expressions like these, all taken from his speech of 8 July 1964, all belonged to the same theme: a 'systematic and destructive programme of action to enslave society' was under way. To Franco, the western world seemed to be disintegrating, lacking faith and ideals, dominated by atheism and materialism.

It was hard for a man who talked in these terms to believe in the value of liberty. 'Liberalism,' he told a veterans' reunion on the heights of Garabitas, in Madrid, on 27 May 1962, 'is the door by which communion enters society. He told the veterans that he saw Spain as 'the key in the political defence of the west.' Against this background, all the speeches he uttered from 1962 to 1964 about political development, renovation, further political progress – and even the assurance, given in his end-of-year message for 1964, that the political consistency which he embodied was not intended to preclude change – seemed no more than talk. Franco held political development back: firstly, because he always put a lot of thought and reflection into his decisions; secondly, because he was afraid of the consequences.

Furthermore, the indecision of the period up to about 1965 on the regime's two main outstanding problems – the succession and the institutions – was to some extent a luxury Franco could afford. There were two reasons for this: first, because with Castiella as foreign minister, Spain's foreign relations had been almost completely normalized, and secondly because of the undeniable success of the new economic policy followed since 1957–59.

Castiella, Foreign Minister from 1957 to 1969, did a highly effective job, even though of his most important targets – the integration of Spain in the European Community and the recovery of Gibraltar – were not achieved. In 1963 the agreement with the USA was successfully re-negotiated: what had started in 1953 as a mere pact at executive level now became a virtual alliance in which the Spanish position was much improved. As one result – among others – it became possible to begin an ambitious programme of modernizing the armed forces in 1964. A measure of détente was achieved with Morocco, leading to the return of Ifni in 1969, though the Sahara question remained: Franco said unequivocally that he would never give the territory up and in 1964 Spain launched a policy intended to safeguard the ethnic and cultural identity of the Saharawis – a policy only jettisoned at the last possible moment, when Franco was already on his deathbed, in 1975.

The policy of friendship with Arab states was maintained, despite the revolutionary changes which had taken place in many of them. Beginning in 1964, Castiella devised a policy for Black Africa: a de-colonization process, tardy and ill managed, was begun in Equatorial Guinea, which became independent in 1969.

In 1962, Spain applied for membership of the European Economic Community. No reply was received but negotiations for a treaty of association were begun in 1967 and successfully completed in 1970. Franco, in any case, was not particularly enthusiastic about joining the Community. At least, he was unwilling to go into Europe at the cost of harm 'to our well being at home', as he said in Valencia on 18 June 1962. He much preferred the idea of a 'Europe of nations' launched by De Gaulle.

From 1960, Spain managed to establish excellent bilateral relations with France and West Germany. The same would have been true of the United Kingdom, and was so for a time until 1964, but Spain forfeited it by raising the Gibraltar question of the UN in that year. Still, the Gibraltar issue did bring the Franco regime one of its biggest successes in the international relations field when, in December 1967, the UN General Assembly agreed to endorse the Spanish arguments and voted in favour of the de-colonization of the territory. When British refused to comply, Spain imposed frontier restrictions and economic sanctions on Gibraltar: the only effect was to strengthen the pro-British sentiments of the people of Gibraltar.

In short, Castiella had consolidated and even extended the now irreversible process of the acceptance of Franco's regime abroad. In 1967, consular relations were even started with the eastern bloc countries.[12]

The years from 1961 to 1964 were outstanding for the Spanish economy. Growth averaged 8.7% a year over the five-year period; price rises were kept down to an annual average of 5.9% while real wages grew by between 8% and 11% annually. The output of electricity rose from 18,614 million kilowatts per hour in 1960 to 31,650 million in 1965. Steel production went from 1.9 million to 3.5 million tonnes. The number of cars produced rose from 39,732 in 1960 to 112,672 in 1964. The volume of imports trebled; exports doubled; the reserves stood at $1,500 million in 1964. Foreign exchange earnings from tourism reached $1,104.9 million in 1965, when the figure of 14 million tourists was first exceeded in a single year.[13]

In 1964 the First Development Plan, drawn up by López Rodó,

came into effect. The second followed in 1968 and the third in 1972. Planning for development became the main political activity of the last fifteen years of Francoism, which had long since discarded José Antonio's national syndicalist ideals. The devotees of development – especially the so-called 'technocrats' of López Rodó's circle, who increased their presence in the governments of 1962 and 1965 thanks to Carrero Blanco – believed that the regime could be made to last if the economy was modernized and expanded. Growth and prosperity would then preserve public order and obviate any danger of social conflict.[14]

So Franco found the last two great slogans of his long rule: peace – celebrated with special pomp in 1964 when the regime completed twenty-five years of power – and the 'State of Works'. The latter was a Spanish phrase coined by Gonzalo Fernández de la Mora, Minister of Public Works between 1970 and 1973, to sum up the thesis that the total transformation of Spain's infrastructure during the Franco years constituted an unanswerable argument in favour of the justification of the regime and of Franco's leadership as Caudillo.[15]

Spain's transformation in those years was profound. Between 1966 and 1971 the economy grew by 5.6% per annum. Output of electrical energy reached 56.484 million kilowatts per hour in 1970. In the same year steel production exceeded seven million tons and more than 450,000 automobiles were manufactured. 21 million tourists entered Spain. Between 1965 and 1972 real wages grew by 7.9% annually. Per capita income was $900 in 1970 and $1,239 in 1972.

Not everything, however, was quite as rosy as official propaganda claimed. It could even be said – by Julián Marías – that Spain was a developed, but badly developed, nation. From 1965, Spain's growth was accompanied by inflation which approached 14% per year. In 1966 a mini-deflation was necessary to keep down prices; the peseta was devalued in November 1967 and wages were frozen for several months. The Spanish economy did not stop growing – indeed, growth continued until the second half of 1974 – but went through a stop-go phase in which periods of growth with inflation alternated with times of deflation and crisis in 1966–67, for example, and 1970–71. From 1965 onwards growth and recession followed each other on a more or less two-year cycle. There were practically no real changes of policy after 1964.

And there were even worse problems. Spain's development suffered from grave deficiencies. Three were fundamental: stagnation of agriculture, gross regional disparities and high rates of emigration from the countryside (almost four million people left the countryside between 1960 and 1970, about half of them bound for Europe). Other problems were almost as serious: the diminishing yield from taxation; the high level of protectionist tariffs; a public sector – the INI so beloved of Franco – which was inefficient and in the red; inadequate social and welfare provision, especially for housing, health and education; speculation in urban land prices; horror stories of urban planning in the tourist areas and big cities; ecological disasters, for example in the industrial rivers.

At least, however, Spain have broken out of underdevelopment. She had ceased to be a rural and agricultural country and was now the homeland of a modern, urban, industrial society with high levels of prosperity and of consumption. The active population in the rural section, which had accounted for 42% of the total workforce in 1960, made up only 25% by 1970. In 1960, only 27.7% of Spaniards lived in cities of over 100,000 inhabitants; in 1975 they amounted to 50%. More than 1.5 million people took up manufacturing work between 1960 and 1970. The metallurgical industries alone went from employing half a million people in 1950 to more than two million in 1970. In that year, manufacturing industry employed 37% of the total workforce and the service sector 38%. Roads, airports, airlines, railways had been overhauled in the previous ten years. The biggest Spanish firm in 1969–70 was the car firm SEAT. Shipbuilding had become the biggest export earner in place of the traditional oranges, oil and wine. In 1960 only 1% of Spanish homes had television, while only 4% had refrigerators and 4% cars. In 1969, 62% had television, 63% refrigerators and 24% cars. These figures would go on rising spectacularly until 1975.

By 1964 development was already a demonstrable fact and economic optimism was at its height. This was the background against which the regime could celebrate 25 years of peace in 1964 in what was also in part an orgy of adulation for Franco's person. The cult of his personality already defied belief: he had been called 'the hero of the hosts of heaven and earth', 'the Leader-priest', the 'chief who could work miracles', 'Caesar and pontiff', 'the man sent from God and made Leader', 'the sword of the Most High', 'the voice of bronze with tones of adamant', the 'Minister of God', 'the inimitable superman' and many other such things.[16] Now the cult went wild. Popular tributes, distinctions, medals, honorary appointments, laudatory phrases, visits in homage and so on rained down on Franco's head. In November, a film in his honour, *This Man Franco* (*Franco, ese hombre*), reached the screens: the director said Franco was 'the best actor I have ever directed'. Even sport bowed in homage and Spain beat the Soviet Union, no less, at a soccer match presided over by Franco, to become European champions in his own favourite spectator sport. It is hardly surprising that Franco himself ended up by believing unshakeably in his Messianic role; as early as 1941 Marshal Pétain, after their meeting at Montpellier on 13 February, said that Franco was too ready to believe he was the Virgin Mary's cousin.

And yet it was just when the twenty-five years of peace were being celebrated that, despite the impressive achievements, evidence appeared of the regime's failure to solve some of the basic problems of Spain. Development brought mixed results. On the one hand, it made Spanish society incomparably more willing to accept a regime that had brought prosperity and created opportunities for material self-improvement; on the other hand, it caused the re-emergence of serious conflicts which put Franco's vaunted peace in jeopardy.

Conflicts were breaking out on several fronts: with workers, students, regionalists – especially Basques – and churchmen. There was no single or co-ordinated movement of protest, nor were all the conflicts equally intense. The aquiescence of most of Spanish society in Francoism was not disturbed; and, indeed, Spaniards generally turned against the minorities which were causing the trouble – particularly against the students and the priests. Nor indeed, was conflict more rife in Spain than in many other western countries. But its every existence seriously impaired the regime's claim to legitimacy.

In chronological terms, the first important signs of conflict were strikes by workers. After a big wave of strikes in the spring of 1962, centred in Asturias but spreading to other provinces, industrial disputes prompted chiefly by successive rounds of wage-bargaining grew ever more frequent; official figures admitted to 777 disputes in 1963 – in a country where strikes were illegal until 1975 – and another 484 in 1965; similar figures were published for subsequent years, with a record level of 1,595 strikes in the strife-torn year of 1970. Barcelona, Asturias, the Basque Country and Madrid, mining, metallurgical industries and building were at first the areas and sectors most affected. Later, around the turn of the decade, strikes spread to new regions, industries and groups of workers. They started up in areas with no tradition of social conflict, such as Galicia (at Vigo and El Ferrol) and Navarre, and in previously unaffected industries, like motor manufacture. They spread to middle class professions like banking, teaching and medicine.

Strife returned to the universities in 1963–64. The student revolt started with a demand for democratic student unions but did not end there. Further demands emerged for democracy in the unversities and in society at large.

Student unrest was important at first only in Madrid and Barcelona. In February 1965 a series of incidents in Madrid culminated in a mass march of students, joined or supported by Professors Aranguren, García Calvo, Montero Díaz, García, Vercher, Tierno Galván and Aguilar Navarro. The following year, representatives of students of Barcelona University, meeting in the safety of a Capuchin friary at Sarriá, founded the Democratic Students' Union (*Sindicato Democrático de Estudiantes*) in open defiance of the official unions. After that, demonstrations, strikes and public disturbances became almost continuous in almost every campus in the country. The incident which most offended the regime was the attack on the Rector's office of Barcelona University in January 1969: a bust of Franco was destroyed.

The re-emergence of regional question in both Catalonia and the Basque Country showed that a sense of national identity in those regions had survived 30 years of enforced castilianization and cultural propaganda. Catalan self-awareness stayed alive thanks to the vitality of the Catalan language and culture in an atmosphere where a strong sense of Catalonia's distinctive identity was preserved by writers, intellectuals, singers, the Church, and even a sporting institution like Barcelona Football Club. There were no violent outbreaks – not even with the trial of Pujol in 1960, nor the protest campaign of the previous year, nor the expulsion in 1965 of the Abbot of Montserrat, Aureli Escarré who had made some unmistakeably anti-Francoist statements to *Le Monde* two years before. Even so, it was clear that Catalan sentiment was widespread in Catalonia as the unrest in Barcelona University revealed.

In the Basque Country, Basque identity was probably more deep-rooted but less widespread than in Catalonia. This was because the language and culture were known only to a minority and because the Basques were more widely and deeply divided over the 'national' question. Nationalist protest, however, became much more violent, chiefly because of the emergence of ETA with its strategy of armed struggle and terrorism. Until 1968 ETA kept to bloodless forms of direct action: bank raids, outrages against symbols of Francoism, hoisting Basque flags, daubing slogans and so on. In 1968 a Civil Guard and a policeman died in separate incidents and an ETA leader, X. Etxebarrieta, was killed in a shoot-out with the Civil Guard. Between 1968 and 1975, 47 people, including the prime minister Carrero Blanco, were killed in ETA outrages, in addition 27 members of the organization were killed during the same period. ETA had also carried out some spectacular kidnaps and the Basque Country had seen innumerable mass protests.

Last but not least, the Franco regime saw unmistakeable signs that the Church was slipping away: the Church that had been instrumental in sanctioning Francoism by defining the war of 1939–45 as a crusade, and had played a vital role in securing international acceptance of the regime between 1945 and 1953. In May 1960 came the letter of 339 Basque priests deploring the lack of freedom; in 1963 the statements of the Abbot of Montserrat to *Le Monde*. At about the same time a number of bishops who sympathized with the underground Catholic workers' movements made public criticisms of the official trade unions.

Friction arose when Spanish censorship banned some progressive texts of Popes John XXIII and Paul VI. The latter, as Cardinal Archbishop of Milan had aroused resentment on a number of occasions, particularly when he pleaded for the life of the communist leader Julián Grimau, condemned and executed in 1963. Franco described his election as pope as 'a ducking'. Some theologians began a dialogue with Marxism; Basque priests declared support for ETA; others, in other provinces, did the same for clandestine workers' organizations or for the students. In May 1966, for instance, some 130 priests marched through the streets of Barcelona – leaving the Spanish public aghast – to protest against the ill treatment of a student leader in detention.

In 1971, the bishops' conference actually passed a resolution indicting the 'crusading' ethos by asking public pardon for having taken sides in the Civil War. In 1973, the bishops published a call for the independence of Church and State.

These conflicts with the clergy came about through the modernization of the Spanish Church, encouraged by the papal nuncios Riberi and Dadaglio. Late and imperfect as this was – the hierarchy remained on Franco's side almost up to the appointment of Cardinal Vicente Enrique y Tarancón as primate of Spain in 1969 – it helped to fashion a new, progressive Church which clashed with the principles and values of the Francoist state.[17]

So Franco faced a series of significant conflicts on a broad front. The workers' strikes raised doubts about whether official syndicates – one of the keystones of Francoism – could be a means of reconciling the working classes permanently to the regime, or even work efficiently in resolving industrial disputes. The Workers' Commissions (*Comisiones Obreras CC 00*) – nerve centres of the working-class opposition and kernel of the communist unions of the future – arose as efficient instruments for labour disputes independent of the official unions. Student agitation showed that there was a gap between the élite of the rising generation and the old authoritarian and reactionary system; the ageing, obsolete regime could not meet the needs of a new, modern Spain. The rise of regional sentiment belied the ideal of a unitary state upholding a single 'Spanish' identity, proclaimed in the Francoist slogan, 'Spain, One, Great and Free!' The parting of ways with the Church imperilled the regime's supposed Catholic legitimacy.

It was in this period that what was probably Franco's most serious deficiency as a ruler came to light: he was incapable of moving ahead fast enough or adapting the institutions of his regime to changes in Spanish society. It was now that the political risks implied in the 'inactivity' and 'prudence' which typified his style and which formerly had brought so much evident success became apparent. Franco had two ways of dealing with strife: either by repression, or with reforms which were too little and too late.

Repression there undoubtedly was. In April 1963, as has been mentioned, the communist leader Julián Grimau was executed. So were the anarchists Delgado and Granados, accused of planting bombs in Madrid, in August of the same year, albeit without the international repercussions caused by Grimau's death.

In the same year the Public Order Court (*Tribunal de Orden Público*) was formed. It went on to try hundreds of prisoners accused of political crimes. Hundreds of students and workers, including the most important figures in CC 00, were detained, arraigned and summarily judged. So were many teachers, including those involved in the events of 1965. It was rare for a university to escape temporary closure from time to time. Police operated inside the universities from 1968.

States of emergency – by which certain rights granted in the *Fuero de los Españoles* were suspended – were declared nine times between 1962 and 1975, three of them nationwide, the rest confined to the Basque Country. By the end of 1968, 189 Basques were in custody and about 30 – rising to 300 the following year – in exile.[18] Fines, and occasional arrests, were imposed regularly on dissident Basque priests from the end of the sixties. Between 1970 and 1973 alone 11 people died in clashes with the security forces in connection with strikes.

The Burgos trial of ETA members in 1970 and prosecution number 1,001, in 1973, of the leading members of CC 00 (Marcelino Camacho, Julián Ariza, Nicolás Sartorius and others), as well as the executions which took place in 1975 and to which we shall turn in due course, seemed symbolic of the regime's increasingly repressive reaction to the conflicts that emerged and escalated as the economy developed.

Franco was not particularly alarmed by strife, at least not to begin with. 'I intend,' he told his cousin Franco Salgado when the Asturian strikes began in 1962, 'to carry on without resorting to violence, and I am willing to concede pay awards as big as can be made without harm to the economy.'[19] And it must be said that he never called in the army, neither then nor in later disputes. Naturally, he felt the government should act vigorously and punish all crimes against public order, but he also realized the need to act calmly and according to the law. 'We must never take any repressive measures', as he said to his cousin à propos of the student disorders of 1865, 'that are not sanctioned by existing laws.' He wanted no 'innocent victims'.[20] When his government was accused of acting weakly over the unrest in Barcelona University in 1966, he explained – again in private conversation with his cousin – that the government could not go around killing students or making war on the clergy. The public order policy he wanted was a combination of vigour, restraint and observance of existing legal rules – which he thought should also be applied when they called for the death penalty or severe prison sentences. He believed unwaveringly that his own policy, at once just and forceful, would be enough to put an end to conflict. But he was not slow in invoking harsher measures, such as the states of emergency in 1968–69 when conflict seemed more threatening. He did so to avoid charges of weakness against his regime, rather than because he was genuinely fearful of the threat.

As for the basic roots of the conflicts, as outlined above, he never understood them. Even so, he always seemed more responsive to the industrial disputes and relatively contemptuous of student unrest which he dismissed as 'adolescent dust-ups' run by 'rebellious' minorities on behalf of the communists. He tended to be tough with the Basques and merely long-suffering with the Church. He was convinced – and rightly so – that his regime had done more for the Church than any other. He felt, accordingly, that the criticisms and accusations levelled by dissident priests and the Catholic press were undeserved. He was scandalized by the growing political interference of the Church and did his best to avoid a confrontation.

He was deeply vexed and angered by Pope Paul VI's request of 29 April 1968 that he should renounce the rights over episcopal appointments which he had been given in the concordat of 1953. He had always exercised the privilege with the utmost prudence and had accommodated the wishes of the popes. In a draft of his letter to Pope Paul there were phrases – subsequently omitted – which showed how he felt: 'Spain feels poorly loved in Rome'; 'our enemies' machinations are succeeding in Rome'; 'Rome's attitude to the Spanish administration is lamentable', etc.[21] In the final version of the letter, dated 13 July 1968, Franco's annoyance seemed tempered. He did not refuse to comply with the Pope's request, but proposed a re-negotiation of the entire concordat of 1953, which would imply that privileges would be revised on both sides – those of the Spanish State and of the Church (which, as we have seen, enjoyed substantial rights). Franco never managed to understand the crisis through which the Church was passing.

Nor did he ever stop believing that the existing machinery of his state was adequate to contain and channel discontent. Therefore he could see no need for any changes. The economic liberalization of 1957–60 was not matched by politcal freedoms as had been hoped when the 1962 government took office. Only two tangible advances were made: the 1966 Press Law, of Information Minister Fraga Iribarne; and a law on liberty of conscience, passed in 1967, after being indefatigably championed for many years by Castiella against the opposition of many government colleagues grouped around Carrero Blanco. This religious liberty had hardly any repercussions on a country that was almost completely Catholic.

The Press Law, on the other hand, restrictive and narrowly interpreted as it was (many publications continued to be hauled into court between 1966 and 1975) made substantial changes in the amount of information available to the public. In 1965 Franco had told Fraga that the press was 'pretty brazen'[22] but he accepted the new legislation, as we have seen, none the less. He did insist on introducing a number of alterations to the draft law, subordinating press freedom to other principles – generally of a moral order – which he thought more important and defining a long list of offences the press could commit: attacks on the Church and the Movement, vindications of communism, publicity for immoral acts, incitement to discontent and disorder, advertising in furtherance of vice and so on. He defended Fraga from the chorus of condemnation that grew among the extremists of the regime and in the Council of Ministers itself when the press took on a newly critical tone in the aftermath of the new law. But he soon became infected by the exasperation and dissatisfaction of his closest collaborators. 'I am fed up,' he told Fraga on 4 November 1966, 'with the way the press seems to wake up every morning asking, "What can we complain about next?"'[23] Other laws were either too late – like the Education Law of 1970, which reorganized schools at all levels and substantially broadened the basic general curriculum – or too little, like the Trade Union Law of 1971. Neither of these, at any rate, prevented further disputes.

Throughout the sixties, Franco was confiding in Carrero Blanco more and more, and delegating responsibility to him. Carrero Blanco was an extremely conservative, passionately religious man, inspired by absolute, unconditional loyalty to Franco, hostile to any notion of easing or liberalizing the regime and dedicated to preserving Francoism intact. Relying on López Rodó and the Opus Dei technocrats – most of whom were liberals only in the economic sense – Carrero was developing his own strategy for assuring the future of the sort of Francoism he believed in: conservative, committed to economic progress, ideologically sanitized. To Fraga Iribarne – the most progressive minister, along with Castiella, of the 1962–69 period – the 1965 government, which was more right-wing than its predecessor, was López Rodó's 'perfect crime'.

Franco was convinced, in any case, that a great part of the Spanish people were behind him. He found the evidence in the crowds that mobbed him on his journeys round Spain. Some of these trips were particularly rewarding: those to Valencia in June 1962, Bilbao in June 1964 and Barcelona in July 1966. 'Now nobody will be able to forget,' he told his cousin after the first of these, 'that Valencia has given a resounding yes to my policies and has truly acclaimed my work as head of state.' On his return from the Bilbao trip he declared, 'It has been an overwhelming experience – something I shall always remember and for which I shall always be grateful. The people of Bilbao have shown that they are with me . . . '.[24]

Franco was in no doubt that Spaniards were living well under his rule – at any rate, that they had never had it so good. He used to say that 90% of the people were behind him. He told the daily *Arriba* on 1 April 1969 that his regime had lasted since 1939 by virtue of popular 'attachment'. Without free elections, it was impossible to put such claims to the test. But Franco obviously could command the unconditional support of a large number of Spaniards, just as he was rejected, instinctively no doubt, by many others who were not free to say so. Above all, Franco could count on the comfortable acquiescence of an important sector of Spanish society: those who had no time for Francoist ideology and who already displayed a modern mentality, up-to-date beliefs, values and ways of life, but for whom Franco's stress on peace, order, work and political démarche retained its appeal.

With the 1965 government, Franco was at last about to tackle the two great outstanding questions for the future of his regime: the drafting of an Organic Law of the State and the appointment of a successor. Franco, who did not like to be rushed over this sort of topic, and who preferred to exclude political problems of a general character from discussion in the Council of Ministers, had at last become convinced of the need to confront them head-on. No doubt the emergence of strife provided cogent arguments for those who thought that these two questions could be put off no longer if the regime was to be given the institutional backbone it needed and if its survival after Franco was to be assured.

On 14 June 1966 Franco called a number of his ministers together. He gave them the text of an Organic Law of the State. He had prepared it on the basis of the numerous memoranda which, as we have seen, had come into his hands in preceding years and, most of all, on the paper submitted by Carrero Blanco and López Rodó. The text was finalized in the course of the summer. Although it was opposed by the men of the Movement, represented in cabinet by Solís, and even by the deputy prime minister Muñoz Grandes, Franco agreed, at the end of October to lay it before the *Cortes*.

Franco introduced the law in the chamber on 22 November 1966. His speech – not a long one – was a summary of what the regime had achieved over its thirty years in power and a meditation on its future. Franco stressed three themes, above all, in the regime's achievements: peace, order – which, as usual, he contrasted with the anarchy and disorder of the years before 1936 – and the spectacular transformation of Spain's economy and society which he illustrated with copious statistics. He summed up as a 'national revolution' all that had been accomplished by his regime and, as he pointed out several times by his own personal commitment. He rejected all claims that the Movement and the crusade were reactionary or intransigent.

As for the future, Franco regarded it as secure precisely because of the regime's great achievements. He presented the proposed Organic Law as the culmination and rationalization of a new order that he had built up since 1938–39, adding a brief gloss on this new order's fundamental laws. One way or another, however, Franco-ism's uneasy political conscience made itself felt in Franco's words. He spent a long time defending the pragmatism of his regime against the democracies' vapid ideology and in proclaiming the validity of his 'organic democracy' against liberal democracy, and in proving that parties were not essential for democracy.

In sum, despite appearances, Franco claimed that his was a state founded on law, that it was open and flexible and that the process of development of its institutions would be perfected by the proposed law. Starting from those assumptions and throwing the full weight of his prestige behind the measure – 'fully aware of my responsibility before God and history', as he said – he asked the *Cortes* to approve the law. He then announced that it would also be subject to a referendum.

And so it was. On 14 December, the Organic Law of the State, (the *LOE, Ley Orgánica del Estado*) was submitted to a plebiscite. This was the second mass vote the regime had organized in the thirty years of its existence. It was preceded by a steamroller campaign masterminded by the Minister of Information, Manuel Fraga. As in 1947, no means of exerting pressure was neglected. Press, radio and television blinded public opinion with clouds of propaganda. No campaign against the proposed law was allowed. The whole of Spain, to the remotest corner, was plastered with posters, stickers and pictures, all bearing Franco's features, exhorting the people to vote. The electors were coerced: officials, employees and workers had to present certificates of having voted before collecting their December pay cheques. In any case, it was all unnecessary. The question in the referendum had been formulated in such a way that a 'yes' was a vote in favour of the LOE and therefore in favour of perpetuating the regime, while to vote 'no' was to vote to leave things as they were – in other words to keep the same regime in power.

The campaign was cleverly managed, so that public opinion became convinced of two things: that it was voting for Franco and at the same time that it was voting for change. Franco himself wound up the campaign by twisting the referendum into a plebiscite on his personal position. On 12 December he addressed the country on television. There was only one theme in his short, impassioned and effective appeal: that it would be right for the nation to grant its vote to the man who had renounced the chance of a life of his own to give himself up, for thirty years, to the service of Spain. 'Here I stand,' he said, 'by the cannon's breech, in the same spirit of service as in the days of my youth, consuming what useful life I have left in your service . . . Is it too much for me to ask you in return to give your support to the laws which, for your good alone and that of the nation, are about to be submitted to your vote?'

A large majority of the people thought it was not too much to ask. Just to be on the safe side, the figures were boosted – though the government denied this – and a result was published that was beyond cavil. Almost 89% of the possible total of 19 million electors voted. 95% of valid votes favoured the LOE. Franco was delighted and even, in view of the result, disposed to embark on further reforms. In his Christmas message that year he talked euphorically of the 'great democratic victory' of 14 December. He thanked the Spanish people for what he characterized as 'the noble, the truly exemplary fashion in which you have been good enough to show your support and trust for me, freely and ringingly.' He promised that the LOE was just the beginning of a new and better era in politics: 'in politics there is no place for intransigence,' he said.

That was what Franco thought. And yet the LOE was not the 'sweeping democratization' he had claimed when he presented the law to the *Cortes*. It was simply a set of administrative rules for the institutional machinery used by the regime. It could have been the beginning of some sort of change, but not of democratic change, because none of the new features it introduced was democratic.

The 'family section' of the assembly, which consisted of about a hundred deputies elected by heads of families, was a parody of parliamentary democracy. Although the LOE recognized the right to 'divergent opinions' ('contrast of opinions' in the official phrase) on matters of policy, it did not authorize political parties. On the contrary, it made the 'Movement' and its National Council – appointed directly or indirectly by the head of state – the only permitted means of channelling political life or subjecting the principles of the regime to scrutiny. This was tantamount to saying that political activity would be tolerated only inside the Movement. Although the offices of head of state and prime minister were treated separately, the former retained formidable powers. The assembly's new power to challenge excesses by the executive (called '*contrafuero*' – an archaic term) did little more than give the deputies – for the most part nominated by the government anyway – a feeble right to refer ministers to questions about the validity of laws and administrative orders; in no sense did it confer power to challenge executive decisions or make the government accountable for them. The LOE was not the new departure Franco claimed, but a cosmetic exercise.

The LOE confirmed that the Spanish state was a monarchy. But it said nothing about the succession. Yet this was the most controversial and intractable problem for opponents and adherents alike. On it, moreover, hung the vital question, 'What happens after Franco?' Soon after the passing of the LOE, the answer to this question would be broached. And just as the law was approved when the regime had been in power for thirty years, so Franco, ever inscrutable, behaved as if he had decided to wait until Prince Juan Carlos reached the age of thirty years before proclaiming him successor in accordance with the stipulations of the succession law. This was to be in 1969; meanwhile, Franco missed no opportunity of bestowing public favours on the prince.

At all events, what triggered off the last political battle over the succession was a statement of the Minister of Information, Fraga Iribarne to the London *Times* in November 1965, treating Juan Carlos's nomination as a foregone conclusion. By then it was already obvious that options which excluded a king – such as a regency or presidency, which were wanted by the diehards of the populist, 'blue' faction, rooted in the Falange and more or less led by the minister Solís Ruiz, – were non-starters.

It was also obvious that even the members of that faction would do whatever Franco said. For instance, the argument of one of their most representative and incisive spokesmen, Emilio Romero, in his *Letters to the Prince* (*Cartas al príncipe*), published in 1964, was that the populists of the Falange would accept the monarchy if and only if the prince respected the ideology of the Movement and if the Movement were somehow built into the future monarchy, perhaps on the lines of the Mexican PRI ('Institutional Revolutionary Party'). The same sort of argument was approached from a similar set of assumptions by the professor of political law, Jesús Fueyo, who said that Franco would be succeeded by 'the institutions'.

This was the background against which new difficulties were now created by Don Juan de Borbón in Estoril. Don Juan was probably resigned to the fact that Franco had already made up his mind in favour of Juan Carlos, when, beginning in 1966, he launched his last campaign in favour of his own title and in defence of his concept of a liberal monarchy of reconciliation. Part of the explanation lies in the appointment to Don Juan's privy council of José María de Areilza, who had been Franco's ambassador in Buenos Aires, Washington and Paris but who had clearly distanced himself from Francoism since 1964: in writings he published between 1964 and 1968 he had expressed the view that Spain's future lay not with the Movement but through the creation of a democratic, pluralist state.[25]

On 5 March 1966 an act of homage to the memory of Alfonso XIII was organized at Estoril. It was a further assertion, clear and unmistakeable, of Don Juan's position as head of the house of Bourbon and, therefore, as legitimate heir to the Spanish throne. On 21 July 1966, the authorities in Spain ordered the confiscation of the monarchist daily, *ABC* – at that time the leading paper in the country – for having published an article, written by Luis María Anson, a young monarchist closely associated with Don Juan.

Under the title, 'The Monarchy that Belongs to All of Us', he argued for a European type of monarchy, democratic and popular – 'belonging to everyone' – in the person of Don Juan. At the end of January 1968 the Infante Felipe, Juan Carlos's son, was born. At his baptism in Madrid on 8 February, Queen Victoria Eugenia, Alfonso XIII's widow, who had not returned to Spain since 1931, was present. So was Don Juan himself.

Franco was not pleased with the resurgence of the pro-Don Juan monarchists. He had sharp words with Areilza in private. His reaction was unwontedly marked. Anson's article struck him as 'tendentious, impolitic and inopportune';[26] when Don Juan landed in Madrid, receiving individuals and delegations as if he were already head of state, Franco was mortified.

This situation was exploited by men like Carrero Blanco, López Rodó, Alonso Vega, Oriol, Silva and others, who from inside the government saw the installation of the monarchy in the person of Don Juan Carlos as the only way of perpetuating Francoism after Franco's death, in a kingdom which, as the principles of the regime demanded, would be 'traditional, Catholic, social and representative'. In July 1967 Franco dismissed the deputy prime minister, Captain General Muñoz Grandes, an army man of great prestige and acknowledged probity, who had enjoyed some degree of influence over Franco. Muñoz Grandes was certainly more open to change than Franco; he had little love for Carrero and the technocrats and he had been seen as a possible successor to Franco by those who hoped for a regency rather than a monarchy. Probably, it ws not because of this that Franco demanded his resignation: Muñoz Grandes was a sick man and he was soon to die. But his replacement by Carrero Blanco gave another boost to the men behind what was called 'Operation Prince'.

Two documents which Franco received from the promoters of the Prince's succession proved decisive. The first, dated 2 October 1968, came from Oriol, the second, of the 21st of the same month, from Carrero Blanco; both were based on jottings by López Rodó. When Franco read Carrero's note, discarding Don Juan, Alfonso de Borbón-Dampierre and Don Carlos-Hugo in turn, and arguing that Don Juan Carlos was the only member of the royal families with the qualities and background necessary to succeed to the throne, Franco made up his mind. 'I'm in total agreement,' he said.[27] Soon after, in December, he expelled the Bourbon-Parma family from Spain – first Don Carlos-Hugo, then Don Javier and the other members. A dynastic dispute that went back to 1833 and which had caused a series of civil wars was effectively over.

There was nothing Don Juan could do, short of making his son refuse the crown. At the end of the day, he could not bring back the monarchy on his own; if Don Juan Carlos turned down the chance to do so, it might have meant the end of all hope of a restoration. On 7 January 1969 Don Juan Carlos made some widely reported statements to the daily *Pueblo*. Fraga Iribarne had put him up to it. The message was that he acknowledged the validity of the fundamental laws of the regime; he was willing to respect them and he declared his willingness to serve Spain at the cost of any sacrifice. The meaning of these statements was clear. Don Juan Carlos would accept the succession. He put the recovery of the throne above the principle of hereditary right, because he appreciated correctly that no other solution was viable or credible in the circumstances created by Francoism.

Franco was highly satisfied with the prince's statements. He told Don Juan Carlos so in person a few days later on 15 January. 'I feel very reassured, Your Highness,' he said. 'Don't let anything distract you now. The whole matter is settled.'[28] Evidently, he had made his choice. Only the date remained to be decided.

This was the only remaining objective of 'Operation Prince' by the spring of 1969, once the government had brought forward to 21 March the lifting of the state of emergency (decreed for three months in January because of student unrest and violence in the Basque Country). The key event now seems to have been the long conversation Franco had with his friend, the Interior Minister Lieutenant General Alonso Vega, on the latter's eightieth birthday on 28 May. The reminder of his own age – Franco was now 76 – convinced him. On the following day Franco let Carrero Blanco know that he would appoint a successor before the summer holidays.

He did so at a plenary meeting of the *Cortes* on 22 July 1969. Previously, on 14 June, he had sent Don Juan a blunt letter informing him of his decision and expressing the hope that he would be able to accept the designation of Don Juan Carlos as the best course for Spain. On 19 July Don Juan released a statement disassociating himself from the monarchy which was shortly to be installed and recalling – with exactitude – that his sole mission over the previous thirty years had been as spokesman and upholder of monarchy, conceived as a liberal and democratic institution. The statement summed up a political course that had never strayed from democratic lines. For Franco, it seemed the unanswerable proof that Don Juan was 'unserviceable', as he said to his ministers at a council held on 21 July.[29]

Franco laid Don Juan Carlos's nomination before the *Cortes* on the following day. His speech, brief and to the point, rested on three contentions: that the Spanish state, constituted as a monarchy, had been born on 18 July 1936 and not before; that Juan Carlos's appointment was to ensure the unity and perpetuity of the Movement; that what was proposed was an 'instauration' not a restoration.

At last Franco had come up with an answer to the question the political class had been asking for years. What he was putting forward was a version of what he had been saying repeatedly ever since 1947: a monarchy founded on the legitimacy of the 18 July. When the assembly approved the designation of Don Juan Carlos to succeed with the title of king – which it did by 491 votes to 19 with 9 abstentions – Franco could rest assured, as he said in his speech, that he had everything 'well and truly battened down' for the future.

Moreover, he was still around. The nomination of Don Juan Carlos was only for when Franco died or became incapacitated. If there was any doubt about his determination to carry on, he dispelled it in his end-of-year message for that same year of 1969. 'As long as God gives me life, I shall be alongside you, working for our fatherland.' God gave him six more years.

7

The Autumn of the Patriarch

'I have seen Franco fishing, walking, leaping from crag to crag and reeling in a nine-kilo salmon,' said the director of the *EFE* Press Agency, Carlos Mendo, at the end of May 1964, in a report on the holiday Franco had spent in Asutrias pursuing his favourite sport. Franco was then seventy years old – an age when leaping from crag to crag is not generally thought normal or advisable.

Yet, from that time on, reports of this kind came thick and fast. From time to time, Franco's doctor, Vicente Gil, would tell the media that his patient's health was splendid. The leader would be shown on television playing golf alongside Joaquín Guimaraens at La Zapateira in the province of Corunna or fishing, in Asturias, up to his waist in the water, as he did regularly until 1973. He went on shooting until the winter of 1974–75, a few months before his death.

Such assertions about Franco's health seemed to protest too much. They were attempts to outdo the growing rumours of the leader's alleged sickness started by Franco is evident ageing from 1964–65 and by some unmistakeable signs of his physical decline.

Until then, Franco's health had always been excellent. He had only had three accidents in his whole life: the wound at El Biutz in 1916; a car crash in 1935 in the province of Salamanca, when the car occupied by Franco and his wife – he never took the wheel – knocked over two cyclists, killing one of them and injuring Carmen Polo; and the shooting accident of 1961. None of these had any long-term complications. Nor did he have much in the way of serious illness. Between 1939 and 1974 he had to take to his bed no more than half a dozen times: two bad attacks of 'flu and occasional minor ailments, dental decay and extractions performed by his friend Dr Iveas (and previously, until 1961, Dr Jacobo Chermant), a bout of food poisoning and in 1973 an inflammation of the intestine, for which he was treated, without need of further aid, by his personal physician Vicente Gil.[1]

'There is nothing wrong with me except that I am 73 years old,' observed Franco to his cousin Franco Salgado on 5 May 1966.[2] This was probably already untrue, though Franco may have been unaware of his condition: at the time, though it was not admitted officially until 1974, he was beginning to suffer from Parkinson's disease, a slow degeneration of the brain brought on by old age and accompanied by muscular tremors, stiffness and general debility. The disease is not completely incompatible with normal life, but it impairs the patient's speed of response and aggravates a tendency to introspection and mental inflexibility. That is what seems to have happened to Franco. At least, he showed all the outward signs of Parkinson's disease: the set features, the weak and monotonous voice (though Franco's voice had always been like that anyway), the unsteady hands, the fixed stare, the stiff body, the slight stoop and so on. This was what fed the adverse rumours about his health.[3]

So in the period after 1964–65 Franco began to take on the image of a weak and frail old man. In combination with his courtesy and affability, this gave him an air of mellowness, even kindness, ill suited to the reality of the despotic, oppressive power, which he continued to wield until 1975.

He was a sick man, ever less lucid with ever slower reflexes. It was true that he could still fish and shoot, and even stand for an hour and a half in pouring rain, as he did at the Victory Parade of 1966. But his ministers began to notice the symptoms of exhaustion. Meetings of the Council of Ministers grew shorter. On 6 December 1968, Franco rose and withdrew from one of them before it was over – the first time he had done such a thing in 30 years. It was not unusual for him to fall asleep occasionally during a meeting; and at most of them he scarcely uttered a word. His rigid self-control could still make him capable of leaving a cabinet meeting for 20 minutes on 12 May 1972 to have two teeth taken out and return to his seat without anyone being aware of what had happened. Yet in the same year, just a week later, he had to be discreetly propped up on a shooting stick to preside at the Victory Parade. His ministers began to get apprehensive about the audiences Franco continued to give, in case the effects of Parkinson's disease made him look pathetic or ridiculous.[4]

Franco's obvious decline was like a symbol of the sclerosis of the regime. At the very least, it seemed odd that a man with a shrivelled and feeble body, failing pulse, unchanging expression and almost inaudible voice should continue to govern a dynamic society like Spain's in the late sixties and early seventies.

Franco had said many times that his regime had been born to restore the Catholic faith and combat the atheism and materialism of the modern world. He did have a genuinely Christian vision of life and society. The family was the cornerstone of social life as far as he was concerned, and he had given ample proof of the fact in his work in government: the introduction of family representatives in the assembly was only one example.

On the other hand, the last word in Francoist political thought was 'development'. In a decade of heady change, it had turned Spain into a secular society given over to an idea of life that was based on pleasure-seeking, permissiveness and consumerism. Of course, the change did not come about abruptly or easily or without qualifications and exceptions. Traditional customs, habits and ways of thought survived. But it was a real and irreversible change.

In 1975, the year Franco died, Spain achieved a per capita income of $2,486. The number of people living in cities of more than 100,000 inhabitants stood at about 75%. Between 35% and 40% of households had cars. In the average family budget 'miscellaneous spending and holidays' accounted for almost as much as food. About 5 million Spaniards now went abroad for their holidays.[5]

A new Spain was taking shape, with towns and industries growing, women going to work, mass tourism and material prosperity together with a dramatic decline of religious observance and priestly vocations. Spaniards were enticed towards consumerism and a notion of prosperity which television, firmly under state control, equated with cars, holidays in the sun, travel, domestic gadgets, foreign aperitifs and expensive scent. The penitential processions and other rituals of Holy Week had been reduced to little more than part of the country's package for tourists: what was most in evidence at that time of year were beaches full of young people in bikinis and shorts.

It seemed hardly possible that an eighty-year old man, sincerely religious and imbued with moral values should rule a society with which he was wholly at odds.

And yet, in some ways, the same sort of contradiction underlay the whole crisis – a crisis of politics and of authority – which the Franco regime faced in the last years of its life. The paradox was profound. Franco's regime was a victim of the social changes it had spawned itself. Or, to put it another way, because of the pace of social change in Spain, political changes were needed which

Franco and his regime could not and would not implement.

Conflicts, which had continued to get worse from 1969 to 1975 were, of course, the catalyst that brought on the crisis. Yet it was basically a crisis within Francoism, provoked by the dilemma of how to adapt the institutions of the regime to cope with Franco's death. The power struggles and differences over the succession only made matters worse. Blas Piñar, leader of the ultra-right wing 'New Force' (*Fuerza Nueva*), founded in 1967, was quite right when he said, 'In Spain, what we are suffering from is a crisis of identity within the state itself.'[6]

The crisis began to become apparent from 1967, giving the lie to Franco's claim that he had 'everything well and truly battened down'. It developed in at least two ways. There was a struggle to control the political process between Carrero and López Rodó, on the one side, and the 'blue' faction inside the Movement on the other – a struggle which was concealed from the public and which did not prevent the contenders from co-operating when neces-sary. At the same time there was a clash between the diehards and those who favoured further change: the focus of this struggle was the further development of the Organic Law of the State and, more particularly, the question of whether political 'associations' should be permitted within the Movement.

The battle for control of decision-making had been brewing ever since the rise of Carrero Blanco, López Rodó and the technocrats during the sixties: it could be observed, for instance, in sporadic outbursts against Opus Dei in press organs controlled by the Movement.

Carrero Blanco and López Rodó had a well defined political programme: strong government, the completion of the process of institutional development, economic progress, administrative reform, installation of the 18 July monarchy with Juan Carlos as successor, and above all a carefully regulated continuity.

The interests of the Movement, which had Solís as a spokesman in the Council of Ministers, were quite distinct: to make the Movement the only vehicle for representing political opinion, if necessary by allowing a variety of associations to be formed within the Movement. The result would be that the National Council of the Movement would become an organ of state higher even than the *Cortes*, with the power to make the government accountable and so to control it. In other words, as has already been suggested, a replica of Mexico's Institutional Revolutionary Party would be created, with institutions of its own – the Movement and the National Council – which would provide a basis of continuity of the regime and of political power.

In a sense, the struggle between these two tendencies which broke out in 1969 laid down lines of battle for the other conflicts that split Francoism over further change and the succession.

Hostility to further change was the policy of the extreme right, made up of a number of different groups: the Falangist old guard, Girón de Velasco's ex-servicemen's association, Blas Piñar's neo-fascist groups, some diehard elements in the army (the 'blue generals' García Rebull, Iniesta Cano and Pérez Viñeta) and some reactionary Catholic and traditionalist groups. Many men of these persuasions occupied prime positions in the corridors of power; they were influential in Franco's circle of intimates; and they had a near-monopoly of emotional allegiance to the *Caudillo*. The diehards saw Francoism as a coherent, flawless system; to modify it, even only slightly, would set off a chain reaction that would bring the whole structure crashing down. They contended that the dangers had been demonstrated by the experience of the sixties. The 'weakness' of the 1962 and 1965 governments and the 'liberalization' introduced at that time – in the Press Law, for example – had led to waves of conflicts and disorder from 1965–66 onwards.

For those who favoured further change, the *aperturistas* or 'openers', the same signs of conflict were evidence of the need for a more open legal and political framework in which divergent opinions (the 'contrast of opinion' as the phrase went) could be peacefully contained and the conflicts which had arisen in the course of social change could be settled. In large part, support for change was a characteristic of the younger generation, the 'third generation' of the regime or 'the Prince's generation' – those born around 1930–40. This was a generation that favoured dialogue and admired western European models; it had played no part in the Civil War; and its members were convinced that Spain's changed society had to be served by a changed political system, which, moreover, to a greater or lesser extent, would have to represent a bridge to some form of democracy.

The presence of these sources of tension in political life, which became well-known as a result of the new press freedoms of 1966, gave the last years of Francoism a semblance of political vivacity never seen before. The growing conflicts with workers, students, Basques and priests added to the excitement.

In the event, however, there was to be no fulfilment of the hopes of further liberalization aroused by the Organic Law of the State in 1966 and encouraged, at times, by Franco's own words, such as his declaration on 30 December 1968 that 'intransigence isn't viable in times like ours.' The diehards won all the battles fought over the interpretation of the LOE. The law on religious liberty (*Ley de Libertad Religiosa*), promulgated on 28 June 1967, triggered a ferocious campaign from the right wing of the regime: all that went through after amendment was toleration, not full liberty, for non-Catholic religions; Spain's status as a Catholic state and nation was moreover, confirmed. In the Organic Law of the Movement (*Ley Orgánica del Movimiento*), promulgated on the same day, after even fiercer debate, the diehard position was more firmly asserted. The Movement was again defined as an 'organization' and not, as in the LOE as a 'communion'. The effect of this was to entrench the power of the formidable bureaucratic apparatus of the Movement and the official trade union, while calling a halt even to the very limited measure of dialogue – limited and solely within the system – that might have been possible under the concept of the Movement as a communion.

The Law on representation of families in the *Cortes* (*Ley de Representación Familiar*), also of 28 June 1967, was again a step back from the LOE. The qualifications it imposed (on the numbers of deputies from each province, the right to vote and so on) robbed the exercise of all credibility. In any case, when the elections were held in November 1967, the Movement's organization – as it now was – grabbed almost the entire family vote. Admittedly, a few independent deputies representing families were returned and they did add a critical voice to the sittings and debates; but the following year, in September 1968, the Interior Minister, Alonso Vega, banned the meetings of a small group of such deputies, known as *transhumantes* – the term for migratory flocks of sheep – who had been joining together to try to plan concerted action.

The statutes of the Movement and of the Association, which came into force in December 1968 and July 1969 respectively, were the work of the minister responsible, Solís. Despite the claims made for them, they did nothing to open the door to the founding of political associations within the regime. They did indeed authorize the formation of associations 'of puplic opinion' but the term 'political associations ' was not admitted; 25,000 members was the minimum number an association was required to have; participation in elections was not permitted; and the associations had to be approved by the National Council of the Movement – rather than being subject, say, to the laws of the land.

Echoing, as it were, the frustrations of reformists at home, foreign policy grew more rigid and futile around 1967–70. Gibraltar came to monopolize the attention of the government or at least that of the Foreign Minister Castiella. On 4 May 1968 the

Spanish government sealed the frontier at La Línea de la Concepción, in response to the British Government's refusal to negotiate de-colonization. The results were counter-productive. The people of Gibraltar were alienated for good and Spain got nothing out of it. In September 1968 negotiations with the United States over renewal of the bilateral agreement, took a similar course. Castiella's demands – $1,000 million in military aid and US support over Gibraltar, which Franco seems to have approved – were a stumbling block. No agreement was reached. The existing pact was extended until September 1970 without any concessions from Washington.

Faced with a great wave of strife (ETA's first fatal attacks in 1968; big workers' marches on May Day in 1967 and 1968; more disturbances at the universities, culminating in the death of a student, Enrique Ruano, in Madrid in January 1969 and the occupation of the Rector's office at Barcelona University a few days later) the government had no reply except to declare a state of emergency in February 1969. So on all fronts the regime seemed to be backtracking from the reforming process begun in 1966.

In reality, Franco had never held out much hope. Phrases coined by him, like the famous one of 30 December 1968 quoted above, were no more than chance remarks. Rather than on any firm or clear promises from Franco, the movement for change, the so-called 'opening' of the regime, fed on its own fantasies and its own hopes.

Franco was not guilty of misleading anybody. When others started talking about 'liberalization' and 'opening up' – terms Franco hardly ever used – he spoke only of 'institutionalization'. What he meant by that was a slow, evolutionary process, which would equip his regime to cope with changing circumstances and with the needs of the time, but which would not change it in any essential way.

Franco explained what was essential in two long speeches made on 17 and 28 November 1967 at the opening of the 9th session of the *Cortes* and the 11th annual meeting of the National Council of the Movement respectively. His minimum criteria were: (1) the National Movement itself, its teaching, its principles and its structure: 'this Movement,' he declared on 28 November, 'has been, is and must continue to be the basis of our legal and political order'; (2) unity: 'I shall never tire,' he proclaimed on the 17th, 'of calling for unity in matters which are vital for the good of this Spain of ours . . .'; (3) authority: 'No changes, of course,' he said on the same occasion, 'can be allowed to affect the maintenance of the principle of authority', a principle which Franco saw as the key to all order, peace and justice; (4) the inadmissibility of political parties: 'It is a mistake,' he warned, 'to think that institutionalization can only happen if the unity of society is broken up into a multiplicity of political parties.' He had said the same thing a little earlier, on 27 April, in Seville: 'If it's political parties they want, under cover of providing for "contrast of opinions", they had better realize once and for all that it is never going to happen.'

As far as Franco was concerned, Spain already had the 'backbone' she was said to need. The state was fully equipped with institutions; the country had been given a solid and effective structure of government. To his mind, the appointment of his successor in July 1969 had rounded off the process. In his message of 30 December 1969 Franco said, 'The Principles of the Movement, changeless in perpetuity, the solidity of the institutional structure of the state, the designation as successor and oath of the Prince of Spain, who has given abundant proof of his loyalty and love of the fatherland, are a sure guarantee of the continuity of our work.'

'Institutionalization' and continuity for the future. These were Franco's replies to the debate that had begun within his regime. Allowing for his pragmatism and prudence, Franco was sticking to his long-term aim: to create institutions that would perpetuate Francoism. He was not a diehard *à outrance*, like some of his henchmen who were now beginning to be known as 'the bunker'; much less, however, was he reconciled to 'opening up' the regime. Faced with the choice between inflexibility and further change, he maintained a rough balance which slightly favoured the former.

This could be seen in changes he made in his governments from 1969 onwards. When he decided to delegate the prime ministership, he chose hard-liners, tried, loyal and trustworthy, such as Carrero Blanco, deputy prime minister from 1969 to 1973 and prime minister from June to December of that year (though he acted as premier throughout that time) and Carlos Arias Navarro, who was appointed to the premiership on Carrero's death.

The formation of a new government in October 1969 seemed predictable and necessary. The 1965 government was exhausted and divided (over the press law, the LOE, strikes, the state of emergency, the succession issue). Franco and Carrero, who was again the key figure in the re-shuffle, had been studying the situation for some time with a view to making changes.

They did not go ahead, however, until a new problem had come to the fore. The was a financial scandal which, by its very nature, seemed to heighten the impression of a regime in crisis and decline which bedevilled Franco's last years. On 10 August 1969

the government admitted that credits given to the Matesa company
for a total of 10,000 million pesetas – an enormous sum at that time
– to guarantee the export of textile machinery, had been
fradulently converted. Several directors of the firm, thought to
belong to Opus Dei, were arrested and put on trial; the Ministers of
Finance, Juan José Espinosa San Martín, and of Commerce,
Faustino García Moncó, seemed to be seriously implicated.

Undoubtedly, the Matesa scandal seriously eroded public
esteen for Franco's regime. Corruption, which had been glimpsed
several times before, was now exposed to full public view. People
felt that the system and the state had been plunged into crisis.
Franco's own response did little to dispel suspicion or allay
rumour. He refused to accept that the affair had discussed men in
high office in the government and the civil service, taking no
notice, when the report of the committee of inquiry into the affair,
implicating a number of high officials, was laid before Franco's
own *Cortes* on 30 June 1970. He sidestepped the issue by including
Espinosa San Martín and García Moncó in a general pardon issued
on 1 October 1970, which relieved them of any penalties they
might have incurred.[7]

Franco was unhappy about the way the Movement's press had
politicized the Matesa scandal: it seemed to be an attempt to
manoeuvre the Opus Dei technocrats out of the government. If so,
it did not succeed. Franco's re-shuffle followed the lines suggested
by Carrero Blanco. The ministers involved in the Matesa affair
were sacked, but so too were others suspected of manoeuvring
against Opus, such as Solís, or those who were said to have
condoned the ploy, like Fraga Iribarne, whose province included
the press.

On 29 October 1969 Franco carried out the biggest re-shuffle in
the history of his long rule. Out of eighteen ministers in the
incoming cabinet, thirteen were new. It was as near as Franco ever
came to picking his government from a single faction, though in
fact it was still quite broadly based. Carrero Blanco, a deputy prime
minister in name, would henceforth act in the premier's role.
From now on, Franco's practical role would be as head of state (as
in reality it always had been: his Councils of Ministers were little
more than administrative committees, save on a few rare occasions, and major issues of national importance were hardly ever
broached at their meetings). At least twelve ministers in the new
government could be classified as belonging to the conservative-
technocratic tendency led by Carrero Blanco and López Rodó:
hence the ribald talk of 'Opus-pocus'.

Institutional development was over; the dilemma of inflexibility or 'opening up' had been posed; the system's capacity to survive intact has been called in question; and the whole Francoist state was facing a crisis of identity. In these circumstances, Franco backed the undiluted, pro-development, conservative and non-ideological Francoism of Carrero Blanco.

Carrero's first concern was to restore government control over all state institutions. This was what was meant by the 'unification of power and co-ordination of functions', which, according to official statements, would be the aim of the new government's policy. With a relatively homogeneous cabinet, Carrero hoped to be able to tackle effectively an ambitious political programme that would bring the crisis of authority to an end and prepare the way for transition to a post-Franco era that seemed ever more urgent. There would be educational reforms, a new trade union law, reflation of the economy after the recession of 1967–69, a new start in foreign policy and a re-structuring of relations between Church and state.[8]

In only two fields did the 1969 government have any success: the economy and foreign policy. The gross domestic product grew by 4.1% in 1970, 4.9% in 1971, 8.1% in 1972 and 7.8% in 1973, albeit at the cost of high inflation, which exceeded 8% in 1971 and 1972 and climbed to 11.4% in 1973. In foreign policy, the new minister, Gregorio López Bravo, for whom Franco had a particularly soft spot, brought Spain out of the mire in which Castiella had left her. In June 1970 he signed a preferential agreement with the European Economic Community. In September he renewed the US military agreements and he arranged for President Nixon to visit Spain in October. He boosted Spain's relations with the Arab countries by supporting Palestinian claims in the Middle East – doubtless with a view to disarming Moroccan claims in the Sahara. He started work on a rapprochement with the eastern bloc states and with China, with which he established formal diplomatic recognition.

For the rest, however, the government found it was up against some serious obstacles, not because the government was the problem, but because of the nature of the regime itself. The 1970 law of the Education Minister Villar Palasí would have been laudable in different circumstances but it did nothing to dampen student unrest, which had been going on for years at variable levels of intensity and which would culminate in a series of major disorders in the universities of Madrid and Valladolid in 1972 and 1973.

The trade union law of 1971 proved unsatisfactory even to many people inside the Movement. Franco's social peace broke down just at that moment. 1,547 strikes were recorded in 1970, 542 in 1971 and 853 in 1973.

What was worse, the lack of a democratic system in labour relations caused many disputes to degenerate into serious clashes between strikers and police. Eight workers were killed in these between 1970 and 1973: three in Granada in July 1970; one in Madrid in September 1971 in a building industry strike; one in Barcelona in November when police tried to dislodge some 7,000 strikers who were occupying the SEAT factory; two in El Ferrol, Franco's native town, in March 1972 and the last the following year in a strike at a nuclear reactor construction site at San Adrián del Besós near Barcelona.

In the Basque Country things were even worse. Between July and September 1970, despite a tough campaign of repression in which 1,953 prisoners were detained in 1969 and 831 in 1970, ETA pulled off a series of spectacular robberies from banks, and private business. On 18 September 1970, at a game of pelota, the Basque national sport, at San Sebastián, Franco – perplexed but un-perturbed – watched as the veteran Basque nationalist Joseba Elósegui made a human torch of himself, following the ritual suicide methods of Buddhist monks.[9]

Soon after, in December, Franco and his ministers had to face a more dramatic event than any in recent times: the trial at Burgos, before a court martial, of 16 members of ETA, including two priests and three women, for whom the prosecution was demanding a total of six death penalties (or nine, if those duplicated are counted) and 752 years of imprisonment.

Franco gave the green light for the trial to go ahead because he and his government wanted to reply to the Basque challenge with a display of force and because they hoped to silence critics on the far right who bemoaned the weakness of the regime. The outcome could hardly have been worse: first, because the new Spain, a modern developed society, could find no reasonable excuse for the repression practised by the regime – something Spaniards had previously been unwilling to acknowledge or which they had complacently overlooked when it was a matter of breaking up students' and workers' demonstrations. Secondly, the trial sparked off an international reaction against Franco such as had not been witnessed since 1946.

The tensions caused by the Burgos trial began before the trial was due to open. The trial was fixed for 3 December 1970. On 21 November, two Basque bishops Cirarda and Argaya published a pastoral letter in which they condemned the laws under which the accused were to be tried and appealed for clemency for those facing death. On 30 November several hundred people demonstrated in Barcelona against the trial and against Franco.

On 1 December a full meeting of the bishops' conference pleaded for the 'utmost clemency'. On the same day, several days of strikes, mass meetings and marches began in the Basque country. Even while General García Valiño was suggesting to the Captain-general of Burgos, General García Rebull, that the trial should be deferred until the court martial's competence to try the case had been established, ETA carried out a daring propaganda coup by kidnapping the West German consul in San Sebastián, Eugen Beihl.

From then on, events moved quickly. The accused turned the trial into a defiant indictment of the regime and a defence of the Basque cause. On 4 December a state of emergency was declared in the Basque province of Guipúzcoa; on the 9th and 10th there were more demonstrations in several Spanish cities; on the 12th 300 well known Catalan intellectuals, including the painter Miró, Tàpies, the singer Raimon, Serrat, and the writer Terenci Moix shut themselves up in the Abbey of Montserrat and issued a manifesto which, as well as condemning the Burgos trial, called for an amnesty and the restoration of democratic freedoms. On 14 December 1970, after several Captain-generals had demanded a firm response from Franco, the government decided to declare a nationwide state of emergency for a period of six months.

International reaction had also been highly unfavourable. From the time the trial opened there had been demonstrations and mass protests in many European cities; Spanish consulates and Iberia offices had been stoned; Spanish ships were boycotted in some ports; the international press and media were unanimous in expressing their revulsion at the trial and the Vatican's own paper called for clemency.

Francoism responded in a way very similar to that of 1946, when the Franco regime was condemned at the UN. Opinion was galvanized in adulation of Franco; national chauvinism was invoked against foreign hostility. On 17 December in the Plaza de Oriente, the huge square in front of the old royal palace in Madrid, Franco acknowledged the tribute of a crowd of hundreds of thousands of people, acclaiming him – and the army with him – and calling for ETA to be punished and the condemned to be executed. Similar demonstrations were organized over the next few days in almost every part of the country.

On the 28th, after two tense weeks of waiting since the end of the trial, in which there had been no relief from tension except for the release of the kidnapped German consul, the court martial gave its verdict. Six of the accused were sentenced to death and the rest to a total of 519 years in prison.

The sentence having been confirmed by the Captain-general of Burgos, Franco assembled his cabinet on the 29th. He took the chair in the uniform of a Captain-general – something he had never done before. Almost the entire government – which had behaved cautiously amid the climate of tension that surrounded the trial – pronounced in favour of commuting the death sentences.

Franco did not reveal his own view, although the ministers thought he seemed to show some signs of relief as they gave their respective opinions. One of them was later to claim that he had even said, 'Thank you very much: you have taken a great weight off my shoulders.' On the 30th, in his end-of-year message, Franco told the country he had decided to exercise his right of pardon and commute the death sentences.[10]

Thus what would have been an irreparable moral and political error was righted. Even so, however, the Burgos trial was a setback for the regime. The unacceptable face of Francoism had again been unmasked; the question of the regime's legitimacy had been re-opened; and Spanish opinion had been polarized. Most of all, in the Basque Country the trial was a real turning-point. Basque national consciousness was re-awakened, as could be seen from the wide-ranging mobilization of opinion that went on throughout the month of December. This was the start of a process that would end, after a few years of agitation and oppression, by alienating the Basques from Franco's regime in large numbers and creating a widespread feeling of revulsion from the very idea of Spain.

This was something Franco was incapable of appreciating. The policy Francoism pursued in the Basque country between 1969 and 1975 was one of the great historic errors of recent times in Spain.

It was at this time, moreover that Franco's social peace broke down for good. To the serious incidents, already mentioned, at Granada, the SEAT plant, El Ferrol and San Adrián del Besós, general strikes were added in Vigo, Pamplona and other places, which were broad-based and violent though without fatalities. This was all far from being 'well battened down'. In 1971, the joint synod of bishops and clergy of all Spain voted in favour of a motion that the Church should ask to be pardoned for having failed to find a reconciling role in the Civil War. Two years later the bishops asked for the concordat of 1953 to be rescinded and for the separation of Church and State.

In 1971–73, ETA (or rather ETA's 'Vth Assembly' – its hard-line, separatist and 'armed' wing) under the command of Eustaquio Mendizábal, known as Txikia, launched its most virulent campaign of violence to date. There were robberies, shootings (four policemen and five terrorists were killed in 1973–73), kidnappings (of the industrialists Lorenzo Zabala in 1972 and Felipe Huarte in 1973), bombings (of trade union offices, Civil War memorials, exclusive clubs, etc.). At about this time the Anti-Fascist Patriotic Revolutionary Front (*Fronte Revolucionario Anti-fascista y Patriótico* – FRAP) emerged – an activist unit, Maoist in ideology, dedicated to the violent overthrow of Francoism. On 1 May 1973 its members assassinated a policeman in Madrid.

It seemed as if Franco's precautions might fail even in connection with the succession. Franco was not pleased when Prince Juan Carlos tried to patch up his relationship with his father, because of the possible political implications. Nor did he welcome reports, like those which appeared in *The New York Times* on 4 February 1970, which portrayed the prince as representing Spain's hope of a democratic future. When Franco heard from Don Juan Carlos's own lips that the prince had dined with José María Areilza, one of the architect's of Don Juan's liberal politics, Franco told him, 'The choice is Your Highness's: you can either be a prince or a private individual.'[11]

More complex were the problems produced by the marriage, at the Pardo Palace on 8 March 1972, of one of Juan Carlos's cousins, Alfonso de Borbón-Dampierre, with Franco's eldest granddaughter, María del Carmen Martínez Bordiú.

The problems arose from the political undercurrents of the marriage. Because of the peculiar significance of the bride and groom, elements opposed to Juan Carlos could see Alfonso de Borbón as an alternative potential king. He had never made any secret of his approval of Franco's Movement and he was held to be a man of right-wing views. A possible point in his favour was that no king had yet been crowned and the future order of succession had therefore not yet been established in Juan Carlos's descendants by hereditary right. This left open the possibility that the assembly could include Don Alfonso among the heirs of Don Juan Carlos, bearing in mind the closeness of their relationship and the fact that Don Alfonso had never concurred in the renunciation of the throne by his father, Don Jaime.

Franco, who had a profound respect for institutions and for the law, probably never considered such a possibility. It is also likely that no one else did more than speculate about it either. Don Alfonso himself declared that he accepted the 'instauration' of Don Juan Carlos, although he also affirmed that he would never renounce what he believed were his own rights.

Franco was, however, offended by the efforts mounted from Don Juan's and Don Juan Carlos's households to deprive the wedding of the status of a state occasion or 'royal marriage' and to prevent Don Alfonso from using the title of prince (which, strictly, could only belong to Juan Carlos). When the Justice Minister, Antonio María Oriol, had a meeting with Franco about it on 1 February 1972, the dictator could not conceal his annoyance. 'I'd like to know who started this manoeuvre,' he said. 'Don Alfonso used to have the title of prince and now that he is marrying my daughter they want to take it away from him.'[12]

Although he accepted the explanations he was given, his disappointment was obvious. Relations between Franco and Juan Carlos cooled further when Don Juan made some new liberal utterances at Estoril on 24 June, at the time of a visit from the prince. This did not, however, prevent Franco on 18 July from signing laws that would give the future king enhanced authority over the institutions of the state from the time of his accession.[13]

Franco, moreover, had jibbed at stripping Don Alfonso of the title of Prince of Borbón; he informed Carrero Blanco of this on 16 November 1972. A very tense meeting between Juan Carlos and Franco held on the 20th of that month, was necessary before Franco relented and agreed instead to the granting of the title of Duke of Cadiz, with the style of Royal Highness, which would also apply to Franco's niece and all the couple's direct descendants. This title clearly underlined Don Alfonso's marginal position in the line of succession to the throne.

The regime went on without settling the political divisions within its own ranks. Carrero, like Franco, recoiled from the idea of bringing a 'legal opposition' back into the system – which was much talked of at the time – seemed to him unnecessary and dangerous. He would not even allow that members of the *Cortes* might co-operate in groups among themselves. He felt that the official syndicate, the family and the municipality provided enough scope between them to satisfy all calls for ideological pluralism.

Given these terms of reference, it was hardly surprising that the new Minister for the Movement in the 1969 government, Torcuato Fernández Miranda, found himself faced with an almost impossible task. When he took office in December 1969 he abolished the National Delegacy for Associations (*Delegación Nacional de Asociaciones*), which seemed to suggest that the Statute of Associations, passed by his predecessor Solís only a few months before, was going to be dropped.

There is no doubt that the new minister understood the need to provide a framework for the diversity of opinion that existed in Spain and to broaden the existing channels of representation. He talked, for instance, of a 'pluriform Movement' and in May 1970 tabled a new plan for associations in which 'associations for political activity' were now to be permitted.

Yet Fernández Miranda, an intelligent man who cannot have failed to realize that political associations would end up as nothing less than parties by another name, was unable convincingly to represent them as a middle way between a full party system and a single party state. The government froze his plan and declared the associations issue shelved. The verbal balancing act Fernández Miranda performed to justify this decision was quite extraordinary. 'To give a simple "Yes" or "No" to associations would be like falling into one of the pharisees' traps. . . . What we have to establish is whether a "Yes" to political associations also implies a "Yes or no" or a "*Not* Yes *but* No" to parties.' The conclusion apparently to be drawn from the minister's riddle-me-ree was that since associations would be parties in disguise there would be no associations. And indeed none was authorized.[14]

The government and the regime were caught in one of the 'pharisees' traps' that Fernández Miranda spoke of. Francoism had no answers to the country's problems. Even men of the regime were now able to see this. In 1971 the former minister Fraga Iribarne published a highly influential book, *Political Progress* (*El desarrollo político*) in which he pointed out the root cause of the crisis the regime faced: that a developed and industrial society like Spain's needed different political institutions and a new political system. Fraga himself was now thinking in terms of an opening towards liberalization with associations, broad channels of representation and a re-structuring of the arguments in favour of the legitimacy of the regime on the basis of democracy. What was more, this was being said by a Francoist whose name figured in every possible combination of what the next government might look like. That was the important thing: the extent of political debate within the regime itself. Areilza, for example, was now writing openly in the papers about 'Spain's road to democracy' and reminding his readers that democracy meant popular sovereignty, accountable government, a genuinely representative legislature and political parties. The arguments for 'opening up' the regime were now being couched in the same language as that of the democratic underground opposition.

The Carrero Blanco government could find no way of resolving the contradictions and dilemmas it had inflicted on itself. To the escalation of conflict in the country, ministers responded by tightening public security measures. In 1971 the 1959 Public Order Law (*Ley de Orden Público*) was revised to increase fines and prison terms for the offences it covered. The daily evening paper *Madrid*, the most progressive organ in the Spanish press, was closed down by the government in 1972 and its offices bombed on 21 April 1973; its editor, Rafael Calvo Serer, who had once been the ideologue of Catholic triumphalism, had to go into exile. Other publications – papers, journals and the publishing houses responsible for them – suffered temporary closures or fines. In 1972 the leading figures in the clandestine union, Workers' Commissions (*Comisiones Obreras*) were arrested, to be tried the following year and sentenced to terms of imprisonment of up to twenty years.[15]

This policy turned out to be futile. We have already seen how unrest among workers, students and Basques were unaffected. The same was true in other fields. The disappearance of *Madrid* failed to awe the press, which ended up as a sort of 'parliament on paper', speaking for the diversity of points of view which were rife in the country and the regime. The clandestine opposition, however, had to pick its way through threats and restrictions to reach public opinion and was still feeling the effects of repression. A group of excellent and famed cartoonists (Mingote, Forges, Chummy Chúmez and others) used the papers to ridicule the inflexibility and antiquated rhetoric of Francoism.

The government itself was split. While Carrero Blanco and the Minister of Public Works, Fernández de la Mora, went public, writing diatribes in the papers under pseudonyms denouncing the call for 'opening up' and exoriating parties, there were other ministers who spoke up for liberalization and political associations. The Minister of the Interior – responsible as such for public order – Tomás Garicano Goñi, told Franco in a memo of 11 September 1972, that the regime's political line had to be re-directed away from extremism towards the sort of change and relief of tension that the younger generation was striving for. A few months later, in a further memo of 7 May 1973, he condemned the 'disproportionate hysteria of the ultras' and told Franco that he thought 'an authentic opening-up' was necessary.[16]

The reaction on the right wing of the regime, among the 'ultras' Garicano Goñi spoke of, showed the depth of the crisis of Francoism while helping to make it even worse. In the *Cortes*, diehard deputies tirelessly conveyed their profound displeasure at any progressive trends in government policy – with López Bravo's efforts to open a diplomatic door to the east, for instance, or with plans to allow the principle of conscientious objection.

In 1971, ultra-right wing violence began to break out. Terrorists of right wing persuasion attacked bookshops or art galleries which were thought to favour leftist tastes in culture or politics. It was the right which whipped up the huge demonstrations in support of Franco in 1970 and on 1 October 1971, and which organized public tributes to the police in May 1973, combined with an implied protest against the 'weakness' of Home Minister Garicano Goñi. The right rejected the idea of political associations outright. The most they would allow – to judge from what Girón de Velasco said in May 1972 – was the interplay of 'tendencies' within the regime. Girón referred to a 'revolutionary progressive' tendency, by which he presumably meant the Falange, a 'conservative and traditional' one (the Catholics) and a third which was 'pragmatic and moderate' – thought to be a reference to López Rodó's line.

Francoists no longer seemed to be agreed on anything except unquestioning loyalty to Franco. A year after the gigantic demonstration of 17 December 1970, the Francoist masses took to the streets again. On 1 October 1971 they were back in the Plaza de Oriente, paying raucous homage to their leader. This time there was no particular reason for the demonstration. It had been put on 'just because', as the intensive propaganda put it. Exaltation of Franco's person – that new form of populist leadership, dependent now on the venerability of an old man – was Francoism's answer to its own irresoluble crisis of identity.

Franco, meanwhile, did not have much to say for himself, though his level of activity remained tremendous. In 1970 he visited Barcelona, Valencia, Saragossa, Cáceres, Jeréz and Salamanca; at the Pardo he received, among others, Presidents Nixon of the USA and Americo Thomas of Portugal. He went on giving innumerable audiences at El Pardo and, in summer at Meirás in Galicia. In his forty years as head of state he received 9,169 individuals and 5,023 delegations comprising 68,596 people.[17] In 1971, however, his travel round Spain came practically to an end and in any case his speeches on these occasions were now limited to the predictable formal utterances.

Franco was caught up in the same contradictions as his regime. In December 1969, for instance, when Fernández Miranda announced his intention of scrapping the Statute of Association, Franco told him, 'Whatever you do, don't shut the door completely: just leave it a little bit ajar.'[18] It was just this sort of ambiguity that helped to keep the crisis going.

'We must have hope – we must have hope,' said Girón de Velasco to Franco's doctor Vicente Gil on 14 November, 1972. 'The man is bound to take action soon. He's got to. We have no other remedy.'[19] The hope of the leader of the ultra-right ex-servicemen's organization was to remain unfulfilled: not only did 'the man' Franco fail to take action; he had no 'remedy' himself, either.

Franco made the last two genuinely political speeches of his life on 18 November 1971, opening the tenth session of the *Cortes*, and on 31 January 1972 at the opening of the twelfth annual meeting of the National Council of the Movement. Once again, it was apparent that not everything was 'well and truly battened down' – a phrase Franco repeated in the speech of 18 November. The proof of this was that Franco, now nearly eighty years old, still felt obliged to explain what his regime and its institutions were.

In the first of the speeches, after summarizing the .assembly's work since 1967 and eulogizing the development that had gone on between 1940 and 1970, Franco homed in on his favourite topics. He stressed his view that development had been achieved thanks to the National Movement and that Spain was a 'social state founded on law'. He characterized his regime with Carrero Blanco's phrase, 'unification of power and co-ordination of functions'. Spain, he reminded his audience, 'as a political entity, is a social, Catholic and representative state which, in conformity with tradition, is constituted as a monarchy.' He spoke of the need to bring the institutions of state 'to perfection' but openly rejected political parties and made it crystal clear that under his regime, divergence of opinion could not be confused with 'political corner-fighting from pre-conceived positions by doctrinaire groups'. He again recalled that the principles of the Movement were, by definition, 'perpetual' and 'unalterable'.

He did not try to deny that Spain had problems, but argued that they had been brought on by fast economic growth and the 'systematic campaigns of subversion' mounted by his enemies. He did insist that Spain was in good political health, that she was already a democracy – a 'practical' and 'organic' democracy and that his 'social state founded on law' was the best guarantee of freedom and justice.

The speech of 31 January 1972 was shorter but no less concerned with matters of definition. Franco's purpose was to define the role of the National Council of the Movement itself and commend the defence of the state institutions to it. He identified as crucial its right to supervize political conduct and its function of setting out the political aims and standards of the regime.

Franco had not really said anything new in either speech. He made this much clear: that he acknowledged no alternative to his own regime; that allegiance to the principles of 18 July must not be evaded and that there could be no political activity outside the Movement.

Perhaps it would be unreasonable to ask more of an 80-year-old man than unshakeable fidelity to his own life's work. But the speeches offered nothing except abstract, formal definitions and an idealized résumé of the work and significance of his regime. The problem was that the regime as he defined it had been outgrown by Spain's dynamic society; as the growing number of conflicts showed, the country was bubbling over with a diversity of political views that could not be contained within the existing structure. The solution did not lie in the regime; the regime itself was the problem.

And so the vacillation and uncertainty continued. The tough action Girón hoped for from Franco was not forthcoming. On the contrary, in his Christmas message for 1972, Franco seemed to incline towards a more open policy. 'We have to get away,' he said, 'from dogmatic judgements and closed minds. Disparity of views or tendencies is not only legitimate but positively necessary.' On 1 March 1973 Carrero Blanco asked the National Council of the Movement to devise 'concrete proposals to broaden the scope for citizens to lend a hand in public affairs.'

Hopes of a new opening were soon dashed, despite the enthusiasm with which Franco's Christmas message was welcomed. In May 1973 FRAP murdered a policeman and a row broke out when the Archbishop of Madrid, Cardinal Tarancón, refused to allow a party of politically motivated pilgrims to enter the capital en route through Spain to the shrine of the Virgin of Fatima in Portugal. In response, the extreme right mounted a fierce campaign which culminated in the mass tribute to the security forces.

Though Carrero Blanco defused the situation with moderation and skill, a cabinet shake-up was needed. In June 1973 Franco re-shuffled the government. The main novelty was the separation of the offices of prime minister and head of state – which seemed inevitable in view of Franco's great age – and the appointment of Carrero Blanco to the premiership. Other important moves were López Rodó's to Foreign Affairs and the arrival of the hard-liner Carlos Arias Navarro at the Ministry of the Interior. In terms of policy, there could be little hope of change. Carrero himself said that the new government's programme was 'to carry on'.

In any event, the government of 11 June 1973 seems to have envisaged a turn to the right as the only way of appeasing the 'ultras' without sacrificing a modest and strictly controlled measure of liberalization. This seems to have been the message of Carrero's speech to the *Cortes* in July and of the 'institutional offensive' promised in October by Fernández Miranda, who had been promoted to the rank of deputy prime minister.

The government's intentions, whatever they were, were still-born. On 20 December 1973, the very day on which the trial of the leaders of Workers' Commissions was due to begin, Carrero Blanco was assassinated by an ETA terror squad. A powerful explosion was set off by three bombs stuffed into a six-metre tunnel under the road surface of Claudio Coello Street in Madrid. The car in which Carrero Blanco was travelling, after attending his usual daily Mass at the Jesuit church, was blown sky-high. The car was lifted more than 30 metres into the air, hurtled over a five-storey building where the Jesuit fathers were housed, and landed in an inner courtyard. Along with Carrero, his driver and his police escort were killed.

Franco heard the news at about ten o'clock that morning, some twenty minutes after the event. The Minister of the Interior Arias Navarro informed Antonio Galbis, one of Franco's aides, immediately after hearing from the police. But until about noon, Franco was led to believe that Carrero had been the victim of an accident. When Fernández Miranda told him that it had been a terrorist attack, Franco, who had a severe bout of influenza at the time, received the news relatively calmly. He took a few steps and said, 'These things happen.' On the following day, however, the anguish the event had caused him was revealed. He broke down and wept – though he composed himself again almost immediately – before calling to order the meeting of his ministers which he had summoned urgently. The ministers decided to confer the posthumous title of 'Duke of Carrero Blanco' on the assassinated premier.[20]

Franco did not attend the funeral, which took place in the afternoon of 21 December in the presence of Prince Juan Carlos, in an atmosphere of high tension and emotion. The ceremony prompted a strident manifestation by the fanatical right, who cheered the Civil Guard and called for the army to take power.

Franco was present, however, at the Requiem Mass on the 22nd in the Church of S. Francisco el Grande, where Cardinal Tarancón officiated; the cardinal had been the target of the diehards' anger at the funeral where cries of 'Tarancón to the scaffold!' had been heard incessantly. Franco was in a highly emotional state. He wept and moaned at intervals during the service and he wept unashamedly at the end when he embraced Carrero Blanco's widow.

Carrero Blanco's death was certainly a severe shock to the

ageing Franco. Carrero had been his closest and most loyal collaborator, virtually his alter ego, since 1941. He had played a crucial part in building up Francoism, in constructing governments, in devising laws and in developing the institutions. Moreover, he had been the key figure in Franco's hopes for the survival of Francoism after his own death.

As the Minister of Public Works, Fernández de la Mora, remarked, 'No harder blow could have been struck at the future prospects of the state of 18 July.' It seemed as if the death of Carrero Blanco would mean the end of Franco's regime; and if that was what people felt, it was precisely because public opinion was aware that Franco was physically exhausted and that his regime had been in the throes of a profound crisis for years.

This was an accurate appraisal. Spain was a Catholic state in which the Church condemned the regime and cries echoed in the streets against the Archbishop of Madrid and the 'red prelates'. It was a state where strikes were banned and where thousands occurred. It was an authoritarian state, driven by its bad conscience to search for some sort of democratic legitimacy.

As 1973 drew to a close, in view of the failure of the security forces to prevent the attack on Carrero Blanco, and in the face of the crisis in which Francoism was marooned, one could almost have applied to Franco's regime what the Italian patriot, Giuseppe Mazzini (1805–72) said of the Genoese authorities a century and a half before: they had every prerequisite of tyranny, except the ability to exercise it.

8
Agony and Death

In his *History of the Civil War* written in 1853, the historian Antonio Pirala explained how, during the transition from absolutism to liberalism which occurred in Spain after the death of Ferdinand VII in 1833, the country rejected as unserviceable the ultramontane and reactionary policies of Calomarde, who was the king's chief minister in 1832. Franco does not seem to have been aware of Pirala's analysis, because when he appointed Carlos Arias Navarro prime minister on Carrero Blanco's death, he committed the same mistake as Ferdinand VII. The political circumstances in which Spain found herself in 1974 had made Carlos Arias equally 'unserviceable' as Calomarde a century and a half before, and this was seemingly borne out with Arias's government between January 1974 and November 1975.

The appointment came as a surprise even to Arias Navarro himself. As Minister of the Interior's in the previous government he had been responsible for the spectacular security failure resulting in Carrero's death. Furthermore the deputy prime minister Torcuato Fernández Miranda had handled the crisis caused by Carrero's death with serenity and skill: there had been no breakdown of order; and no repressive measures such as might have been feared, especially in view of the tough directives issued by the Commander of the Civil Guard, General Iniesta Cano, which the government had promptly revoked. It was natural to think of Fernández Miranda as the man best placed to take over from Carrero.

Yet it was not to be. There was fierce opposition to Fernández Miranda from men of great influence with the regime, like Girón and Alejandro Rodríguez de Valcárcel, president of the *Cortes* since 1970. Nor was he a figure close to the magic circle of the Pardo, where decisive influence could be exerted by the small ring composed of Franco's wife, Carmen Polo, his son-in-law the

Marquess of Villaverde, his physician Vicente Gil, his adjutant Navy Captain Antonio Urcelay and the deputy head of the Military Household, General José Ramon Gavilán. In any case, Fernández Miranda made little effort to secure the job for himself, either because he did not want it – he seems to have been subjected to a certain amount of family pressure – or because in the circumstances he thought his appointment was a certainty.

Franco, however, quickly ruled him out. Fernández Miranda was a professor of constitutional law with a subtle and complex mind and Franco always mistrusted intellectuals who, he thought, had no practical aptitude for power: the case of Marcelo Caetano, Oliveira Salazar's successor in Portugal since 1969, seemed to prove this. In some circles it was already being said that Fernández Miranda would 'dig the regime's grave' as he was widely thought to be one of the best men available to steer Francoism towards some sort of constitutional reform.

But that was not what Franco was looking for. So when Fernández Miranda sounded his leader out about his chances at a meeting on 24 December 1973, four days after the attack on Carrero, Franco cut him short with shrewdness undiminished by the nervous condition brought on since Carrero's death. 'Excuse me,' he said, 'but are you trying to imply that I should have your name included in the list of three to be submitted by the Council of the Realm?' That was clear enough. Fernández Miranda's name was not on the list, which was made up of Carlos Arias Navarro, José Solís Ruiz and José García Hernández; therefore, he could not be chosen.

Franco did not make up his mind until 28 December. He passed the intervening days in an agitated condition, visibly unnerved and uncomfortable, wilting under the pressure from his intimate circle. Carmen Polo was particularly jumpy during the critical period; she was afraid that unless the new prime minister was a man of vigour, they would all end up like Carrero Blanco. Franco was dithering in the face of a decision he knew to be crucial and for which he was utterly unprepared.

Until the 28th he was inclined to favour is old friend and former minister, Admiral Pedro Nieto Antúnez, who until then was also favoured by Doña Carmen. But he yielded to counter-pressure that Antúnez was regarded as too old – he was 76 – and irresolute. He changed his mind probably only at the last moment, when even the president of the assembly and of the Council of the Realm, Rodríguez de Valcárcel, was waiting expectantly for Franco's orders to elect Nieto Antúnez. The last-minute views of Antonio Urcelay, Franco's adjutant, and Doña Carmen in favour of Arias settled the matter. 'Tell them to include Carlos Arias in the list of three,' Franco ordered Valcárcel, in Doña Carmen's presence, on the morning of the 28th. On the same day in the afternoon, the Council, summoned by Valcárcel, obediently presented its list, in which nothing mattered but the name Franco had wanted.[1]

Thus Franco appointed his second and last prime minister by means of a personal, autocratic choice, influenced by no considerations beyond the recommendations of his circle of confidantes. In political terms the appointment made sense. Of the men closest to the Pardo, Arias looked best equipped with the resilience needed to do what Carrero had been unable to do: to 'carry on'.

Arias's appointment satisfied almost nobody outside the 'bunker' of the regime. For the supporters of an 'opening up', the reformists and the clandestine opposition, as well as for ever more demanding public, Arias identified with repression because of the severity he had shown as a public prosecutor in Málaga during the Civil War and because of the many years he had spent with Alonso Vega as Director General of Security.

Franco had therefore opted for a hard-line policy. He had not completely jettisoned the programme of seeking to secure continuity by restrained and prudent means, and leaving some room for changing circumstances to be accommodated as agreed with Carrero. On the contrary, Arias would, for example, authorize political associations in December 1974, and legalize strikes in April 1975, with Franco's support. But Franco now rated the assertion of authority higher than any other priority. Law and order, rigorously and vigorously maintained, seemed to him the indispensable pre-condition of any further 'opening up'.

Arias formed his government in January 1974. He retained eight ministers from Carrero Blanco's cabinet but he got rid of López Rodó and the technocrats, who had been in power since 1957. He brought in figures from the Movement and from the Falangist tradition and introduced some new men, who were little known to the public but who had worked with him in their previous posts (Antonio Carro, José García Hernández, Valdés y González Roldán, Rodríguez de Miguel). A surprising inclusion was one of Fraga's men, Pío Cabanillas, as Minister of Information.

The new government had to begin by dealing with two urgent problems: law and order, brought to the fore by the attack on Carrero, and the economic crisis that had begun to emerge in the second half of 1973. Inflation was running at about 14% per annum and the trade deficit stood at $4,500 million dollars, although the gross industrial product still managed to grow by 10.1% in the course of the year and the industrial workforce by 2.4%.

The basic problem facing Arias was, however, the same as had bedevilled the regime since 1967 at the latest: that of what course political development should take. This was now exacerbated by the question, ever more openly asked, of whether Franco should hand over power to Prince Juan Carlos in his lifetime and so make the transition easier. Arias – without going into all the good and bad moves he made during his premiership – turned out to have more talent for politics than had been supposed and he was well aware that Carrero's rule between 1969 and 1973 had shown that the intransigence of 'immobilism' was impossible and that the problems of the country – and above all the survival of the regime – called for some new form of consensus.[2]

The difficulty for Arias lay in finding the right balance between total commitment to Franco and his system, and evolution towards this new consensus, which he regarded as inevitable. Thus his two years in power were to consist of a series of swings back and forth, advances and retreats. Arias never seemed able to get the dose right. His combination of progressive talk and oppressive mea-sures satisfied nobody. Indeed, he vexed the 'bunker', disillu-sioned the progressives, revived the spirits of the underground opposition and stimulated the spread of political consciousness through Spanish society – so much so that there were times when those familiar 'demons' of the Spanish character, which caused Franco so much concern, seemed to have escaped from hell, to rage, albeit not entirely unchecked, over the country.

Arias Navarro took the political class, the regime and the whole country by surprise in his first speech to the *Cortes* on 12 February 1974, by announcing a detailed programme, which promised, a genuine 'opening up' of the regime over a specified period. This was drawn up by a young politician from Soria called Gabriel Cisneros. The key point of the speech was the prime minister's promise that national consensus, which hitherto had found expression 'by way of consent' to what Franco did, would henceforth make itself felt 'by way of participation' in the political process. This formula, which implied the emergence of associa-tions and a broader scope for political life, was what in more general terms came to be called 'the spirit of the 12 February'. Franco must have shared in the general astonishment, but he did not demur. He merely counselled caution. 'Go easy, Arias,' he said.

It was possible to tell from indirect evidence what were the public opinion and mood, for the effect of the speech of 12 February was to revitalize political life. Extraordinary interest and enthusiasm were aroused – more than by any other political event connected with the official life of Francoism. Arias got the unanimous support of those who favoured political change and the whole-hearted applause of a press corps surprised by the liberal and tolerant attitude of the new Information Minister Pío Cabanillas.

Indeed, from 1974 Spain enjoyed a degree of press freedom unprecedented in the previous history of Francoism; this helped in turn to make a significant contribution to the resurgence of interest in politics – and in democracy – in the country. The success of a review like *Cambio 16*, with a weekly sale of almost half a million copies, reflected the revival of political consciousness a desire for political change in part of Spanish society. Some months after Arias's speech, Emilio Romero, editor of *Pueblo*, the organ of the official unions, commented ironically on the transformation that had occurred while displaying at the same time the anxiety it had caused on the Francoist right. 'My distinguished colleagues of the press,' he wrote, 'were high on liberalization and "opening up" like junkies in a hashish den.'[3]

To Cabanillas's opening up of information was added the so-called 'opening up of culture' by the man in charge of popular culture, the historian Ricardo de la Cierva. Spain discovered the female nude on the cinema screen at the theatre and in the press. This caused disgust in Franco's close entourage, and not without irony: the lifestyle of Franco's grandchildren, for instance, was as emancipated as that of the rest of the younger generation of the upper middle class; as such, it was a negation of the public and private morality practised and preached by Francoist orthodoxy and by Franco in person. The press, meanwhile, reported fully and frankly on strikes, politics and terrorism. Even the views of the leaders of the clandestine democratic opposition appeared frequently in articles and interviews published in Spanish papers and reviews.

True, the government did suppress the meetings and political activities of the opposition; and Cabanillas's liberalization still had some conspicuous limitations which became more marked when he was removed and replaced by León Herrera in October 1974. Basically, however, the existence of moderate opposition groups – Christian democrats, liberals, social democrats and socialists – was tolerated. By May 1975 the journalist Pedro Calvo Hernando could claim that all educated Spaniards were now familiar with such names as Felipe González, who had been elected Secretary of the Spanish Workers' Socialist Party (*Partido Socialista del Obrero Español* – *PSOE*) at a party conference, held in exile in France in October 1974; or the social democrat Dionisio Ridruejo, who had been the true inspiration of the opposition at home since the fifties; and the Christian democrats Ruiz-Giménez and Gil Robles.[4]

The freedom of the press and the toleration of the opposition were irreversible steps forward. But that was all that was to remain of the gradual progress towards the democratization of the regime promised by Arias on 12 February. His policy tacked continually from inspiring speeches to disappointing initiatives, from encouraging promises to repressive crackdowns. The speech of 12 February was followed by two serious crises: the house arrest of the Bishop of Bilbao, Monsignor Añoveros, for having published a defence of the use of the Basque language on 24 February; and on 2 March the execution of a young Catalan anarchist, Salvador Puig Antich, accused of taking part in the murder of a policeman in Barcelona.

The 'Añoveros incident' exacerbated Church-State relations that were already in a bad way. The Spanish bishops and the Vatican supported the Bishop of Bilbao. It was said that Pope Paul vi had a Bull ready excommunicating Franco himself – the man Cardinal Herrera Oria had once called 'the sword of the Most High' and 'minister of God' – and the entire government in the event of the bishop being expelled from Spain. The execution of Puig Antich sparked off a new series of demonstrations and protests throughout Europe and profoundly angered the Spanish opposition, which was powerless to act at home.

Franco forced Arias to retreat over the Añoveros case, strictly forbidding him to break with the Church. He went on trying to avoid a showdown with the Church – the conflict he was most afraid of – however much the clergy's attitude to his regime embittered and distressed him.[5] He said nothing, it seems, on the case of Puig Antich. However one looked at it, the government had suffered grave losses. It was even said (by Gabriel Cisneros) that the Arias government in three months had forfeited as much goodwill as a government might normally expect to lose in three years.

It was because of this erosion of support that all the government's efforts to restore its credibility proved useless; the efforts peaked on 22 April when Cabanillas made a speech in Barcelona, talking once again of a new start, of liberty, of toleration, and of putting an end to state control of the press. What was more, the minister waved a traditional Catalan liberty cap in a gesture of acknowledgement of Catalan distinctiveness which was without precedent in the history of the regime.

It all proved useless for two main reasons. First, the Francoist bunker was digging in – with undoubted sympathy from Franco himself – in anger at the freedom of the media, alarm at events like the Portuguese revolution of April 1974, and anxiety at the escalation of unrest and violence. In 1974 twenty people were killed by acts of terrorism – 12 of them in an attack on the Rolando Café in Madrid; violence broke out at 69 political meetings or marches; there were 96 robberies by terrorists, 168 acts of sabotage, and 37 bombings. Secondly, Arias was too much of a Francoist and a reactionary at heart to go through with the democratization of Francoism: that is why he resembles Ferdinand VII's minister Calomarde.

The Portuguese revolution of 24 April led to an offensive by the Francoist right against the government and particularly against the information policy of Cabanillas. Franco himself remarked soon after to López Rodó that the Spanish papers' treatment of events in Portugal, welcoming unreservedly the collapse of Salazar's state, had been 'a propaganda exercise in reverse'.[6]

On 28 April in the daily *Arriba*, Girón published a manifesto which came to be called 'the Girón Broadside', denouncing press freedom and warning that the right would not allow the Civil War to be forgotten or the regime or Franco to be betrayed. A few days later, Blas Piñar made a reference to the 'pygmies of the regime' who had infiltrated it in order to subvert it. This was taken as an allusion to Cabanillas, a man of no great physical stature. Piñar called those papers which had sent reporters to Paris to cover a press conference by the Communist Party secretary Santiago Carrillo 'the gutter press'.

On 13 June the Chief of the General Staff, General Manuel Díez Alegría was relieved of his post. He was the great white hope of the liberal wing of the armed forces, the man the opposition saw as a potential 'Spanish Spínola', who like the Portuguese general, would step in to bring the dictatorship to an end. On the 15th the reaction that had overtaken the language Arias used could be noted in a speech in Barcelona. Backsliding on his message of 12 February, Arias emphasized the leading role of the Movement and proclaimed it conterminous with the people. His point was clear enough: the spirit of 12 February could be allowed to mean nothing distinct from or inconsistent with the regime and the Movement. As Emilio Romero smugly said in his new role as the mouthpiece of Francoist orthodoxy, folk who fancied the spirit of 12 February would now have to light their candles and look for it under their rocking-chairs.

Such was the state of affairs when Franco's health and age intervened, flooding Spanish politics with all the uncertainty and tension that could be expected when the head of a power-structure so thoroughly personal as Franco's is suddenly no longer there. On 6 July 1974 Franco woke up with pain and an inflamed swelling in his right foot. His doctor, Vicente Gil, suspected a case of thrombophlebitis – that is, a blood-clot in a vein – and was inclined to blame the long hours Franco had spent sitting in front of the television watching football matches from the World Cup series in West Germany. Then it was discovered that the cause of the blood-clot was an abscess which had formed under a callous in one of Franco's toes.[7]

As the case was so serious, Dr Gil called in Doctors Francisco Vaquero, Ricardo Franco Manera and Rivera López. The diagnosis was confirmed by analysis and the doctors agreed, after consulting the prime minister, that Franco should be referred to a clinic. He entered the Francisco Franco Provincial General Hospital in Madrid on the 9th reluctantly – he would have preferred to be treated at the Pardo – after Vicente Gil had explained the gravity of his condition to him.

Franco was ensconced in Room 609 at the hospital. Carmen Polo took the adjoining room. A large team of doctors and nurses was in attendance. It was decided not to operate – Franco had thought they would do so – and a course of heparin treatment was followed. Treatment for Parkinson's disease was also administered and every imaginable kind of analysis and probe was carried out – into the digestive system, the prostate gland, the rectum, the heart and so on. To avoid the danger of an embolism, the Marquess of Villaverde – who returned from a trip to the Philippines on the 14th to join the medical team – ordered a special apparatus which had to be brought from another hospital to be installed.

Franco faced his hospitalization and treatment with his usual tranquillity, even with resignation. He received no one except Arias, Prince Juan Carlos – both of whom visited him daily – José Antonio Girón, who was a close friend and political associate of Dr Gil, and members of his family. He never complained about the treatment and behaved towards all the staff who attended him with his customary courtesy and charm. He even made the occasional joke. He responded well to medication and his pulse and heart-rate seemed normal. The swelling quickly began to subside, enabling him to go for walks in the corridor in order to stimulate the circulation. On the 16th, it was decided to switch to treatment with orally administered anti-coagulants. The doctors' optimism was apparent.

On the political front, no action was taken at first. Before entering hospital, Franco had told the prime minister, Arias Navarro, and the president of the *Cortes*, Rodríguez Valcárcel, that they should prepare the decree under which, in accordance with article 11 of the LOE, the prince would assume the functions of head of state. Arias agreed and presented the decree for Franco to sign. It was the prince himself who was against it, partly in deference to Franco but partly also because he was afraid of finding himself in the anomalous position of a successor who was not yet king, a temporary understudy with no clear role.[8]

Franco did not go to the commemoration of 18 July at La Granja. He spent the day watching a television film about his own life. The emotional strain it caused, combined with a break in the heparin treatment, brought on a very serious relapse which put paid to the doctors' optimism. Franco was very unstable throughout the 18th, with a high pulse and low blood pressure. At dawn on the 19th he had a serious stomach haemorrhage. It was possible to contain this, but the deterioration of Franco's condition raised anew the question of whether to operate. At Doña Carmen's request, Father Bulart administered supreme unction as a precaution.

The question of the transfer of power was also raised. Despite the opposition of the Marquess of Villaverde, Arias handed Franco the decree by which Prince Juan Carlos would take over the functions of head of state. Franco signed it, saying only that the law had to be observed.

In the end, Franco did not have the operation. The treatment followed the recommendations of the Marquess of Villaverde, Franco's son-in-law, whose differences of opinion with Vicente Gil led to stormy scenes that almost reached the point of physical violence. On the 22nd there was another flaming row, this time between the irascible Gil and the prime minister because of the doctor's belief that Arias had failed to uphold his authority as Franco's official physician against what he regarded as Villaverde's affronts. Gil was replaced as official physician soon afterwards by Vicente Pozuelo. In further consultations among the doctors, it was felt that of the various dangers by which Franco was threatened – haemorrhage, embolism, etc. – the worst was an operation. The doctors therefore decided to revert to treatment with anti-coagulants, massages and walking. More uncomfortable probes were made to see whether there could be any other reason for the haemorrhage. It was even thought, on the evidence of some tests, that Franco might have a tumour in the rectum.

Yet Franco managed to rally and survive the crisis. On the 25th he was already much recovered; on the 26th he even discussed business with the prince, Arias and several ministers for three hours. On the 30th, the medical team, in which the influence of the Marquess of Villaverde was prominent, gave the go-ahead for Franco to leave the hospital and return to the Pardo. He did so at mid-morning, to applause from the many people who had gathered around the hospital, smiling and emaciated after losing four kilos in weight.

He was not yet cured, however. He was even to feel the pains in his foot again a few days after leaving hospital. The team of seven doctors who were looking after him did not call the treatment off until 31 August, and Juan Carlos continued to perform the duties of head of state until 2 September.

When Franco's new personal physician, Vicente Pozuelo Escudero, took over on 31 July 1974, he found the leader not only weak and voiceless, but depressed and terribly drained. Depression was perhaps the biggest obstacle to the patient's total recovery.

Pozuelo began a simple but effective course of psychotherapy, which, given Franco's authority and venerability, looked almost like a sacrilegious joke. He made him march around his room, behind closed doors, in time to martial music, keeping step with the beat. He made him do Swedish exercises. He borrowed a set of aircraft boarding steps from Iberia airways and installed it in the garden of the Pardo so that Franco could practise on it before flying to his country house at Meirás on 16 August.

At Meirás, Pozuelo kept up the treatment. Franco was given some speech therapy sessions to help him get his voice back. On 13 September, the day after resuming his official duties, he played a game of golf in the interlude of a working day which began, at his usual time of 8.30 a.m. and went on until after midnight. His extraordinary willpower and determination had re-asserted themselves. Franco was relatively agile and alert. He kept fully up to date on national and international politics and had meetings with aides and colleagues. On 9 August, while he was still at the Pardo, a council of ministers had been held there with Prince Juan Carlos in the chair; there was another on the 30th at Meirás, again chaired by Juan Carlos. On both occasions, Franco welcomed the ministers, had private meetings with the prime minister and the prince, and appeared almost fully recovered, save for his voice, which was still weak.[9]

Franco had told his doctor that his removal to a hospital would be a political bombshell, and it was. But an even bigger surprise came on 2 September when it was announced that Franco would resume his duties as head of state. The surprise became stupefaction when more details emerged, because it appeared that Franco had said nothing about the move at Meirás the day before. Apparently, Arias first heard the news on the telephone from the Marquess of Villaverde. It was also said that Franco's only words on the subject were 'Arias, I'm better now,' uttered in his almost inaudible voice. The prince first heard about it when he arrived at his usual summer residence in Majorca on 1 September where he too received the news by telephone.

The most generous explanation was that Franco was acting from a sense of duty, or perhaps from altruism in not wanting to leave the prince to face the grave problems of terrorism, the Sahara question – which the Moroccans had now brought out into the open – and the behaviour of the opposition. On 30 July the Communist Party, with the collaboration of a few individual politicians and independent groups who between them were not very widely representative (Rafael Calvo Serer, Antonio García Trevijano, the Carlists, Tierno Galvan's small socialist party, etc.) had met in Paris to set up a democratic junta as a potential democratic alternative to Franco's regime. An ungenerous way of explaining Franco's resumption of power was to see it as the crowning act of his long enjoyment of autocracy, the final proof of his determination to hang on to power to the last.

Probably several of these explanations were right – and not as mutually exclusive as might appear. Franco was probably also influenced by the apprehension felt by members of his family circle – not counting his daughter, Carmen, who did not want him to resume power – and by the 'bunker': they were afraid that Franco's removal would help to open the door to a process of political development which would gradually introduce a new regime. Above all, however, it was the very nature of Franco's regime that made his decision inevitable. When he had said, time and again, that his rule would be for life, he had not been indulging in rhetoric. He meant, in effect, that he was the regime and that the regime would die with him. A two-headed set-up, with Don Juan Carlos on the throne, and Franco in retirement at Meirás, was almost unthinkable and – though this is pure speculation – it seems likely that the situation would have been intolerable.

Franco returned to Madrid on 9 September of that same year 1974 and took up the normal work of the head of state again. This was only a little time after he had told his physician that his dearest wish for the previous ten years had been to retire to a Carthusian monastery.[10] He was still attended daily by Dr Pozuelo, who had thought up a new form of therapy to improve Franco's voice and reflexes by making him extemporize speeches. Franco and his doctor tried out 'pretend' audiences. Franco made up little dialogues according to whatever it was the doctor was pretending to be – trade union leader, chairman of a scientific delegation, or whatever. Franco was given a minute to reply. The exercise amused him and he rounded off his improvizations, like his real audiences, with a cry of 'Viva España!'[11]

López Rodó, who was ambassador in Vienna at the time, visited him for 35 minutes on 11 September and found him physically well, mentally alert and with the same good memory as ever. Fraga, also an ambassador, representing Spain in London since November 1973, had visited him at Meirás on 25 August, when he seemed relaxed and welcoming but 'obviously done for'.[12]

Franco had clearly recovered some of his old vigour. On 4 October 1974, his saint's day, for example, he remained on his feet to greet no fewer than 427 people. He was back to his usual routine of ten or twelve audiences a day with soldiers and civilians on Tuesdays and Wednesdays. During the winter of 1974–75 he took up shooting again, enduring the inseparable cold, and tiredness, to the risk of his health. In May 1975, jointly with Prince Juan Carlos, he opened the May Fair – an occasion which always gave him pleasure. He took the salute at the Victory Parade and on the 31st received President Ford of the United States. He also went to the charity shield football match and the cup final. On 11 July he opened the Museum of Contemporary Art and on the 18th he presided once more at the reception at La Granja. He even did some fishing in the lake in the grounds. That August, on his last summer holiday at Meirás, he was playing golf again and fishing aboard the yacht *Azor*.

He also put up with some painful moments. In December 1974 he had to have a broken tooth removed and for almost a month bore without complaint the swelling and pain caused by the new plate that had to be fitted. In January 1975 he had to take to his bed with a slight infection of the gall bladder and prostate gland caused by exposure to cold while out shooting. On 25 March he had a minor attack of phlebitis which was overcome by the usual treatment. In June three more teeth had to come out.

Quite apart from all this, the real problem was, of course, how far an old man could continue to exercise power while suffering from Parkinson's disease, having just survived a serious phlebitic thrombosis, and while under constant medical supervision with frequent therapy sessions. Ambassador Fraga was filled with 'revulsion' – his word for it – at the thought of the country left in the hands of a ruler utterly unable to cope. The historian de la Cierva, who called on Franco in October 1974, soon after resigning from his job in charge of popular culture, was left with the feeling that the leader 'was now no more than a puppet controlled by other people.'[13]

What is certain is that once Franco had resumed his powers,

Spain lived in a state of complete uncertainty and apprehension. The proof of the rapid disintegration of a regime was everywhere: the proliferation of political clubs, the rise to the surface of an opposition that could no longer be kept underground, the abandonment of Francoism by many of its adherents, the government's own gyrations. Francoism was a regime adrift and Spain a country on the watch, where everything hung on the death – not yet announced but always awaited – of its leader.

In the circumstances, the prime minister, Arias Navarro decided to try to re-activate the 'spirit of 12 February'. In his first statement after Franco's resumption of power, on 10 September, Arias announced that there would be political associations in Spain by January 1975.

Arias's initiative was rewarded with a horrifying ETA outrage. A bomb exploded in the Rolando Café in Madrid, where many policemen used to gather, killing twelve people. The stridency of the ultra-right wing 'bunker' increased. 'Mr Prime Minister,' wrote one of the ultra spokesmen, Blas Piñar, in a famous article, 'we are counting ourselves out of your policies . . . We will not obey you and we will not go with you.'

Arias came back with one of his typical U-turns. He sacked Cabanillas on 29 October, with the approval and perhaps at the insistence of Franco. Something unprecedented happened next – another sign of the depth of the crisis – when the Finance Minister, Antonio Barrera de Irmo, resigned in sympathy, along with a number of high officials of reformist persuasions (Marcelino Oreja, Ricardo de la Cierva, Francisco Fernández Ordóñez, etc.). Arias wanted to balance Cabanillas's dismissal by sacking two of the 'blue' ministers – the Minister for the Movement, Utrera Molina, and the Justice Minister, Ruiz-Jarabo. Franco, however would not hear of it, pointing out that they were men of great loyalty.[14]

As was said at the time, the crisis of 29 October marked the end of the political line of 12 February. The Statute of Associations which Arias presented in December 1974, and which was approved in the National Council of the Movement on the 16th of that month with 95 votes in favour and only three abstentions, was disappointingly limited. It did allow associations and provided for them to compete in elections. But it continued to insist that an association had to have at least 25,000 members – and, what was more, had to be distributed over at least 15 provinces – and the National Council of the Movement was still left a right of veto. Once again, the aim was to allow associations only from within the Movement. That meant the automatic exclusion of the entire democratic opposition; and without the opposition, the democratization of the system would stand condemned as a farce.

Even had Arias's statute been more generously drafted, it is doubtful whether the opposition would have accepted it. The democratic junta brought together by the communists in July 1974 demanded a 'democratic break' with the old regime as the only way forward towards democracy; it rejected the planned monarchy of Don Juan Carlos and argued for a provisional government to grant an amnesty, legalize parties and call a referendum to decide on the future nature of the state.

Moderates in the democratic opposition were more cautious. In 1974–75 the socialists were still in favour of a republic, but figures from the social democrat, liberal and Christian democrat parties continued to pay visits to Estoril to see Don Juan, whom they saw as representing hopes of a monarchy that would dismantle Francoism after Franco's death.

In any case, the moderate opposition, which joined forces in July 1975 in the Platform for a Democratic Consensus (*Plataforma de Convergencia Democrática*), was as firm as the junta in refusing to co-operate with Arias Navarro's initiative. Two months before Arias laid his Statute of Associations before the *Cortes*, the main socialist party, the PSOE, at its thirteenth congress, held in France in October 1974, had voted for a complete break with the existing regime. Its demands – amnesty, democratic freedoms, free elections within twelve months were unacceptable to Arias. At a meeting held in Valencia in June 1975, the Christian Democrats spoke of 'democratic change' and elections for a constituent assembly. In April Ridruejo demanded constitutional reform.

Already in February 1975 Arias had rejected even the mere suggestion for a reform of this nature. Far from contemplating an amnesty, in April he again declared a state of emergency in the Basque Country, which was more rigorously repressive than any the Basques had previously endured. Dialogue between Arias and the opposition was, therefore, out of the question.

It was the refusal of reformists within the regime to accept the 1974 Statue of Associations which finally brought about the collapse of Arias's efforts. For instance, the 'Tacitus' group – composed of young Catholics who had been arguing since 1973 for an 'opening up' of the regime, using the columns of the daily *Ya* – regarded the statute as 'the statute of those who are opposed to associations'. One of the leading figures in the group, Marcelino Oreja, was among the three members of the National Council who abstained in the vote. Another, Juan Antonio Ortega y Díaz Ambrona, argued that 'democratic evolution', with democratic freedoms and free elections, would be a third way between the continuation of the regime and the break demanded by the opposition.

Fraga Iribarne took a long time to make up his mind. While he was still ambassador in London he unleashed a fury of activity in Spain; from December 1974 his overriding objective was to create a broad association of what was called 'the modern evolutionist right', to include Areilza, Silva Muñoz, the 'Tacitists' themselves, Cabanillas, and such, with a programme of reforms that would allow Spain to be gradually transformed into a democratic state.

It was Franco himself who vetoed Fraga. Apparently, in January 1975 when Nieto Antúnez brought Franco the plans of the proposed association which Fraga had drawn up, the leader asked, 'And what country is this supposed to be for?'[15] Soon after, on 17 February, Nieto told Fraga that the Pardo's views on associations could be summed up in two negatives: 'No to clashes between rival tendencies' and 'No to Fraga'. On 25 July Fraga had an opportunity to explain his plans directly to Franco at Meirás. Franco listened but made no reply.[16] So Fraga gave up trying to found an association. Instead, he started a foundation for political studies (FEDISA) organized as a limited company. From October 1975 he used the columns of *ABC* to his plan for reforms that would lead to a democratic legitimacy.

Arias's initiative had failed. Nine months after the passing of the statute only eight political associations had been registered, six of which were Falangist; five were uncomprisingly against further change and only one, the puny Spanish Social Reform group (*Reforma Social Española*), led by Manuel Cantarero del Castillo, clearly favoured reform.

There was a further, more disturbing development. In June 1975 the 'blue' wing of the Movement founded the Union of the Spanish People (*Unión del Pueblo Español* UDPE), the only association with more than the required 25,000 members. It was chaired by Adolfo Suárez, close collaborator of the new Minister for the Movement, Fernando Herrero Tejedor, who had taken office in March, and presumably enjoyed the minister's support. It could also count on the Movement's press and radio network. UDPE seemed to the great association of those who favoured a continuation of Franco's work into the future – a Spanish equivalent of French Gaullism. In practice, it gave the lie to the government's promise of political neutrality.

So the move to political association had failed. Meanwhile, the picture throughout the country had go steadily worse. The economic crisis had emerged clearly in the second half of 1974.

Labour unrest had intensified. In 1974 all records were broken for numbers of disputes, man-hours lost and numbers of strikers. The first two months of 1975 witnessed one of the worst waves of strikes in the history of Francoism.

In spite of everything Franco still had confidence in Arias and in March 1975 gave him the go-ahead for another ministerial re-shuffle, though not without expressing his displeasure at the second set of changes within five months.

Arias seemed to be cutting the 'blue' patches out of his cabinet by replacing Utera Molina and Ruiz-Jarabo, encouraging people to believe that the government might yet recover the impetus to reform. More disillusionment followed almost at once, in June, when Herrero Tejedor, Utrera's replacement, died in an accident. Prompted by Franco himself, Arias brought back José Solís Ruiz, one of the most unmistakeably 'blue' men in the movement, whose appointment seemed like the return of a relic of the past.

Terrorism continued. 1975 was probably the most violent year since the days of the post-war maquis. Between January 1974 and July 1975 200 violent acts were recorded. Between March and October 1975 11 policemen and Civil Guards were killed in attacks by ETA in the Basque Country and FRAP in Madrid.

The funeral of the murdered security men became violent ultra-right demonstrations: in one of them, the cars of the ministers were attacked. At almost all of them the chant went up of 'Iniesta, Iniesta,' the name of the Ex-Commander of the Civil Guard who the diehards hoped would bring the army back to power.

On 25 April 1975, as already mentioned, a state of emergency was declared in the Basque Country. 2,000 people were arrested in the new few days. Gangs of vigilantes sewed terror among the ordinary population. Relations of suspected ETA members, people known for their Basque sentiment, some priests, the lawyers of those in detention, all found themselves hounded and assaulted and their property attacked. Moreover, a man and wife were killed on 14 May in Guernica when the Civil Guard opened fire during the attempted arrest of an ETA activist who also died, as did a sergeant of the force. Later, in September, a young man was killed during a demonstration in San Sebastian. On 12 May the right organized a tumultuous demonstration of patriotic fervour in Bilbao.

As if this were not enough, in Estoril on 14 July, Don Juan issued a statement in which he forecast that in Spain, as in Portugal 'the end of an era of absolutism is at hand'. 'In my own position,' he said, 'as the present trustee of the Spanish monarchy, which is of enduring political value, I have not thought it right to submit to the personal power, widely applied and inflexibly exerted, of a man who was originally raised to command by his comrades-in-arms for the accomplishment of a particular and limited task.'[17] This personal allusion to Franco was a thunderbolt. Franco's reaction was explosive. On 19 June the government banned Don Juan, head of the dynasty, father of the man who since 1969 had been Franco's chosen successor and future king, from all Spanish ports, airports and frontier posts. Don Juan Carlos was informed by telephone. He did not hear from Franco or Arias Navarro, as might have been thought proper: he was told by the governor of the Balearic islands.

Soon after, on 30 July 1975, news broke of the arrest of nine professional soldiers – a major and eight captains, – an unaccustomed event under the Franco regime. They were accused of belonging to the Democratic Military Union (*Unión Militar Democrática* – (UMD)). Hard-line elements in the army thought of the UMD as equivalent to the Portuguese democratic military movement which had overthrown the dictatorship a year before. The feeling that Francoism was falling apart was now unchecked.

The Arias government responded by adding enormously more repressive measures. On 26 August an Anti-terrorist Decree was promulgated, imposing the death penalty on terrorists or their accessories in the event of their activities causing the deaths of security offices or other public servants. Only three days later two members of ETA, Ángel Otaegui and Juan Antonio Garmendia were condemned to death; by the end of the month 11 death sentences were pending – three for ETA men and 8 for FRAP – and hopes were high that the number would increase thanks to the spectacular success that summer of police operations against ETA, which brought two of the most important leaders of the organization into custody: Pedro Ignacio Pérez Beotegui, known as 'Wilson', and José Antonio Múgica Arregui, 'Ezquerra'.

Franco was again faced with a situation like that of December 1970 at the time of the Burgos trial. On that occasion, Laureano López Rodó, a member of the government, told the deputy prime minister, Carrero Blanco, that it would be wrong to sully Franco's image before the world and before history, by making him appear in his old age as a hard and implacable man who sentenced his enemies to death.[18] That sort of sensibility was no longer to be found in 1975 and it was thought that terrorists had to be paid in their own coin. Five of the 11 awaiting execution (the ETA members Ángel Otaegui and Juan Paredes Manot and the FRAP men José Luis Sánchez Bravo, Ramón García Sanz and José Humberto Baena) went to their deaths on 27 September. In the other six cases the sentence was commuted.

Franco, at the end of the day, was a believer in tough measures against terrorism. When he heard of the horrific slaughter at the Rolando Café in Madrid, he remarked to his physician, Vicente Pozuelo, 'Can you tell me why we are going to respect the human rights of these murderers – vicious creatures who have violated those of their victims? These destroyers of society have to countered with the utmost vigour. Either we finish them or they finish us.'[19] It seems likely that the double escalation of terrorism by ETA and FRAP in 1975 confirmed him in his views: he must have known the likely outcome of the decree of 26 August, which had been agreed at a meeting of the Council of Ministers he had chaired four days before at his house in Meirás.

But the cabinet meetings that led to the 11 death sentences, and the immediate international reaction against them, which began in mid-September, exterted a terrible toll on Franco's emotions. Dr Pozuelo came later to believe that this was the moment when the decline began that would lead to his death.

Pozuelo observed that in the few days prior to 27 September Franco was a changed man. 'He lost weight continuously for several days,' he later wrote. 'He was on edge all the time and hardly able to get to sleep normally.' The pressure on Franco and his government was intense. Pope Paul VI and the Spanish bishops begged for mercy; various foreign governments made formal pleas for the commutation of the death sentences. From mid-September mobilization against the sentences – strikes, demonstrations, mass meetings, petitions, sit-ins, occupations began against the sentences not only in the Basque Country but all over Europe. Once more, Spanish embassies, consulates and offices abroad became the targets of international anger.

The Spanish government was unwilling to give in to those pressures. On Friday 26 September the Council of Ministers opted for a judgement of Solomon in which five sentences were confirmed and the rest commuted. Franco, who had enclosed himself in almost total silence, ratified the government's final decision. His doctor reported: 'he was emaciated; he was still losing weight, but he seemed more resolved than ever.'[20]

The executions of 27 September 1975 caused an impressive outburst of revulsion across Europe and, inside Spain, in the Basque provinces of Vizcaya and Guipúzcoa where the strikes and tension continued into the first days of October. There were rowdy demonstrations against the Spanish regime in many cities; Spanish embassies were attacked and invaded; that in Lisbon was destroyed by a fire lit by demonstrators. A number of countries withdrew their ambassadors from Madrid. Mexico called for Spain to be expelled from the UN. Since 1947, Francoism had never been in such bad odour. On 1 October an unknown terrorist cell the 'Anti-fascist Revolutionary Groups of 1st October' (*Grupos Revolucionarios Antifascistas Primero de Octubre* – GRAPO), killed three policemen in Madrid; ETA murdered three Civil Guards at Oñate in the province of Guipúzcoa on the 5th, and a few hours later Ignacio Echave, brother of a well known ETA activist, was murdered by vigilantes.

As so often before, Francoism once more took to the streets to acclaim its leader, again repudiated by international opinion which forty years of effort had still not brought round. On 1 October 1975 the Plaza de Oriente in Madrid again gave shelter to a crowd of hundreds of thousands who cheered Franco to the echo in defiance of a world they dismissed as hostile and ill informed. Amid cries of 'ETA to the scaffold!' and amid placards that read, 'We don't want change: we want a firm hand,' Franco, now shrivelled and quavering, spoke for the last time to the multitude of his followers. He did not disappoint them. In a weak and halting voice, forming his words with difficulty, he was still able to encapsulate his thoughts on what was happening in a few crisp words. 'All this,' he said, returning to that political obsession of his, 'is the work of a conspiracy by leftist freemasons from among the ranks of the politicians, in a squalid alliance with communist and terrorist subversives in society at large, which does us honour even as it sullies them.'

Franco was finished. When he withdrew from the balcony of the royal palace where he had made his speech, he collapsed into the arms of the Cardinal-primate, Monsignore Marcelo González, where he stayed for a few minutes, weeping, overcome by emotion.[21]

A few days later on 12 October, Columbus Day (when Spain celebrated her links with the rest of the Hispanic world), Franco felt unwell. To begin with, it looked like the start of 'flu. At dawn on 15 October he woke suddenly, afflicted by pain and a terrible feeling of pressure. He had suffered a heart attack, as his doctor, Vicente Pozuelo, feared, hurrying urgently to the Pardo, and as Drs Castro Fariñas, Gómez Mantilla, Mínguez, Vital Aza and Franco's son-in-law, Cristóbal Martínez Bordiu, Marquess of Villaverde, confirmed.

Franco seemed normal despite the heart attack and was unwilling to cancel his audiences for that day, although the doctors, through Vital Aza, told him what was wrong and recommended that he should have absolute rest. He replied that he would do what they asked only after the close of the meeting of the Council of Ministers on the 17th.

So that was what happened. On the 16th Franco had a meeting with Arias and the Foreign Minister Pedro Cortina Mauri. They examined the Sahara problem. The Moroccans had taken the case to the International Court the previous December, but now that the court had found in favour of Saharan self-determination, they were preparing the 'green march' – a sort of pilgrimage of conquest – to take over territory which was still under Spanish sovereignty. Franco was inclined to stand firm but he was probably at the same time unwilling to go to war. On 8 October he had sent his envoy General Gavilán to Rabat and obtained an assurance that there would be no war from the Moroccan king, Hassan II.

Franco was still determined to take the chair in cabinet on the 17th. But he did so with three electrodes taped to his chest and connected by cables to a monitor in an adjoining room where several doctors kept watch. He refused to hold the meeting in his bedroom or attend it in a wheelchair. 'It is essential for me,' he told the doctors, 'to be in my place.' The whole scene was symbolic of the determination he had always shown to remain 'in his place' until the end. He did so now, though he suffered a number of cardiac fluctuations during the meeting – irregular contractions, a mild heart attack.

Despite this, Franco passed the night of the 18th peacefully. It was probably then that he wrote his will, which he handed to his daughter Carmen a few days later. On Sunday the 19th, however, he had another heart attack. He was fully aware of what was happening. 'It's getting to the end,' he told one of his aides. But he rallied, went to mass and was able to watch a football match on television in the afternoon.

The following day he received Arias Navarro, Prince Juan Carlos and the president of the *Cortes*, Rodríguez de Valcárcel in order to discuss the problem of handing over power. Don Juan Carlos would not agree to another interim arrangement; he wanted power to be handed over only on irreversible terms. At one point Arias told him that he could not bring himself to say to Franco that the end had come and that the moment of succession had arrived.

On Monday 20 October Franco had another heart attack but he rallied yet again and on the 21st and 22nd there were no further incidents. In the early hours of the 23rd, however, he had a sudden relapse as the result of a further and more serious cardiac arrest which was repeated on the 24th. The weekend of the 25th and 26th October was spent in great alarm and anxiety. The cardiac arrest that had caused the crisis had been followed by water on the lungs, intestinal paralysis, stomach haemorrhages (caused by the treatment for Parkinson's disease) and other complications. On the

27th dropsy appeared – an abnormal build-up of liquid in the digestive system – and an inflammation of the liver. A probe produced bleeding. The X-rays seemed to suggest a perforation of the peritoneum.

Despite the seriousness of his condition Franco was still conscious – and, what was more, conscious of the state he was in. He could talk to his family and to the numerous doctors who had been added to the team until the Pardo looked like a temporary hospital. On the 25th Fr Bulart gave him the communion and unction of the sick. It was Franco himself who commanded, on the 30th, that Article 11 of the LOE be applied and Don Juan Carlos take up the duties of head of state. He was probably convinced that this time the transfer of power was irreversible.

The first clinical bulletin was released to the public only on the 21st and not until the 24th was a full medical account issued. From then on there was no doubt of the gravity of Franco's condition. Previously, lack of information had meant that all sorts of rumours and guesses had been flying around; henceforth, there would be constant interest and tension in the media, medically well informed but politically speculative – sometimes wildly so, as with the guesses which were offered on the exact day and time when Franco might be expected to die.

Until 3 November Franco's medical condition remained stable but critical. That night he suffered a severe haemorrhage which left him on the brink of death. The doctors decided on a life-or-death operation in the sick bay of the guard house of Pardo palace.

Franco did not want to have the operation, which Dr Hidalgo Huerta performed, but his position was desperate. On the 5th he had to undergo dialisis because of urinary problems. When he began to haemorrhage he had to be removed urgently to the La Paz Clinic in Madrid and undergo a second operation – again, a life-or-death affair. The operation lasted four hours; he needed more than six litres of blood and a large part of his stomach was removed.

Franco demurred at his second operation. He suffered badly. He was heard to murmur phrases like 'How hard this is to bear!' 'Please let me be,' and 'My God, how hard it is to die!' He was on a drip, sedated with pain-killers, with assisted breathing, on two rounds of dialisis a day, with probes in his stomach to counteract the dropsy. On the 15th he had another huge haemorrhage and acute peritonitis. Hidalgo Huerta had to operate again.

Franco had entered the last phase of his long and painful agony. His level of consciousness was now very low. He had lost more than 20 kilos. Some of the medical team and some members of the family – apparently his daughter Carmen and his grand-daughter Mariola – only wanted him to be left to die in peace. On the 18th he was being kept at a constant temperature of 33 degrees, having completely lost consciousness. His abdomen was enormously swollen. That night he suffered further haemorrhages and a brutal attack of peritonitis. It was decided not to operate again and a course of blood transfusions alone was begun.

It was the end. He died of heart failure brought on by the peritonitis at 5.25 in the morning of 20 November 1975. The final medical bulletin was overwhelming: Parkinson's disease, mio-cardiac arrest, stomach ulcers with massive haemorrhaging, peritonitis, acute renal failure, thrombophlebitis, bronchial pneumonia, endotoxic shock, irremediable heart failure.[22]

Franco died only two months after the scandal and crisis brought on by the executions of September 1975. He was fully conscious of his impending death when he met it with undeniable dignity and serenity. His death-bed agony was terrible and perhaps unnecessarily prolonged.

But there were elements of that agony that recalled, at times, the ridiculous plots of Valle-Inclán, the author who had once been Franco's favourite. The incessant intrigues of politicians and Francoist notables in the corridors of the Clinic of La Paz; the prayerful throngs and penitent crowds that gathered at the Pardo or La Paz, composed of genuinely pious souls who hoped to achieve the impossible cure with their prayers and oblations; the veritable miracle-workshop set up in the patient's own sickroom where the arm of St Teresa was installed – a relic Franco had treasured since the Civil War – with the mantle of the Virgin of the Pilar, Patroness of Spain, brought specially from Saragossa. The contrast between all this and the sophistication of the medical attention Franco received seemed to symbolize the Spain Franco ruled: a modern society under a traditional Catholic state.

What was happening in the Sahara was also strangely symbolic. The Spanish government did not want war: they probably intended to abandon the territory to a UN administration. In any event, Don Juan Carlos's first act as head of state was to present himself at El Aaiún, capital of Spanish Sahara, on 1 November 1975 to re-assure the Spanish forces and to explain Spain's posture in the face of the imminent 'green march' which had in fact been announced for 7 November. On that very day, the minister Antonio Carro arrived to Agadir to give the Moroccans assurances on new agreements – there had already been preliminary discussions – in exchange for the calling off of the march.

Once this had been achieved, Spanish policy on the Sahara did an about-turn. Self-determination for the Saharawis, which had been the consistent policy until then, was abruptly dropped. On 14 November an agreement was signed in Madrid which amounted to the cession of the territory by Spain to Morocco and Mauretania. Probably, in the circumstances with which Spain was beset, it was by no means the worst solution. But from the perspective of the life story of Franco – the man who said that without Africa he would not have been able to understand himself – it seemed as if Spain was hurrying headlong away from that continent, as though anxious to rid herself for ever of that same Africa that had nourished the career of the soldier who had ruled her for forty years.

Franco left his will behind him, the last document from his hand. Arias read it to his fellow Spaniards, when, deeply moved, he made the official announcement of the Caudillo's death. It was a short, sincere document. Its simplicity and message alike reflected Franco's personality, his sincere Catholicism ('I have wished to live and die a Catholic. I glory in the name of Christ and it has been my constant will to be a faithful son of the Church, in whose bosom I am about to die'); there was his idea of patriotism ('. . . Spain, whom I love to the last moment of my life, which, as I now know, is near'); his autocratic paternalism ('I beseech you to persevere in unity and in peace . . . Do not falter in the search for social justice and culture for all the citizens of Spain and make this your highest objective'); his tendency to over-simplification and obsessive notions of politics ('Never forget that the enemies of Spain and of Christian civilization are on the alert . . . Preserve the unity of the lands of Spain'). It even showed his obstinacy in refusing to understand pluralism and diversity of political views: he asked pardon for himself and pardoned his own enemies, but said that he hoped and believed that he had had none 'who were not enemies of Spain' – as if to differ from Franco were equivalent to being an enemy of Spain.

On 17 November 1967 Franco said that neither he nor his regime could be dismissed as a 'parenthesis' in Spanish history. 'We *are* that history,' he declared. And so it was, until 20 November 1975. Perhaps one could adapt what the young Italian liberal intellectual Piero Gobetti (1901–26) said about Fascism in Italy, and say that Franco and his regime were much more than an historical episode, of greater or lesser interest, like any other: like it or not, they were – at least, from the perspective of the mid-1980s they seemed to be – the history Spain had written for herself.

For this very reason, posterity will look back on them for a long time to come not, as Franco prophesied on 24 December 1966, with 'admiration and respect' but with impassioned interest and divided and conflicting views.

Nor could it be otherwise. It will be possible to argue about the causes of the rising of the 18 July, about Franco's personal reasons for taking part, about the nature – whether more properly totalitarian or authoritarian – of his regime. There will no doubt be debates over the right and wrong judgements Franco made as head of state and head of government, over his relations with Hitler and Mussolini, over his conduct during the Second World War, over the choices he made in forming his various governments, and over the policies they pursued in different fields. There will be scope for controversy over the extent of repression and the breadth of social support on which Francoism could call. It will even be possible to explain and understand the reasons that moved the Francoists to follow him. But there is one fact that will never be disputed: Franco established the most enduring dictatorship of nineteenth- and twentieth-century Spanish history, a personal dictatorship, which lasted for forty years and which by its very existence provoked revulsion in the liberal and democratic value-system of its day.

While that same value-system continues to imbue our own way of looking at things, Franco, who said that he was accountable only to God and history, will suffer, like it or not, by a majority verdict, the latter's adverse judgement.

Notes

In order to keep these notes short, Franco's speeches are cited only by date and place of delivery. The speeches were collected at intervals until 1970 in volumes entitled *Discursos y mensajes del Jefe del Estado*, published by the Dirección General de Información; thereafter they appeared one by one, issued by Ediciones del Movimiento. The quotations come from these editions.

Notes to Chapter One

1 I. Prieto, *Discursos fundamentales* (Madrid, 1975), p.257.
2 Another sister, Pacita, died at five years old. Franco's parents were Nicolás Franco Salgado-Araújo and Pilar Bahamonde Pardo. Franco was baptised on 17 December 1892 in the church of San Francisco at El Ferrol. His father, a ship's purser, left his family when he was promoted and moved to Madrid, something Franco was always to resent. See F. Franco Salgado-Araújo, *Mis conversaciones privadas con Franco* (Barcelona, 1976), p.174.
3 L. Suárez Fernández, *Franco y su tiempo* (Madrid, 1984), i, 145.
4 See especially J. Busquets, *El militar de carrera en España* (Barcelona, 1971), pp.141–47.
5 The book first appeared, as stated, in 1922. A recent edition is Comandante Franco, *Diario de una bandera*, ed. M. Aznar (Madrid, 1976).
6 *El Debate*, 26 January 1923.
7 See the anthology of views on the subject in F. Franco, *Pensamiento político de Franco* (Madrid, 1975), i, 77–93.
8 Interview in *Estampa*, 29 May 1928, reproduced in R. de la Cierva, *Francisco Franco: un siglo de España* (Madrid, 1973), i, 214, 278, 293.
9 See Franco's speech on the unveiling of General Primo de Rivera's monument in Jeréz, 30 October 1970 in *Pensamiento político de Franco* (Madrid, 1975), i, 197.
10 F. Franco Salgado-Araújo, op. cit., p.184.
11 Franco's rules for his cadets are reproduced by almost all biographers. See for instance J. Arrarás, *Franco* (Valladolid, 1939), pp.150–1.
12 See Franco's own account in G. Hills, *Franco: the Man and his Nation* (London, 1967), p.157.
13 R. de la Cierva's explanation of Franco's behaviour in 1917 seems convincing. Op. cit. i, 122ff.
14 e.g. see what Franco said to his cousin on 29 June 1965. F. Franco Salgado-Araújo, op, cit., p.452.
15 Ibid., p.425.
16 Quoted in R. Baón, *La cara humana de un Caudillo: 401 anécdotas* (Madrid, 1975), p.110.
17 For Franco's conduct in October 1934 see L. Suárez Fernández, op. cit., pp.246–8.
18 J.M. Gil Robles, *No fue posible la paz* (Barcelona, 1968), pp.233–64.
19 L. Suárez Fernández, op. cit.

Notes to Chapter Two

1   F. Franco Salgado-Araújo, *Mis conversaciones privadas con Franco* (Barcelona, 1976), p.526.

2   The original members of the junta were Generals Cabanellas (chairman), Saliquet, Mola, Ponte and Dávila and Colonels Montaner and Moreno Calderón. On 30 July 1936 Franco and Naval Captain Francisco Moreno joined; on 18 August General Gil Yuste; on 19 September Generals Orgaz and Queipo de Llano.

3   On Franco's designation as head of state, see R. de la Cierva, *Francisco Franco: un siglo de España* (Madrid, 1973), i, 506–28, and P. Nourry, *Francisco Franco: la conquista del poder* (Madrid, 1976), pp.369–95.

4   *Palabras del Caudillo, 19 de abril 1937–31 de diciembre 1938* (Barcelona, 2nd ed., 1939), p.214.

5   Franco's statements in J.E. Díez, *Colección de proclamas y arengas del Excmo. Sr. General D. Francisco Franco, Jefe del Estado y Generalísimo del Ejército salvador de España* (Seville, 1937), pp.86, 92.

6   It included Andrés Amado, Mauro Serret, José María Pemán, Joaquín Bau, Eufemio Olmedo, Alejandro Gallo and José Cortés, as heads of the various departments (Finance, Public Works, Culture and Education, Industry, etc.) with General Fidel Dávila as chairman of the junta and Generals Fermoso and Gil Yuste appointed Governor-general and Secretary for War, respectively.

7   See the speech in J.E. Díez, op. cit., pp.50–5.

8   Quoted by R. de la Cierva, op. cit., p.584.

9   Because of the nature of this book, the events of the war are considered only in relation to Franco's life. I do not attempt even a rough outline of the conflict. My analysis of the war is based on the usual bibliography of the subject, which is very extensive. Critical apparatus has therefore been omitted. Suffice it to say that H. Thomas, *The Spanish Civil War* (Harmondsworth, 1965) remains the best overall treatment of the topic; the numerous monographs of Colonel Martínez Bande are essential reading on military aspects; the controversial little book of R. Salas Larrazábal, *Los datos exactos de la guerra civil* (Madrid, 1980) is of great value; and for Franco in the war, the biography of R. de la Cierva, already cited.

10   The article, the statement to *ABC* and Franco's Salamanca speech in *Palabras del Caudillo*, op. cit.; on Serrano Suñer's work see his books *Entre Hendaya y Gibraltar* (Madrid, 1947), pp.17–32 and *Memorias* (Barcelona, 1977), pp.181–209.

11   *Palabras del Caudillo*, p.230.

12   General Gómez Jordana was Foreign Minister. General Fidel Dávila, who had taken over from Mola in command of the Army of the North, took on the Defence Portfolio. Two former Primo de Rivera men (Andrés Amado and General Martínez Anido) entered the Ministries of Finance and Public Order; two technicians (Peña Boeuf and Juan Antonio Suances, a sailor and childhood friend of Franco) at Public Works and Commerce and Industry; a Falangist, Raimundo Fernández Cuesta, Secretary General of Franco's umbrella organization at Agriculture; a Traditionalist, the Count of Rodezno, at Justice; a Monarchist, Sainz Rodríguez, at Education; a Serrano man Pedro González Bueno, at Organisation and Trade Unions.

Notes to Chapter Three

1 See L. Ramírez, *Francisco Franco, La obsesión de ser, la obsesión de poder* (Paris, 1976) and Carlos Castilla del Pino, 'Psiocopatología de un dictador', *El Viejo Topo*, extra no. 1 (1976).

2 The whole letter is in L. López Rodó, *La larga marcha hacia la Monarquía* (Barcelona, 1977), pp.520–2.

3 J. Giménez-Arnau, *Yo, Jimmy: mi vida entre los Franco* (Barcelona, 1981), p.76. There is a great number of anecdotes about Franco's private life in R. Baón, *La cara humana de un Caudillo* (Madrid, 1975).

4 F. Franco Salgado-Araújo, op. cit., p.280. Franco defined his regime as a system of personal power in a statement to *The Observer* on 5 July 1959.

5 L. López Rodó, op. cit., pp.229–30.

6 F. Franco Salgado-Araújo, op. cit., p.443.

7 See L. Suárez Fernández, *Franco y su tiempo* (Madrid, 1984), ii, 116, n.44.

8 On this point, see the MS notes cited ibid., iii, 52–9.

9 The debate is summarized in D. Sueiro and B. Díaz Nosty, *Un imperio en ruinas: historia del franquismo (1)* (Barcelona, 1985), pp.146–63.

10 The text is in X. Tusell, 'Relaciones secretas Franco-D. Juan', *Actualidad Económica*, 4 May 1976.

11 Bibliography on Spain in the Second World War is very extensive. See R. Serrano Suñer, *Entre Hendaya y Gibraltar* (Madrid, 1974); J.M. Doussinague, *España tenía razón 1939–45* (Madrid, 1949); R. Garriaga, *La España de Franco*, 2 vols (Barcelona, 1976); Angel Viñas et al., *Política comercial exterior en España 1931–75*, 2 vols (Madrid, 1979); *Revista de Occidente* (October, 1984). The biographies of Franco by R. de la Cierva and L. Suárez Ferández, cited above, are essential, as are those of B. Crozier, *Franco: historia y biografía*, 2 vols (Madrid, 1975), G. Hills, *Franco, the Man and his Nation* (London, 1967) and J.W.D. Trythall, *Franco* (London, 1970).

12 In addition to the works cited in the previous note, see R. de la Cierva, *Hendaya, punto final* (Barcelona, 1981) and R. Serrano Suñer, *Memorias* (Barcelona, 1977), pp.283ff.

13 J. Tusell and G. García Queipo de Llano, 'Franco y Mussolini: las relaciones hispano-italianas en la II Guerra Mundial', *Revista de Occidente* (October 1984), pp.101–17.

14 Hoare wrote *Ambassador on Special Mission* (London, 1946).

15 On Franco's relations with Don Juan, see Tusell's article and López Rodó's book, both already cited.

16 S. Ellwood, *Prietas las filas* (Barcelona, 1984), pp.125ff; the conversation between Franco and Varela is in López Rodó, op. cit., pp.503–7.

17 See C.J. Hayes, *Wartime Mission in Spain* (New York, 1945)

18 R. Baón, op. cit., p.140.

19 J. Tusell, *Franco y los católicos: la política interior española entre 1945 y 1957* (Madrid, 1984).

20 Ibid., p.99.

21 According to L. Galinsoga, *Centinela de Occidente: semblanza biográfica de Francisco Franco* Barcelona, 1956), p.387. On the UN censure see R. de la Cierva, *Historia del franquismo: aislamiento, transformación, agonía (1945–47)* (Barcelona, 1978), pp.13–42.

22   *Palabras del Caudillo* (op. cit. ch. 2, n.4), p.302.

Notes to Chaper Four

1   Text in *La voz y la obra de Francisco Franco, Caudillo* (Madrid, 1983), p.19.
2   L. Suárez Fernández, *Francisco Franco y su tiempo* (Madrid, 1984), iv, 175.
3   G. Brenan, *The Face of Spain* (London, 1950), p.11.
4   J. Tusell, *Franco y los católicos: la política interior española entre 1945 y 1957* (Madrid, 1984), pp.84–93.
5   R. Soriano, *La mano izquierda de Franco* (Barcelona, 1981), p.60.
6   Jakim Boor, *Masonería* (Madrid, 1952), p.11.
7   Ibid., p.74.
8   On Franco's foreign policy, see J.M. Armero, *La política exterior de Franco* (Barcelona, 1978).
9   On Spanish-us relations see A. Viñas, 'Autarquía y política exterior en el primer franquismo (1939–59)', *Revista de Estudios internacionales*, and *Los pactos secretos de Franco con Estados Unidos* (Barcelona 1979); L. Suárez Fernández, op. cit., iv.
10 Ibid., pp.417–49.
11 As well as A. Viñas, *Los pactos secretos*, L. Suárez Fermández, op. cit., v is essential reading.
12 The best treatment of Franco and the Catholics and therefore of the Concordat is Tusell's book (op. cit. n.4). See also Suárez Fernández, op. cit., 79–100.
13 v.s., nn.9 and 11.
14 Quoted G. Hills, *Franco: the Man and His Nation* (London, 1967), p.416.
15 Cited J. Tusell, op. cit., p.60.

Notes to Chapter Five

1   *Palabras del Caudillo* (op. cit., ch. 2, n.4), p.310.
2   On Francoist economic policy throughout this chapter see M. Jesús González, *La economía política del franquismo (1940–70)* (Madrid, 1979); J. Ros Hombravella et al., *Capitalismo español: de la autarquía a la estabilización (1939–59)* (Madrid, 1973); A. Viñas et al., *Política comercial exterior en España (1931–75)* (Madrid, 1979); J.A. Biescas and M. Tuñón de Lara, *España bajo la dictadura franquista* (Barcelona, 1980); J.L. García-Delgado, *El intervencionismo económico del primer franquismo en su perspectiva histórica. Coloquio: España bajo el franquismo* (Valencia, 1984).
3   All preceding quotations from *Palabras del Caudillo*, op. cit., pp.25, 168, 174, 286, 302.
4   J. Verges, *La seguridad social española y sus cuentas* (Barcelona, 1976).
5   V.s. n.2.
6   On the re-appearance of popular culture after the war, see F. Vizcaino Casa, *La España de la posguerra 1939–53* (Barcelona, 1975) and M. Vázquez Montalbán, *Crónica sentimental de España* (Barcelona, 1971).

7   V. Fernández Vargas, *La resistencia interior en la España de Franco* (Madrid, 1983), pp.210–11.

8   F. Franco Salgado-Araújo, *Mis conversaciones privadas con Franco* (Barcelona, 1976), pp.317 and 319.

9   Ibid., p.308.

10   G. Brenan, *The Face of Spain* (London, 1950), p.110.

11   See L. Suárez Fernández, *Franco y su tiempo* (Madrid, 1984), v, 211–61; J. Tusell, *Franco y los católicos* (Madrid, 1984), pp.367–84; F. Jáuregui and P. Vega, *Crónica del antifranquismo* (Barcelona, 1983), i, 186ff; J.L. Abellán et al., 'Nace la oposicion interna', *Historia del franquismo: Diario 16*, ch. 25.

12   F. Franco Salgado-Araújo, op. cit., pp.158, 172, 176 etc. On Morocco see V. Lezcano Morales, *España y el norte de África: el protectorado en marruecos (1912–56)* (Madrid, 1984), p.197ff.

13   See Arrese's own version in *Una etapa constituyente* (Barcelona, 1982) and Javier Tusell's (op. cit., pp.387–453) and L. López Rodó, *La larga marcha hacia la Monarquía* (Barcelona, 1977), pp.120–35.

14   On the new government, as well as works cited in the previous note, see R. de la Cierva, *Historia del franquismo* (Barcelona, 1978), ii, 153ff.

15   Quoted J. Tusell, op. cit., p.403.

16   V.s. n.2.

17   F. Franco Salgado-Araújo, op. cit., p.294. The remark about turning communist is in M. Fraga Iribarne, *Memoria breve de una vida pública* (Barcelona, 1980), p.106.

18   R. Baón, *La cara humana de un Caudillo* (Madrid, 1975), p.81.

19   R. Rossanda, *Un viaje inútil* (Barcelona, 1984), p.30.

20   X. Tusell, *La oposición democrática al franquismo* (Barcelona, 1977), p.388ff.

21   R. Rossanda, op. cit., p.38.

Notes to Chapter Six

1   E.g. in statements to *Arriba* of 22 January and 27 February 1955.

2   M. Fraga Iribarne, *Memoria breve de una vida pública* (Barcelona, 1980), p.124.

3   L. López Rodó, *La larga marcha hacia la Monarquía* (Barcelona, 1977), pp.145–8.

4   F. Franco Salgado-Araújo, *Mis conversaciones privadas con Franco* (Barcelona, 1976), pp.40, 52, 106, 156, 208, 214 etc.

5   L. López-Rodó, op. cit., pp.166–84.

6   Ibid., p.186ff.

7   Ibid., p.202.

8   Ibid., p.232.

9   M. Fraga Iribarne, op. cit., p.135.

10   L. López Rodó, op. cit., p.228.

11   M. Fraga Iribarne, op. cit., p.145.

12   See, e.g., F.M. Castiella, *España ante las Naciones Unidas* (Madrid 1968); P. García, *España-Mercado Común: una integración problemática* (Barcelona, 1977); J.C. Pereira, *Introducción al estudio de la política exterior de España (siglos XIX y XX)* (Madrid, 1983).

13   V.s., ch.5, n.2.
14   See López Rodó's own book, *Política y desarrollo* (Madrid, 1971).
15   'El Estado de obras' was an article by Fernández de la Mora in *ABC* of 1 April 1973.
16   See the anthology of hyperboles in C. Fernández, *El general Franco* (Barcelona, 1983), pp.311–24.
17   On the conflicts see P. Preston, ed., *Spain in Crisis* (London, 1976); X. Tusell, *La oposición democrática al franquismo* (Madrid, 1977); G. Jáuregui, *Ideología y estrategia política de* ETA: *análisis de su evolución entre 1959 y 1968* (Madrid, 1981); J. A. Biescas and M. Tuñón de Lara, *España bajo la dictadura franquista (1939–75)* (Barcelona, 1980); F. Jáuregui and P. Vega, *Crónica del antifranquismo* 2 vols (Barcelona, 1983); F. Urbina et al., *Iglesia y sociedad en España 1939–75* (Madrid, 1977).
18   S. Vilar, 'La oposición a la dictadura franquista', *Historia de España: Historia 16*, xiii, 82. See also J. de Esteban and L. López Guerra, *La crisis del Estado franquista* (Barcelona, 1977), pp.139–48.
19   F. Franco Salgado-Araújo, op. cit., p.340.
20   Ibid., p.446.
21   L. Suárez Fernández, *Franco y su tiempo* (Madrid, 1984), viii, 41–2.
22   M. Fraga Iribarne, op. cit. p.141.
23   Ibid., p.183; see Franco's own notes in L. Suárez Fernández, op. cit., vii, 228–9.
24   F. Franco Salgado-Araújo, op. cit., pp.342, 426.
25   See J.M. de Areilza, *Escritos políticos* (Madrid, 1968), p.182ff.
26   F. Franco Salgado-Araújo, op. cit., pp.478–9. López Rodó, op. cit. is indispensable for everything connected with the 'long road to the monarchy'.
27   López Rodó, op. cit., p.279.
28   Ibid., pp.291–301.
29   Ibid., pp.363, 316–86.

Notes to Chapter Seven

1   On Franco's health see E. Salgado, *Radiografía de Franco* (Barcelona, 1985), p.208ff; V. Gil, *Cuarenta años junto a Franco* (Barcelona, 1981).
2   F Franco Salgado-Araújo, *Mis conversaciones privadas con Franco* (Barcelona, 1976), p.469.
3   F. Salgado, op. cit., pp.220–2.
4   On Franco's latter days, see *Franco visto por sus ministros* (Barcelona, 1981) and the books of López Rodó and Fraga Iribarne cited for previous chapters.
5   J.F. Tezanos, 'Cambio social y modernización en la España actual', *REIS*, no.28 (1984).
6   Quoted in *Ya*, 10 October 1967. I discuss the last phase of Francoism in R. Carr and J.P. Fusi, *Spain from Dictatorship to Democracy* (London, 1981) and in 'La década desarrollista (1959–69)', *Historia de España: Historia 16*, xiii (Madrid, 1983). The sources and bibliography on which the arguments of this chapter and the next depend can be found there.
7   On Matesa, D. Sueiro and B. Nosty, *Las corrupciones del poder: historia del franquismo (2)* (Barcelona, 1985), pp.276–83, and López Rodó, *La larga marcha hacia la Monarquía* (Barcelona, 1977), pp.403–4.

8   L. Carrero Blanco, *Discursos y escritos 1943–73* (Madrid, 1974), p.165ff.
9   On strife in the last years of Francoism see F. de Jáuregui and P. Vega, *Crónica del antifranquismo (2)* (Barcelona, 1981), p.239.
10   On the Burgos trial, E. de Blaye, *Franco and the Politics of Spain* (Harmondsworth, 1976), pp.281–323; the ministerial comment comes from L. de la Fuente, in *Franco visto por sus ministros* (op. cit., n.4), p.239.
11   López Rodó, *La larga marcha hacia la Monarquía* (Barcelona, 1977), p.401.
12   Ibid., p.416. López Rodó's is easily the best account of this topic.
13   As well as López Rodó, see L. Suárez Fernández, *Francisco Franco y su tiempo* (Madrid, 1984), viii, 279.
14   V.s., n.6.
15   On the crisis see P. Preston, ed., *Spain in Crisis* (London, 1976) and J. de Esteban and L. López Guerra, *La crisis del Estado franquista* (Barcelona, 1977).
16   Garicano's notes are in López Rodó, op. cit., pp.424–5, 441.
17   Quoted V. Pozuelo Escudero, *Los últimos 476 días de Franco* (Barcelona, 1980), p.108.
18   R. Baón, *La cara humana de un Caudillo* (Madrid, 1975), p.148.
19   V. Gil, op. cit., p.55.
20   On the attack on Carrero and its consequences see *El País* Equipo de Investigación (Ismael Fuente, Javier García, Joaquín Prieto), *Golpe mortal: asesinato de Carrero y agonía del franquismo* (Madrid, 1983).

Notes to Chapter Eight

1   On the appointment of Arias Navarro see *Golpe mortal* (op. cit., ch.7, n.20), p.281ff; V. Gil, *Cuarenta años junto a Franco* (Barcelona, 1981), pp.151–63.
2   On the aims and formation of the Arias government see the account of A. Carro in *Franco visto por sus ministros* (Barcelona, 1981), p.312; on the whole Arias period, E. Romero, *Prólogo par un rey* (Barcelona, 1976), J. Oneto, *Arias entre dos crisis 1973–5* (Madrid, 1975) and R. de la Cierva, *Crónicas de la transición: de la muerte de Carrero a la proclamación del Rey* (Barcelona, 1975).
3   E. Romero, 'Luz verde', *Pueblo*, 19 June 1974.
4   P. Calvo Hernando, 'Opinión personal', *Gaceta Ilustrada*, 11 May 1975.
5   L. Suárez Fernández, *Francisco Franco y su tiempo* (Madrid, 1984), viii, 364–6.
6   L. López Rodó, *La larga marcha hacia la Monarquía* (Barcelona, 1977), p.469.
7   V. Pozuelo Escudero, *Los últimos 476 días de Franco* (Barcelona, 1980), p.125; on the thrombophlebitis see V. Gil, *Cuarenta años junto a Franco* (Barcelona, 1981), pp.167–85.
8   L. López Rodó, op. cit., pp. 463–4.
9   Franco's recovery in V. Pozuelo, op. cit., pp. 29–102.
10   Ibid., p.158.
11   Ibid., pp.112–16.
12   M. Fraga Iribarne, *Memoria breve de una vida pública* (Barcelona, 1980), p.333; L. López Rodó, op. cit., pp.468–70.

13   R. de la Cierva, *Historia del franquismo: aislamiento, transformación, agonía (1945–75)* (Barcelona, 1978), p.415; pp.415–66 should be consulted on the last year of Francoism.

14   Account of A. Carro, loc. cit., pp.354–6.

15   R. de la Cierva, op. cit., p.423.

16   M. Fraga Iribarne, op. cit., pp.349, 363.

17   L. López Rodó, op. cit., p.477. On the Arias period, as well as works cited above, n.3, see R. Carr and J.P. Fusi, *Spain from Dictatorship to Democracy* (London, 1981). pp.195–217.

18   L. López Rodó, op. cit., p.406.

19   V. Pozuelo Escudero, op. cit., p.112.

20   Ibid., p.210.

21   Account of J.M. Sánchez-Ventura in *Franco visto por sus ministros* (op. cit.), pp.424–5.

22   The basic source on Franco's last illness is V. Pozuelo, op. cit., pp.215–53; also see R. de la Cierva, op. cit., pp.453–66; Yale, *Los últimos cien días* (Madrid, 1975) and J. Oneto, *Cien días en la muerte de Francisco Franco* (Madrid, 1975).

Biographical Notes

Abd el-Krim el-Khatabi (1882–1963): adviser to the Department of Native Affairs and a local judge. Leader of Moroccan resistance, defeated by French and Spanish arms in 1926.

Alonso Vega, Camilo (1889–1971): professional soldier. Fought in Moroccan war. Instrumental role in preparing and launching the insurrection of July 1936. Became general during Civil War. After the war, appointed to the National Council of Franco's umbrella Movement. Commander of Civil Guard 1943–55; deputy in the Francoist *Cortes* 1942–69; Interior Minister 1957–69. Member of Council of Realm.

Arias Navarro, Carlos (born 1908): lawyer. Imprisoned in the republican zone at the start of the Civil War, joined the nationalist forces at the fall of Málaga. In charge of the security network 1957–65. Mayor of Madrid 1965–73. 11 June 1973 appointed Minister of the Interior by Carrero Blanco. After the latter's assassination, became first civilian prime minister of the Franco regime. 11 December 1975, after Franco's death, confirmed in office by Juan Carlos to become the first prime minister of the monarchy. Resigned 1 July 1976.

Arias Salgado y de Cubas, Gabriel (1904–62): Deputy Secretary of Education and censor. Minister of Information and Tourism 1951–62.

Azaña Díaz, Manuel 1880–1940: Public Notary 1909. Left two years later for Paris for further study. Contributor to *El Imparcial* and *El Sol*; editor of literary review *La Pluma*. Founded the Republican Action party (*Acción Republicana*) in 1925. President of the Madrid Athenaeum 1930. Member of the Revolutionary Committee which helped bring the republic into being. Minister of War under Alacalá Zamora's provisional government, then prime minister in the provisional and first elected governments of the republic till resignation in 1933. Imprisoned 1934 for alleged participation in the Catalan rebellion. Founded the Republican Left (*Izquierda Republicana*) with Marcelino Domingo. Led Popular Front after 1936 elections. President of the Republic after Alcalá Zamora's deposition. Fled to France in 1939. Resigned before the end of the war.

Besteiro Fernández, Julián (1870–1940): socialist intellectual. Vice-chairman of socialist trade union UGT 1914. Vice-chairman of the Socialist Party (PSOE) 1915. Opposed revolutionary attempt to overthrow monarchy. President of republican Constituent Assembly 1931. At PSOE conference of 1932 defeated by Largo Caballero in elections for party leadership. Member of Council of National Defence that tried to negotiate an honourable settlement in 1939. Arrested and sentenced to 30 years in security prison. Died in Carmona gaol 1940.

Borbón, Juan de (born 1913): son of Alfonso XIII and Queen Victoria Eugenia. Had to cut short studies at San Fernando Naval College when his father went into exile at the start of the Second Republic. Completed naval training in England. Became heir to the throne 1932. Married María de las Mercedes de Borbón y Orleans 1935. Lived in Rome where his eldest son Don Juan Carlos was born, and in Portugal, where he wrote a number of manifestos in favour of democratization of the Spanish regime. Reached agreement with Franco for Juan Carlos to study in Spain. After Franco's death resigned his rights to the throne in his son's favour.

Borbón, Juan Carlos de (Juan Carlos I, King of Spain): born Rome 5 January 1938, eldest son of Don Juan de Borbón y Battemberg, Count of Barcelona. Grandson of the last king of Spain, Alfonso XIII. Early education at Marianist Fathers' school, Fribourg, Switzerland. When his father reached agreement with Franco, Juan Carlos arrived in Spain for the first time in October 1948, at ten years of age, and continued his education at the Instituto de San Isidro, Madrid. Entered Saragossa Military Academy 1955; commissioned ensign of infantry 1956. Entered naval college at Marín 1956, graduating 1958 with rank of naval ensign. A course at the Air Force General Academy at San Javier, Murcia, followed, where he obtained the rank of Flying Officer. Madrid University 1959–61. On 14 May 1962, at 24 years of age, married Princess Sophia of Greece (daughter of King Paul and Queen Frederica) in Athens. The couple set up home in the Zarzuela Palace near Madrid. Juan Carlos was proposed by Franco as successor to the headship of state, with the title of king, at a full meeting of the *Cortes* on 22 July 1969. The *Cortes* approved the nomination; Juan Carlos was officially proclaimed and the title of Prince of Spain was conferred upon him. Henceforth took place of honour alongside Franco at all official events. In July 1974, when Franco was incapacitated by thrombophlebitis, the prince assumed the duties of head of state. On 3 September, withdrew from his role when Franco resumed his place as head of state. One year and three months later, when Franco was again severely ill, Juan Carlos again took over his duties. On 22 November 1975, after taking the oath, he was proclaimed King of Spain, with the name and style of Juan Carlos I. From that day on the king proved himself a determined advocate of the introduction of democracy to Spain, as demonstrated by his stand at the time of the attempted military coup of February 1981.

Calvo Serer, Rafael (born Valencia 1916): at the age of 20, elected president of Valencian Federation of Catholic Students. Joined Opus Dei. Won Chairs of Philosophy (1942) and History (1946), University of Madrid. Joined privy council of Don Juan de Borbón. Editor of *Arbor* 1951–3, under the state's 'Higher Council of Research' (*Consejo Superior de Investigaciones Científicas*). Kept the evening daily *Madrid* going 1966–71. When the paper was closed down he went into exile in Paris, where, with Santiago Carrillo and other political figures, he founded the Junta Democrática in 1974.

Calvo Sotelo, José (born Tuy (province of Pontevedra) 1983): state attorney. Member of Maura's conservative party. In charge of local administration 1923. Helped to draw up municipal government statute of 1924, bringing more civilian elements into the regime. Work as Finance Minister included introduction of state petrol monopoly. Exiled on proclamation of Republic. Returned to Spain 1934, when amnesty granted for those who had been ministers under the dictatorship. Founded the right-wing parliamentary alliance, Bloque Nacional. Assassinated 13 July 1936.

Carrero Blanco, Luis (born Santoña, Santander 1903): graduated from naval college. Took part in Moroccan War 1924–6. Teacher of tactics at School of Naval

Warfare. When Civil War broke out, took refuge in Mexican and French embassies until able to cross to the nationalist zone in 1937. Made Chief of Staff of Cruiser division in nationalist fleet and head of operational section of Naval Staff in 1939. Promoted Captain 1940, Admiral 1966. Under-secretary of prime minister's office 1941; deputy prime minister 1967. Prime minister 1973. Killed in ETA bomb attack 20 December 1973.

Casares Quiroga, Santiago (1884–1950): lawyer. Member of the revolutionary republican movement. Signatory of Pact of San Sebastián. Deputy in the Constituent Assembly for ORGA (Galician Autonomous Republican Organization), which merged with Acción Republicana to form the new Izquierda Republicana (Republican Left) party in 1933. Navy Minister in first republican cabinet 1931; Home Minister a few months later till move to Justice Minister in 1933. Became prime minister when Azaña was made president of the republic in 1936. On outbreak of military rebellion resigned in favour of Martínez Barrio. Left for France when Civil War broke out. Died in exile in Paris 1950.

Castiella y Maíz, Fernando María (1907–76): law professor. Volunteer with the Blue Division. Foreign Minister 1957. Applied for Spanish membership of EEC 1963, leading only to Treaty of Association 1967. Signed renewed US Spanish Accord, but unable to agree a re-negotiated renewal in 1969. Resigned to take up his Madrid Chair again that year.

Fernández Cuesta, Raimundo (born Madrid 5 December 1896): lawyer. Appointed Secretary-general and member of the Political Committee of the Falange by José Antonio Primo de Rivera 1934. Falangist candidate for Madrid and Jaén in 1936 elections. Franco named him secretary general of the Movement. Minister of Agriculture in Franco's first cabinet 1938. Later Minister for Justice and for the Movement. Member of Council of the Realm, National Council of the Movement and of the *Cortes*. Became president of the political association Frente Nacional Español when it was formed and remained its head when it became the Falange Española de las JONS.

Fraga Iribarne, Manuel (born 1922): Doctor of Law and Political Science. Professor of the Theory of the State and of Constitutional Law. Clerk of the *Cortes*. Minister of Information and Tourism 1962–9. Ambassador in London 1973–5. On returning to Spain became Minister of the Interior. President of the Democratic Reform movement (*Reforma Democrática*) in 1976. Presided over formation of the conservative party Alianza Popular. Deputy for Madrid since 1977. Was a member of the Constitutional Commission and chief parliamentary spokesman for AP. At the end of 1978 organized the conservative electoral alliance Coalición Democrática, whose lists he headed in the 1979 and 1982 general elections. Leader of the opposition until resignation in 1986.

Franco Bahamonde, Nicolás (1891–1977): Franco's elder brother. Naval officer.

Franco Bahamonde, Ramón (born El Ferrol 1896): Franco's brother. Matriculated Infantry Academy 1911, commissioned 1914. In 1926 piloted the seaplane *Pius Ultra* from Palos to Buenos Aires, winning world-wide popularity.

Political maverick. When Civil War broke out was air attaché in Washington. Returned to command the nationalist air force base in the Balearics. Disappeared while flying along Majorcan coast 1938.

Franco Polo, Carmen, Marquesa de Villaverde. Duquesa de Franco. Franco's daughter. Married Cristóbal Martínez Bordiú 1 August 1950. Seven children.

Gil Robles y Quiñones, José María (1898–1980): Professor of Constitutional Law, 1922. Took part in creation of the Confederación Española de Derechas Autónomas, CEDA, the right-wing Catholic electoral alliance, of which he became president. Minister of War in Lerroux's sixth government May 1935. Went into opposition when the Popular Front triumphed at the polls. In exile 1936–53. Member of Don Juan's privy council till 1962 when he was dismissed for taking part in the Munich Congress. Founded the Christian Social Democratic party (*Democracia Social Cristiana*). On 13 March 1975 launched the Popular Democratic Federation (*Federación Popular Democrática*), of which he was elected president. The Christian Democrat caused collapsed completely in the 1977 general election.

Girón de Velasco, José Antonio (born 1911): law degree. Led Valladolid Falangist militia before the Civil War. By the end of the war he was a member of the National Council of the Movement. Apointed National Delegate for ex-servicemen 1939. Minister of Labour, Member of National Council of the Movement, deputy in the *Cortes*. Since 1974, president of the war veterans' association.

Goded Llopis, Manuel (1882–1936): took part in Moroccan War. Promoted general after the landings at Alhucemas. Transferred to the reserve following army mutiny of 10 August 1932. Inspector-general of the Army and Director-general of Aviation in the War Ministry under Gil Robles in 1935. When the Popular Front came to power he was made Captain General of the Balearic Islands in order to get him away from Madrid. Led rising of 19 July 1936 in Palma, Majorca. Left for Barcelona on the same day to take control of the rising there. Failed and was arrested. Sentenced to death by court martial and shot at Barcelona, 12 August 1936.

Gomá y Tomás, Isidro (1869–1940): Succeeded Cardinal Segura as Archbishop of Toledo. Cardinal 1935. Gave unconditional support to nationalists. At Franco's request, drew up the *Collective Letter of the Spanish Bishops*, supporting the Burgos government, in 1937. Offered a theological justification of the war and approved its being called a crusade.

Herrera Oria, Angel (1886–1968): lawyer. Journalist and Catholic propagandist. Founder-editor of *El Debate* 1910. After proclamation of the republic in 1931, founded daily *Ya*. Left editorship of *El Debate* to organize and lead the Catholic political lobby Acción Católica. Had great influence over this movement, the Catholic press and the CEDA of Gil Robles. Received Holy Orders 1940. Bishop of Málaga 1947. Cardinal 1965.

Kindelán Duany, Alfredo (1879–1962): took part in Alhucemas landings and became Head of Aviation under the monarchy. Proclaimed Franco Leader of Spain in Salamanca. Appointed Air Force Chief by the Junta of National Defence. At the end of the war, became Captain General of the Balearics and Catalonia. Later moved increasingly towards favouring the return of the monarchy, which led to his removal to the Canary Islands. Re-habilitated 1944.

Largo Caballero, Francisco (1869–1946): Secretary-general of UGT for twenty years. UGT's representative on the Revolutionary Committee, 1930; found himself opposing Besteiro, who maintained that the party should not co-operate in the establishment of a bourgeois republic. Minister of Labour in the government of 1931. President of the party 1932. His shift to the left won him the soubriquet of 'the Spanish Lenin'. Became prime minister as Franco's forces advanced on Madrid, at the head of a government combining all the elements of the Popular Front. He was also Minister of War. Communist pressure brought about his resignation. Removed from his positions in the party and the union. Left for France January 1939. The Vichy government put him under arrest and the Germans interned him in the Oranienburg concentration camp. Liberated by Polish units in April 1945. Died Paris, March 1946. Buried alongside heroes of the Paris Commune. Remains transferred to the civilian cemetry, Madrid, 8 April 1978.

Lerroux, Alejandro (1864–1949): journalist. Editor and editor-in-chief of the daily *El País*. Founded the papers *El Progreso*, *El Intransigente* and *El Radical*. Republican deputy for Barcelona in 1901 *Cortes*. Re-elected 1903, 1905. Highly influential with the Barcelona proletariat. Because he advocated a unitary republican state, he parted company with the Catalan nationalists and founded the Radical Party. Left in the wilderness by financial scandals. Returned to politics after the 'tragic weeks' of 1909, as a moderate liberal. Became Foreign Minister on coming of the republic. Headed six republican governments between 1933 and 1935, with support from CEDA. Exiled during Civil War to Portugal, from where he wrote expressing support for Franco. Returned to Spain 1947 and died two years later.

Lister, Enrique (born 1907): emigrated to Cuba with his father 1927 and joined Cuban Communist Party. Returned to Spain 1930 and elected head of the Miscellaneous Trades' Syndicate. Studied and worked in Moscow 1931–4. Commanded Vth Regiment, formed by the construction workers' union. Played an important part in the battles of Teruel, Guadalajara and the Ebro. After the defeat, returned to Moscow for six years. Became general in Russian, Polish and Yugoslav armies. Member of Spanish Communist Party from 1935 and of its politburo from 1946 to 1970, when he was expelled for his differences with the central committee. Founded the Spanish Workers' Communist Party (*Partido Comunista Obrero Español*) 1973. Returned to Spain 7 November 1977.

López Rodó, Laureano (born 1920) Professor of Administrative Law. Outstanding member of Opus Dei. Devised the Plan of Economic and Social Development. Minister-commissioner of Economic and social planning. Foreign Minister. Member of the National Council of the Movement by nomination of Franco. Deputy in *Cortes*. Represented Barcelona at the first party conference of Alianza

Popular. Elected deputy in the general election of June 1977. Resigned from chairmanship of AP in Catalonia 15 January 1979.

Martín Artajo, Alberto (1905–79): close associate of Cardinal Herrera Oria. Secretary-general, later president of Acción Católica. Foreign Minister 1945. Served twelve years in the post, breaking the ring of diplomatic isolation. The high point of his achievement was the 1953 mutual aid and co-operation pact with the US, with the Concordat of the same year, and Spain's admission to the UN in 1956. President of the Catholic press and propaganda organization Asociación Católica Nacional de Propagandistas.

Martinez Bordiú, Cristóbal, Marqués de Villaverde (born 1922): Doctor of Medicine, specializing in throat surgery in the fifties. Married Carmen, Franco's only daughter. Meteoric career brought him the directorship of the cardiovascular unit at the La Paz hospital complex, where he conducted Spain's first heart transplant operations in 1968.

Miaja Menant, José (1878–1958): professional soldier. After fighting in Morocco, promoted general 1932. Despite having belonged to the *Unión Militar Española (UME)*, he remained loyal to the Republic when the war broke out in 1936 and was War Minister in Martínez Barrios's cabinet. In November became chairman of the Junta de Defensa de Madrid, which organized the Battle of Madrid. Later, he was commander of the Army of Central Spain and overall commander of the central and southern army groups. Accepted presidency of the Junta of Casado, formed to try to negotiate peace, March 1939 and shortly afterwards went into exile in Mexico, where he died.

Millán Astray Terreros, José (1879–1954): much wounded professional soldier. Founded the Spanish Legion and the Foreign Legion in 1920. Promoted general 1932. Joined National Movement 1936 and ran the nationalist press and propaganda office in Salamanca.

Mola Vidal, Emilio (1887–1937): professional soldier. Distinguished service in combat in Morocco after 1909. Director general of state security 1930 – arrested and prosecuted when the monarchy fell. Exonerated but discharged from the army. Wrote his memoirs (*Memorias de mi paso por la Dirección General de Seguridad*) and *El pasado, Azaña y el porvenir* to justify his conduct. The amnesty of 1934 allowed him to return to his career. Posted to Pamplona March 1936. Became main organizer of rising of July. Leading member of the Burgos Junta. Won control of a large part of the north of the country and organized the first columns to advance against Madrid. Commanded in the northern campaigns. Died in an air crash, 3 June 1937.

Moscardó Ituarte, José (1878–1956): Colonel in command of the Central Gymnastic School of Toledo when the Civil War broke out. Held out with his men in the Alcázar of Toledo for two months until the arrival of the Nationalist forces. Posted to command Soria Division October 1936. Commander, Army of Aragon 1938. Campaigns in Catalonia and central Spain. Head of Franco's military household. National Delegate for sport.

Muñoz Grandes, Agustín (born Madrid 1896): career soldier and politician. Served with distinction in Morocco. Left Madrid for Nationalist zone when war broke out. Served in Catalan campaign. Secretary-general and Minister of the Movement 1939. Commanded Blue Division 1941. Lieutenant-general 1942. Minister of War, Captain-general and Chief of the General Staff. Also at times deputy prime minister and vice-chairman of the Council of the Realm.

Negrín López, Juan (1892–1956): physician and politician. Distinguished pupil of neurologist Ramón y Cajal. Completed medical training Leipzig. Professor, Madrid University. Joined PSOE 1929. Appointed that year to organize and run the committee in charge of building the new Madrid University campus. Deputy in the Cortes of 1931. Minister of Finance in Largo Caballero's government and succeeded him as prime minister May 1937. Formed government of republican unity April 1938. Left for France on 6 March 1939, where he continued to head the government in exile.

Nieto Antúnez, Pedro (1898–1978): Director of studies, Naval Gunnery School 1935. Rear Admiral 1950. Second-in-command of Franco's military household. Promoted to admiral and made Minister for the Navy in 1962. Deputy in the *Cortes*. Member of the National Council of the Movement.

Polo y Martínez Valdés, Carmen (born 1902): married Franco October 1923. One daughter.

Portela Valladares, Manual (1868–1952): member of Liberal Party. Civil Governor of Barcelona. Minister of Development. After the October uprising of 1934, Lerroux made him Governor-general of Catalonia and subsequently Minister of the Interior. Formed two successive governments with the unrealized aim of getting ready for new elections and forming a new electoral alliance of the centre; when war broke out he went abroad, while placing himself at the republican government's disposal in 1937.

Prieto y Tuero, Indalecio (born Oviedo 30 April 1883): family moved to Bilbao where he began work as a typist on *La Voz de Vizcaya* and later as a sub-editor for *El Liberal*, a republican paper which he ended by owning and editing. Joined Socialist Party and helped found Socialist youth movement. Elected successively member of the provincial administration, city councillor and deputy in the *Cortes*. Signatory of the Pact of San Sebastián. Minister of Finance and Public Works in the republican government. Exiled because of his involvement in the October rising of 1934. Returned to Spain after the electoral victory of the Popular Front. Upheld the alliance of republicans and socialists and supported the replacement of Alcalá-Zamora by Azaña. In Civil War, Minister for Naval and Air Affairs under Largo Caballero, Minister of Finance under Negrín. Resigned in opposition to increase of communist influence. Founded the Spanish Liberation Committee in Mexico in an attempt to being socialists and republicans together to re-establish a credible republican government-in-exile. After the war organised the Committee for Aid to Spanish Republicans in exile.

Primo de Rivera y Orbaneja, Miguel (1870–1930): entered Military Academy 1884. Action in Melilla, Cuba, Philippines and Moroccan campaigns. Led coup of

13 September 1923 with Alfonso XIII's connivance. Prime Minister. Formed military government and suppressed democratic rights. Concentrated executive and legislative power in his own hands and interfered continually with the courts. Founded Patriotic Union 1924 as the party of his regime. He could only count on the army and the extreme right, since, despite his gestures towards other groups, his authoritarian measures alienated most of Spain's political forces. Until the crisis of 1929 the economy boomed and he fulfilled his promise to end the Moroccan campaigns. In 1925 he installed a civilian government. Plots against the regime multiplied. Finally, after failing to obtain adequate assurances of support from the regional army chiefs, he felt obliged to resign on 28 January 1930. Went into exile in Paris, where he died soon after.

Primo de Rivera y Sáenz de Heredia, José Antonio (1903–36): law degree. After the collapse of the dictatorship, he leapt to the defence of his father, General Primo de Rivera. Joined the Monarchist Union 1930. Unsuccessful candidate in 1931 elections. Disillusioned with parliamentary liberalism, he moved towards nationalist, anti-liberal, anti-Marxist, totalitarian ideas. Founded the Spanish Falange in 1933. Elected deputy for Cadiz on the right-wing slate in the elections of November 1933. In February 1934 the Falange merged with the national-syndicalist lobby JONS. At its first conference in October of the same year the new combined movement set out its 27 points and José Antonio was made sole leader. He failed to obtain a seat in the 1936 elections. A month later he was arrested in Madrid and transferred to Alicante goal. From there he announced his support for the military rising. He was charged, with his brother Miguel, with influencing the rebellion and sentenced to death by a people's court. Executed 20 November Alicante.

Queipo de Llano Sierra, Gonzalo (1875–1951): career soldier. Fought in Cuba and Morocco. Exiled 1928 because opposed dictatorship of Primo de Rivera. Of republican inclinations, took part in Cuatro Vientos mutiny of 1930. On proclamation of Second Republic, became the president's head of military household. Resentful of a demotion he approached Mola. The generals in charge of the conspiracy chose him to lead the revolt in Andalusia. He procured the surrender of Seville to the Nationalists. As commander of the Army of the South, he took part in the capture of Málaga and was conspicuous for his highly aggressive propaganda broadcasts.

Ridruejo, Dionisio (1912–75): poet. Joined the Falange when very young and held high office in the organization: provincial chief in Valladolid, 1937; head of the national propaganda network 1938. Founded the review *Escorial* 1940. Joined Blue Division. His critical posture and discontent with the Franco regime were soon revealed. For the letter he wrote Franco in July 1942 he was gaoled in Ronda and Catalonia. It distanced him permanently from Francoism. The 1956 crisis saw him gaoled again. In the sixties he taught in the US. Founded a social democratic party (*Unión Social Demócrata Española*) 1974. Apart from his poetry, his prose works include *Escrito en España* and *Casi unas memoriales*.

Rojo Lluch, Vicente (1894–1966): prominent strategical brain of Republican army. As Major in 1936 he remained loyal to the Republic. Became Chief of Staff of the Madrid Committee of Defence. Organized the 'popular army'. Promoted general in September 1937. Planned the offensives at Brunete, Teruel and the Ebro. After the occupation of Catalonia, went into exile in Paris, Argentina and finally Bolivia. Returned to Madrid 1957, court-martialled and sentenced to life imprisonment. Though the sentence was suspended, he was subjected to controls and restrictions which, together with his poor health, left him in virtual house-arrest until his death on 15 June 1966. His *Alerta a los pueblos* describes the Catalan collapse and *Así fue la defensa de Madrid* the organization of the resistance of the capital.

Ruiz-Giménez Cortés, Joaquín (born Hoyo de Manzanares, Madrid, 1913): read Law at Madrid University and held important posts in the Catholic students' union. At outbreak of war, arrested and detained in Madrid gaol. Escaped to Nationalist zone. Joined army 1937 as officer of engineers and served under Muñoz Grandes. After the war, became city councillor for Madrid and chairman of the international Catholic organization Pax Romana, a post he held till 1946. As a member of the Institute of Political Studies he had an active part in drafting the fundamental laws. Ambassador to the Holy See 1948 with the job of negotiating a concordat. Minister of Education 1951. His reformist policy led to his dismissal at the time of violent incidents on the campus in 1956. Founded review *Cuadernos para el diálogo* in 1963, to which Christian Democrats and Marxists contributed. After Franco's death, formed the 'Democratic Left' Party (Izquierda Democrática) which joined forces with Christian Democratic parties for the 1977 elections, without winning a single seat. In December 1972 the *Cortes* approved his nomination as Ombudsman.

Sainz Rodríguez, Pedro (born Madrid 1897): Monarchist loyal to Alfonso XIII. Professor at Oviedo and Madrid Universities. Deputy in the *Cortes* representing Acción Española, 1933. Important role in Burgos, as Sanjurjo's link-man, in the initial stages of the Civil War. Later sent by Mola to Rome to try to get Italian planes to bring soldiers from Morocco to the peninsula. Minister for Education in Franco's first cabinet, reformed all the republican legislation on the subject to restore Catholic Education. Resigned at the end of the war and went to Lisbon to serve in Don Juan's privy council. Returned to Spain 1968. Academician in the Academies of the Language and of History and author of numerous scholarly works, and of his memoirs, *Testimonio y recuerdos*.

Sánchez Mazas, Rafael (born 1894): lawyer. One of the founders and intellectual progenitors of the Falange. Minister without Portfolio after the war.

Sanjurjo Sacanell, José (1872–1936): career soldier. Promoted Lieutenant-general and made head of the military High Commission in Morocco, 1925. Three years later given command of the Civil Guard. Accepted the lawfulness of the republic on 14 April 1931 but rebelled in Seville on 10 August 1932: the rising collapsed in Madrid and Seville. Court-martialled and sentenced to death for mutiny, commuted to life imprisonment. Two years later the Lerroux government pardoned him and he went to Estoril. In 1936 he approved Mola's plans and accepted the leadership of the generals' insurrection, but he was killed in a plane crash on 20 July in Portugal on his way to Spain.

Segura y Sáez, Pedro (1880–1957): Archbishop of Toledo and Primate of Spain.

Cardinal 1927. Under the republic, issued a number of pastoral letters criticizing the new regime. Expelled from Spain to Rome by the provisional government in May 1931. He inspired the collective pastoral letter of the Spanish bishops in August 1931, drawing attention to the 'serious defects' of the republican constitution. As Archbishop of Seville during the Civil War and after, well known for his conservative and monarchist sympathies; conspicuous in the forties for his teachings and pastoral letters on Christian sexual morality.

Serrano Suñer, Ramón (born 1901): law degree. Member of corps of state attorneys. Head of the youth section of Acción Popular; CEDA member of the republican *Cortes*. Friend of José Antonio Primo de Rivera. Franco's brother-in-law. After the outbreak of the Civil War, he escaped from Madrid to Salamanca, in the Nationalist zone, where he worked to unify the various organizations that supported the uprising. Interior Minister 1938–40. As Foreign Minister after October 1940 he was overtly pro-Axis but avoided committing Spain to intervention. He was abruptly dismissed – largely for reasons of domestic politics – in September 1942. His foreign policy is defended in his *Entre Hendaya y Gibraltar* (revised ed. 1973), *Entre silencio y propaganda: la historia como fue Memorias* (1977).

Solís Ruiz, José (born Cabra, Cordova, 1913): read law. Took part from the first in the insurrection of 1936. As second-in-command of a Falangist militia unit he was among the first provisional officers to be recruited. After the war, as Technical Secretary of the 'vertical' official syndical organization, he organized the first Workers' Congress. Member of Council of the Realm and National Delegate for Trade Unions. Secretary-general of the Movement. Restored to the post of Minister of the Movement in Arias Navarro's government. Three days after Franco's death he became Minister of Labour in the first government of the monarchy.

Ullastres Calvo, Alberto (born Madrid 1914): law degree. Professor of Business Studies. Member of Opus Dei. Head of Acción Católica in his youth. Fought with Franco in Civil War. Minister of Commerce 1957. With Mariano Navarro Rubio, Finance Minister, he drew up the stablization policy which brought the post-war era of attempted autarchy to an end. Began Spain's contacts with the EEC and made her first application to join. Removed from office in 1965, as ambassador to the EEC negotiated Spain's Treaty of Association with the community in 1970.

Yagüe Blanco, Juan (1891–1952): military career in Africa. Played part in suppressing the 1934 rebellion in Asturias, commanding troops of the regular army and the Foreign Legion. Lieutenant-colonel 1936. Go-between for Franco and Mola. Led the insurrection against the republic and Ceuta and commanded the Legion in Spain. Later disembarked on the south coast of the peninsula at the head of men of the Legion and the Moroccan forces. Took Mérida and Badajoz. Led the advance on Madrid. Supported Franco's nomination as head of state. Promoted General 1937. Action on Aragonese and Catalan fronts in command of the Moroccan army corps. Air Force Minister 1939.

A *note on terms*

Carlists See Monarchists.

Captain General The highest rank in the Spanish army. Captains General were the commanders of the major military regions.

Cortes the Spanish Parliament. Under the Second Republic, deputies were elected; under Franco they were largely nominated 'from above'.

Falange A loose gouping of authoritarian Nationalist parties under the leadership of José Antonio Primo de Rivera until his execution in November 1936, and subsequently led by Manuel Hedilla. Fused with the Carlists by Franco in April 1937 to form the FET de las JONS.

Fuero Originally a medieval term for a grant of liberties and privileges to a region or corporation, used by Franco to give a specious democratic cover to grants of 'liberties' to his subjects.

Integrists A dissident group of Carlists who put the installation of a quasi-theocratic monarchy above the dynastic claims of the Carlist pretenders. 'Integrism', therefore, is used to describe the ideology of the extreme Catholic right.

Monarchists Since the 1830s monarchists were divided between Carlists, Catholic conservatives who supported the claims of Don Carlos (1788–1855) and his heirs against the 'liberal' monarchy of Queen Isabella (1830–1904) and her heirs. Under Franco monarchists were divided between Carlists (now called Traditionalists) and the Alfonsine monarchists who supported the claims of Don Juan, son of Alfonso XIII who had left Spain on the declaration of the Second Republic. Most Alfonsine monarchists came to support the restoration of a democratic monarchy.

Movement, the An amalgam of all the different groups which supported Franco in 1936, which came to play the part of the single party in a totalitarian regime.

Municipality Spanish municipalities were the basic organ of local government and often included the surrounding rural area.

Opus Dei A lay brotherhood of committed Catholics who aimed to influence university and political life. Many of the 'technocrats' of the 1960s came from their auspices, though they fell from influence in 1973.

Organic Laws The fundamental laws of the Francoist constitution.

Glossary of abbreviations

CEDA *(Confederacion Espanola de Derechas Autonomas)* A nationwide confederation of Catholic right wing parties founded in March 1933. Its core was Acción Popular, and it was essentially the conservative right party committed to the corporate state.

CCOO *(Comisiones Obreras)* Illegal trade unions in the 1950s formed by Communists, Catholics and Marxists. Legalised in 1977.

ETA *(Euzkadi Ta Askatasuna)* Basque separatist clandestine revolutionary organization formed in 1959. Responsible for the assassination of Admiral Carrero Blanco.

FRAP *(Frente Revolucionario Antifascista Patriotico)* Revolutionary left faction which emerged after 1968, involved in terrorist activities after 1973.

GRAPO *(Grupo Revolucionario Antifascista Primero Octubre)* Left wing terrorist group created in 1976.

INI *(Instituto Nacional de Industria)* State controlled body regulating industry, based on Italian model IRI.

LOE *(Ley Organica del Estado)* Law defining structure of Francoist state.

PSOE *(Partido Socialista Obrero Espanol)* The Socialist party of Spain, founded in 1879.

SEU *(Sindicato de Estudiantes Universitarios)* University Students' Union.

UDPE *(Union del Pueblo Espanol)* A Gaullist type political association formed in 1975 by prominent Francoists, faded out in 1976.

UGT *(Union General de Trabajadores)* Socialist trade union, with particular strength in Madrid, Asturias and the Basque area.

UME *(Union Militar Espanol)* Secret monarchist organization within the army.

Brief Chronology of Events

1892		Francisco Franco Bahamonde born at El Ferrol
1898		USA defeats Spain – end of colonial empire
1923	13 September	Military coup by General Primo de Rivera
	22 October	Franco's marriage to Carmen Polo Martinez Valdes
1931	14 April	Proclamation of Second Republic
1932	10 August	Sarjurjo's failed coup
	1 November	Centre-right win elections
1935	15 February	Franco becomes head of Morocco army
	May	Franco becomes Chief of Central General Staff ·
1936	16 February	Popular Front wins election
	18 July	Civil War begins
	27 September	Liberation of Toledo
	18 November	Franco receives recognition from Italy and Germany
1937	19 April	Totalitarian decree
	26 April	Bombing of Guernica
1938	9 March	Labour Rights Law
	22 April	Press Law
	25 July – 16 November	Battle of the Ebro
	29 September	Munich meeting: Chamberlain, Daladier, Hitler and Mussolini
1939	27 February	Francoist regime recognized by Great Britain
	27 March	Spain joins Anti-Comintern Pact
	28 March	Franco's troops enter Madrid
	31 March	Friendship treaty with Germany
	1 April	Civil War ends
	8 May	Spain withdraws from League of Nations
	4 September	Spain declares neutrality in World War
1940	16 October	Serrano Suner appointed Foreign Minister
1941	13 June	Spain declares non-belligerency
	22 October	Hendaye meeting between Hitler and Franco
1942	3 September	Serrano Suner dismissed
1943	17 March	Cortes opens
1945	19 March	Don Juan's Manifesto against Franco
	17 July	Fuero de los Espanoles
1946	12 December	USA recommends diplomatic boycott of Spain
1951	1 March	Barcelona tramway strike
1953	27 August	Concordat with Vatican signed
	20 September	Base agreement with USA
1955	14 December	Spain admitted to UN
1956	February	Student discontent. Dismissal of Ruiz Gimenez and Fernandez Cuesta
1957	25 February	Franco forms sixth government, including Opus Dei technocrats
1959	22 July	Stabilization Plan announced
1962	9 February	Spain opens negotiations with EEC

1962	April – June	Students' and workers' unrest. State of emergency in Basque provinces and Asturias
	5 – 6 June	Spanish opposition joins in Munich meeting
1963	20 April	Execution of Grimau
	28 December	First Development Plan
1964	30 October	Intellectuals protest against repression in Asturias mining strikes
1965	23–25 February	Student demonstrations in Madrid. 5 professors dismissed from university
1967	21 September	Admiral Carrero Blanco appointed Deputy Head of Government
1968	18 March	Fraga Iribarne's Press Law
	22 November	Organic Law of State
1969	22 July	Franco presents Juan Carlos as his successor
1970	3–28 December	Burgos ETA trial
1971	19 October	CCOO leaders arrested
1973	8 June	Carrero Blanco appointed Prime Minister
	20 December	Carrero Blanco assassinated
	29 December	Arias Navarro appointed Prime Minister
1974	12 February	Arias Navarro announces 'opening' of regime
	29 July	Opposition forms Democratic Junta
	29 October	Dismissal of 'liberal' Minister of Information, Pio Cabanillas
	23 December	Law of political associations
1975	April	State of emergency in Basque provinces
	June	Moderate opposition forms Platform of Democratic Convergence
	21 September	5 ETA and FRAP members executed
	20 November	Franco dies
	22 November	Juan Carlos crowned king

Index